Rethinking the Administi

Brian,

In admiration
of your work!

Best,

Bill Resh

JOHNS HOPKINS STUDIES IN AMERICAN PUBLIC POLICY
AND MANAGEMENT
Manuel P. Teodoro and David M. Konisky, Series Editors

Rethinking the Administrative Presidency

Trust, Intellectual Capital, and Appointee-Careerist Relations in the George W. Bush Administration

William G. Resh

JOHNS HOPKINS UNIVERSITY PRESS   BALTIMORE

Johns Hopkins University Press
2715 North Charles Street
Baltimore, Maryland 21218-4363
www.press.jhu.edu

Library of Congress Cataloging-in-Publication Data

Resh, William G., 1973–
  The administrative presidency : trust, intellectual capital, and appointee-careerist
relations in the George W. Bush administration / William G. Resh.
    pages cm. — (Johns Hopkins studies in American public policy and management)
  Includes bibliographical references and index.
  ISBN 978-1-4214-1849-0 (paperback : acid-free paper) — ISBN 978-1-4214-1850-6
(electronic) — ISBN 1-4214-1849-5 (paperback : acid-free paper) —
ISBN 1-4214-1850-9 (electronic) 1. Executive power—United States.
2. Administrative agencies—United States—Management. 3. Executive
departments—United States—Management. 4. Trust—Political aspects—United
States. 5. Bush, George W. (George Walker), 1946–. 6. United States—Politics and
government—2001–2009. I. Title.
  JK516.R3726 2015
  973.931—dc23   2015008450

A catalog record for this book is available from the British Library.

*Special discounts are available for bulk purchases of this book. For more information, please
contact Special Sales at 410-516-6936 or specialsales@press.jhu.edu.*

Johns Hopkins University Press uses environmentally friendly book materials,
including recycled text paper that is composed of at least 30 percent post-consumer
waste, whenever possible.

To those public servants who "fight for the ideals and sacred things of the city both alone and with many."

—Athenian Oath

Contents

Series Editors' Foreword

Politicians, pundits, and the general public may be excused for often forgetting that the president of the United States is supposed to be an executive; the president's role as initiator and crafter of public policy in the legislative process tends to overshadow his role as the nation's chief executive officer. Mid-level appointments and management directives are not the stuff of stump speeches or State of the Union addresses.

A president overlooks his executive functions at his peril, however. His policy agenda is only as good as his administration's ability to turn the organizational apparatus of government—including its legions of career bureaucrats—to his will. That isn't easy.

A scholarly and political conventional wisdom has developed around the idea that bureaucratic careerists are consummate conservers interested in defending the status quo against popularly mandated presidential action. In this view, the president's appointees must advance the president's agenda through careerists who are recalcitrant at best, and saboteurs at worst. Proceeding from this adversarial posture, the normative prescription for appointees is to exclude careerists from the process of policy formulation and use them to implement isolated policies with little sense of the president's broader policy agenda. Keep careerists in the dark about the president's true agenda, and they won't be able to subvert it, goes the reasoning. The result of this pervasive distrust is what Sanera (1984) has called "jigsaw puzzle" management, where careerists focus on individual pieces while intentionally kept ignorant of the appointees' strategic aims.

William G. Resh's *Rethinking the Administrative Presidency: Trust, Intellectual Capital, and Appointee-Careerist Relations in the George W. Bush Administration* questions the fundamental assumption of inevitable distrust between appointee and careerist. In this careful study of the George W. Bush administration, Resh approaches the managerial presidency from an organizational theory perspective and shows how a president's activist agenda can be carried forward effectively by appointees through optimistic trust in career bureaucrats. With a deft mixture of interviews and quantitative analysis of survey data, Resh shows that rather than dividing and isolating careerists from the president's strategic ends with "jigsaw" management, *successful* Bush administration appointees built managerial "joists," or interlacing systems of interpersonal trust and mutual support between political and organizational actors. By regarding careerists as experts and professionals rather than adversaries, those appointees effectively tapped careerists' expertise.

The kind of trust that characterizes Resh's joist-building appointees is not Pollyanna naiveté. Indeed, Resh argues that the "joist management" that some Bush appointees employed was a rational and calculated means of leveraging careerists' intellectual capital in pursuit of the administration's policy goals. With this argument, Resh challenges directly the received wisdom on presidential management and offers a profound revision to it. Presidents with ambitious policy agendas should urge their appointees systematically to build trust with their careerists, not corner and quarantine them. In short, Resh has shifted the scholarly discourse on the managerial presidency and rewritten the presidential playbook.

By contributing to the study of politics, public policy, and public management, this volume fits squarely with the purpose of the Johns Hopkins University Press series Studies in American Public Policy and Management. We encourage work that addresses contemporary American public policy and management issues with theoretically rich and empirically robust research. Books in the series take up public policy, politics, public administration, and/or public management. We proceed from the premise that public policy effectiveness is inevitably linked with public management and administration, and that public policy, administration, and management are irreducibly political.

Contributions to Studies in American Public Policy and Management generally center on the United States and on issues that are national in scope, but we are also interested in projects that deal with policy and management at the state and local levels. Books in the series are written for a scholarly audience of academics and students but also have an eye toward application and relevance to working policymakers and public administrators.

We hope that the books in the series advance academic thinking while

enlightening our understanding of how to address pressing public policy
and management challenges effectively.

Manuel P. Teodoro
Texas A&M University
David M. Konisky
Georgetown University

Acknowledgments

I would like to thank all the students, staff, and faculty at the three institutions that have been so instrumental to my career and who have supported my efforts to write and publish this book over the last five years. First, I would like thank my colleagues at American University's School of Public Affairs (SPA) for their support and collegiality. My experience at SPA was shaped by wonderful teachers, brilliant classmates, and attentive members of the staff. Foremost, I thank my mentor, Robert Durant, for his patience, guidance, and generosity. I aspire to be half of the scholar that he is. Second, I thank the members of Indiana University's School of Public and Environmental Affairs (SPEA) for championing my professional development and allowing me to start my career at their fine institution. One can only hope to have the level of collegiality and support that I received at SPEA. This book and my career would not have been possible without the friends, mentors, and colleagues I had in Indiana. I thank you all from the bottom of my heart. Third, I sincerely thank the University of Southern California's Sol Price School of Public Policy (Price). I have found a welcome— and warm!—home in Los Angeles and at Price. My Price colleagues and the School's leadership are of the same exceptional quality that I have been spoiled to expect by this point. I am thrilled to be part of Price's bright future and to continue the excellence in public affairs research and teaching that it has long established. I would like to thank my colleagues in the Bedrosian Center for Governance Research, in particular, for their support. However, the entire Price faculty, staff, and leadership have been instrumental to my smooth transition and in allowing me to finish this manuscript on schedule.

I would like to thank George C. Edwards III (Texas A&M University) and *Presidential Studies Quarterly* (Wiley Press) for their permission to reprint parts of "Appointee-Careerist Relations in the Presidential Transition of 2008–2009" (Resh, 2014) in chapter 5 of the present text. I am indebted to Matthew Dull and Patrick Roberts (Virginia Polytechnic University, Alexandria) for their partnership in a data collection effort of appointee vacancies that was central to this work. I am also appreciative of the research assistants from both Indiana University and Virginia Tech who assisted in those efforts. I would also like to thank the following scholars who provided input to this book through direct or indirect advice, or who provided general substantive support. In no particular order, I thank Patricia Sykes, Laura Langbein, David Pitts, Ed Stazyk, Nathan Thompson, William Harder, Christine DeGregorio, James Thurber, and Bob Tobias from American University; George Krause from the University of Pittsburgh; Bert Rockman and David Reingold from Purdue University; David Lewis from Vanderbilt University; Karen Hult from Virginia Tech; John Marvel from George Mason University; Tony Bertelli from New York University; Hal Rainey and Tima Moldogaziev from the University of Georgia; Jim Perry, Sergio Fernandez, Michael McGuire, Shahzeen Attari, Justin Ross, John Graham, Lanlan Xu, Sameeksha Desai, Ashlyn Nelson, Denvil Duncan, Claudia Avellaneda, and Julia Carboni from Indiana University; Pam McCann, Jack Knott, Elizabeth Graddy, Raphael Bostic, and Christian Grose from the University of Southern California; Ken Meier and William West from Texas A&M University, Zach Oberfield from Haverford College; Saba Siddiki from Indiana University–Purdue University Indianapolis; Charles Fairchild from the University of Sydney; David Nixon from the University of Hawaii; Michael Bauer from the German University of Administrative Sciences, Speyer; and James Pfiffner from George Mason University.

I am also exceptionally grateful to the blind reviewers whose input strengthened my work considerably. Moreover, I could not have asked for a more supportive or insightful pair of editors than Johns Hopkins University Press Studies in American Public Policy and Management series editors, David Konisky and Manuel Teodoro. Their direction through this process was practical, erudite, and patient. Their choices for blind reviewers struck me as more than carefully considered, given the feedback I received. I could not have asked for more insightful reviews, and their own assessment of my work and their input was of equal sophistication. I owe Manny, in particular, a debt of gratitude for the "joists versus jigsaws" metaphor that brings together the theme of this work. David's steady and reassuring guidance throughout this process was equally valuable and appreciated. I would also like to thank Johns Hopkins University Press editorial and faculty boards and their staff, including Kelley Squazzo, Juliana McCarthy, and Catherine Goldstead. The Press has lived up to its eminent reputation as a leader in political science and public affairs scholarship through the professionalism they have exhibited throughout this process. Also, I sincerely thank Nicole Wayland for her keen eye, professionalism, and patience.

Finally, I thank my mother, Ann C. Resh Mummert, and all of my family and friends. My accomplishments are theirs. All mistakes and omissions are solely mine.

Rethinking the Administrative Presidency

Introduction

As President Barack Obama entered the final Congress of his presidency facing majority opposition in both chambers of the legislature and ostensibly an opposing ideological majority in the United States Supreme Court, the legislative success of his administration's policy agenda seemed largely in the rearview mirror of his two-term tenure. Thus, as is common to most "lame duck" presidents, the president presumably looks toward bolstering his presidential legacy through his role as chief executive of the US federal bureaucracy. Reliance on this role in domestic matters during one's second term is common, as presidents seek to concentrate on implementation issues and leverage administrative power to ensure short- and long-term alignment of agency actions to their respective policy preferences and legacy. An important question explored in the following pages is to what extent this is possible, given the formulation of goals and implementation of the management initiatives taken by political appointees on behalf of the president leading up to that point. But this book tackles matters that are even more fundamental to the functional governing of the US executive branch, and these matters are seemingly generalizable across presidencies (Posner & Radin, 2014): Why do presidents face so many avoidable managerial dilemmas across the entirety of their administrations, but especially toward the end of their administrations when a president's administrative goals might be more explicit and better aligned with his appointed leadership's prerogatives than during the first term?

This work helps open the "black box" of organizational behavior in US federal executive branch agencies by examining one critical aspect that facilitates the connection between politicization and performance: the relations between appointed and career executives. By coherently modeling these relationships using original and secondary data, I reveal a mechanism by which efforts at political control actually harm agency performance. I examine the "administrative presidency"—the collection of managerial and personnel strategies that are typically employed by modern presidents to "exert control over the executive branch in order to ensure that their policy preferences will not be subverted, intentionally or otherwise, by [career] officials unsympathetic to those preferences" (Rockman, 1986). I do so from the seldom-analyzed perspective of careerists in the executive branch—illuminating the importance of intrapersonal and intraorganizational trust in the context of federal agencies and linking a contextually based definition of trust to intellectual capital development as a precursor to successfully advancing presidential agendas administratively. Specifically, I investigate the means and extent by which the George W. Bush administration (during its second term) was able to increase the reliability and reduce the cost of information to achieve its policy goals through administrative means—namely, the strategic use of presidential appointment powers.

In turn, I test the degree to which the variables that produce intellectual capital are moderated by the political and organizational dynamics within which organizational actors are embedded. The empirical models in this study are constructed using data from several interrelated sources, including the Office of Personnel Management's (OPM) Federal Human Capital Survey (FHCS) and a National Academy of Public Administration survey of career members of the Senior Executive Service (SES). In doing so, I apply statistical analyses that are not common in the study of the administrative presidency. Importantly, I also interlace evidence culled from over a dozen interviews of career executives and managers, as well as political appointees. The research highlights the importance of functional relationships between careerists and appointees in the interest of advancing robust policy and the narrower prerogatives of presidents and their appointees.

This book puts forward a rather simple, but important, argument that presidents (and, by proxy, their appointees) commonly start from the premise of distrust when they attempt to control agencies. In doing so, these control efforts communicate distrust to the career bureaucracy, further diminishing trust throughout the hierarchy. Like trust, distrust is reciprocated and has "trickle-down" effects through lower managerial levels of the hierarchy. Thus, the decline in trust reduces information sharing between careerists and appointees and hurts agency performance—in terms of both "objective" performance and the president's ability to see through his policy prerogatives administratively. Importantly, I theorize and model the moderating effects of politicization and other organizational-level factors on appointee-careerist trust that more accurately capture the contingent nature of these relationships.

Therefore, the roles of trust in appointee-careerist relations and informational exchange become critical subjects for analysis in studies of presidential control of the bureaucracy. It is unlikely that information is shared that would be helpful to all participants in a low-trust environment. Information is necessary for presidents to translate their policy goals into outcomes, and information is necessary to prevent harmful agency failure. This book refines, elaborates, and extends important aspects of the conventional wisdom associated with traditional approaches to the study of the administrative presidency. This includes evidence of the paradoxical effects of administrative strategies premised on distrust of careerists, of the need to reconsider if Bush's use of these strategies actually reflected a more contingency-based approach than previously thought, and of the utility and importance of incorporating previously untapped research in related fields when studying the administrative presidency.

The first chapter provides a review of the existing scholarship addressing the "administrative" or "managerial" presidency, especially the evolution of the use of appointments as a strategic resource for presidential policymaking. It offers an intellectual background to the research questions developed in later chapters, and it delivers important context to the implications of the study's findings. It also introduces the theories that propose the appointment of presidential loyalists as either a theoretically logical or normatively prescribed method of bureaucratic control. The chapter ends by identifying, through past scholarship on the administrative presidency, the repeated emergence of trust between appointees and career executives as a critical factor in the success of the tool's strategic application.

I argue that despite its central importance, the construct has either been only implicitly identified or assumed as a critical factor. Still, even when appointee-careerist trust is explicitly identified as being critical to the success of a president to see through his policy preferences administratively, I find that the construct has seldom been properly defined, and its effects on organizational outcomes has never been expressly or systematically tested.

Also absent in this research is how the administrative presidency affects careerists' trust in political appointees and what that means for information flow from careerists to appointees and vice versa.

The second chapter explores the concept of trust in previously unexplored ways in the literature on the managerial or administrative presidency by offering an integrated model of the relationship between trust and administrative strategies. I examine the construct by providing a brief review of the scholarship on trust in organizations, generally—spanning the fields of public administration, organization theory, management, and political science. I find that there is little in the way of studies on trust in organizations that examines how relationships between actors at higher levels in an organization affect the perceptions and performance of actors at lower levels of the organization. Second, as it relates to the administrative presidency, I argue that the logic of the politicization strategy is based in traditional economic exchange theories of intraorganizational relationships, such as agency theory, that undervalue the efficiency of interpersonal trust. I demonstrate the link between the development of trust among actors at executive levels to an organization's collective intellectual capital. Finally, the chapter highlights the importance of embeddedness attributes to the strength of that relationship.

The second chapter also presents a theoretical model, derived from the preceding discussion. I develop a model that connects a carefully defined conceptualization of trust among stratified organizational actors within public hierarchies to the development of an organization's intellectual capital. From this model, I advance a series of hypotheses that are tested in the subsequent chapters.

Throughout the three succeeding empirical chapters, I supplement the discussion and analysis with semistructured interviews conducted of career managers, executives, and political appointees in the federal executive branch from July 2010 through February 2012. Interviewees were selected on the basis of their management rank in select agencies (namely, the Department of Education and the Department of Agriculture) and respective roles in policy development and implementation. The agency selections are two departments in which policy outcomes aligned with the Bush administration's "big government conservatism" policy goals. They also provide variation in the administration's purported objectives. The agency from the Department of Agriculture is a small regulatory agency for which the administration's alleged intent was to reduce regulatory impacts on large agribusiness—one that involved a concomitant proliferation of agency rules and regulations of purportedly pro-business orientation. The Department of Education provides an example of the administration's attempt to leverage and enhance administrative capacity to see through an expanded role of the federal government for a policy that has had lasting and controversial impacts on education policy across the United States.

Chapter 3 discusses the data collection and findings from the first empirical analysis of the study. This chapter uses FHCS 2006 and 2008 data to examine the relationship between trust and intellectual capital. The focus of this chapter is on how to best match empirics to the theory proposed in chapter 2. This chapter provides descriptive analysis and explores the importance of measurement in terms of using secondary and administrative data in exploring such a complex of cognitive, psychological, and organizational constructs. The chapter also offers a brief introduction and overview to readers on the utility and appropriateness of the multilevel statistical modeling approach used in the empirical chapters that follow.

Chapter 4 delivers a fuller empirical conceptualization of both "trust" and "intellectual capital" than typically has been employed in the administrative presidency scholarship. Notably, I employ a hierarchical linear model (HLM) where the level-one dependent variable is individual perceptions of the organization's capacity for intellectual capital development (i.e., "intellectual capital capacity"). At level two, the intercept is allowed to randomly vary across agencies and is modeled as a function of various embeddedness attributes of the agencies. The coefficient on the trust variable is modeled as a function of level-two covariates that capture various embeddedness attributes (including the construct of "appointee layering") while also including the dyadic trust between career senior executives and appointees in the respondent's respective agency (i.e., "stratified trust") as a level-two covariate.[1] I, therefore, explain in this chapter the systematic effects of appointee layering and the relationship between career executives and political appointees by measuring the relative impact that trust at the highest levels within an organization has on the development of trust among lower-level career officials (i.e., middle managers).

The findings suggest that the trust that is established between appointees and careerists at the executive level of a respective agency has a "trickle-down" effect on the development of institutional competence in that organization as a whole. I also find that politicization has a negative and direct impact on intellectual capital. While this finding seems accordant to structural reform prescriptions that argue that the federal government should reduce the overall number of political appointees,[2] the findings more profoundly speak to why the motivations that underlie presidential administrative strategies and the interpersonal relations that develop among career and political executives as a result are a more imperative direction for analysis. These findings indicate that it is necessary to understand the dynamics of intraorganizational, interpersonal relationships in order to understand the effect that appointee-careerist relations have on organizational outcomes.

Chapter 5 moves the discussion from the effects of stratified trust on the organization as a whole to a policy implemented across agencies that sought to leverage the institutional expertise of career executives toward the administration's explicit priorities. In doing so, I present a second empirical model, which includes the operationalization of the variables, data collection, univariate analysis of warranted variables included in the study and the comprehensive results of the inferential statistical model. The analysis involves a multilevel logistic regression of survey responses in which explicit knowledge exchange is the dichotomous dependent variable, with "encapsulated interest" (i.e., the willingness to depend on another actor based on the potential benefit for both actors to engage in a mutually reinforcing relationship) as the main independent variable of interest. I utilize a 2008 National Academy of Public Administration (NAPA) survey of career SES members on presidential transitions (a project on which I was a consultant). I discuss many of the relevant qualitative and univariate statistics produced in that study. The chapter examines the Bush administration's preparations for the presidential transition of 2008–2009. In doing so, I am able to isolate the encapsulated interest among career executives and political appointees in order to investigate determinants of explicit policy knowledge exchange in an area of implementation for which career executives are particularly suited.

This policy area (transition preparation) provides a sensible point to conduct my analysis because it is one that was simultaneously implemented across agencies, in a largely universal manner, and intended to be carried out according to a centralized presidential mandate from the White House to political appointees. Importantly, the mandate from the White House explicitly directed Bush appointees to work *with* career executives in formulating implementation plans and carrying out implementation. The analysis in chapter 5 also serves as a logical point for empirically examining these relationships because the survey instrument provides conceptual measures that capture the more narrow aspects of "encapsulated interest" (as opposed to a fuller conceptualization of trust) as it was established between career executives and political appointees leading up to transition implementation. I use a model where the dependent variable is explicit knowledge of transition preparation—a policy that required agencywide expertise and efforts. Covariates include respondent characteristics to improve accuracy of the estimates.

The evidence from chapter 5's analysis suggests that information exchange was dependent on the degree to which careerists' interests were encapsulated in the appointees' own. In other words, Bush appointees seemed to be carrying out what Heclo prescribed as a "contingently cooperative" strategy (Durant, 1992; Golden, 2000; Heclo, 1978). At the same time, the evidence shows that a large number of SES personnel were kept in the dark on policy decisions in which the White House explicitly insisted on their participation. Thus, the evidence suggests that selective recruitment and ideological identification of appointees do not necessarily make self-executing commands implicit within the executive branch. So, while not conclusive, the evidence shows that no existing account of managerial strategies is completely accurate.

Finally, chapter 6 provides a summary review of the findings, my interpretation of these findings and their implications for administrative strategies for advancing presidential policy agendas, the generalizability of the theory and findings to the Obama presidency and beyond, and promising next steps in this area of research. When all is said and done, readers will garner an understanding of the administrative presidency that incorporates previously unexplored insights from cognate fields that bear on this important topic. In the process, they can weigh the findings and interpretations of a wide-ranging analysis testing a set of hypotheses derived from a multidisciplinary, scholarship-based, theoretical model of the impact of appointee-careerist trust on the development of organizational intellectual capital. My hope is that the framework and analyses I offer will contribute to our knowledge of the effectiveness and limitations in presidents' attempts to align administrative power to advance their policy agendas. Optimally, it will also spawn future research that takes the study of the administrative presidency in new directions. But, most importantly, I hope to bring some truth to the power of personnel policy within the highest reaches of executive branch agencies.

1

The "Black Box" of the Administrative Presidency

Every tool is a weapon—if you hold it right.

—Ani DiFranco, *My IQ* (1993)

As legislatures delegate policymaking authority to the executive branch, and as political executives seek to advance their own policy interests through hierarchical authority over the permanent career bureaucracy, "it is quite uncertain how that authority will be exercised" (Krause, 2009, p. 538). In the US federal government, these responsibilities largely fall to a cadre of individuals who are appointed by the president. Modern presidents can make more than 4,000 appointments to jobs that range from Senate-approved, executive appointments in the Executive Office of the President (EOP) and executive branch agencies to upper- and middle-management levels throughout the federal bureaucracy.[3] Utilizing this function as an administrative strategy is based on the assumption that appointees wield extensive powers within agencies by (1) rewarding or punishing careerists' behavior and compliance with presidential agendas and (2) establishing internal reorganization strategies that "alter the skill mix" in accord with presidential priorities by fast-tracking positions symbolizing those priorities and shifting the responsibilities of tenured career executives (Durant & Resh, 2010).

As an essential element of any "administrative presidency" (Nathan, 1983), it is critical to both our descriptive understanding of the presidency as an institution and to any normative interest in effective executive governance to determine the degree to which the appointment strategy effectively aligns the expert and institutional knowledge of the career bureaucracy with the president's interest in a given policy area (Rudalevige, 2009). A fundamental tenet of the administrative presidency has been that careerists cannot be trusted to be responsive to presidential policy agendas (Moffit, 2001; Sanera, 1984). And while it is typically claimed that applying the tools of the administrative presidency is motivated by appointees' distrust of careerists to faithfully carry out those agendas (Ban & Ingraham, 1990; Pfiffner, 1991a), scant research exists on the extent to which applying the tools fosters distrust of (or diminishes trust in) political appointees among careerists.

We simply do not know the extent to which wielding the tools of the administrative presidency provokes responsiveness, furthers distrust, or promotes agency effectiveness. The literature today is largely atheoretical beyond principal-agent or game-theoretic models that are incapable of capturing the complexity of the Madisonian system in affecting the success or level of difficulty in advancing presidential policy agendas administratively (Bertelli & Lynn, 2006). By the same token, prior empirical research has not examined in theoretically grounded and statistically sophisticated ways *when* various tools are used and *if* various factors intervene in accelerating or mitigating the use and effect of trust on organizational effectiveness. Nor has it incorporated and integrated with prior research on the administrative presidency the insights of cognate fields such as public administration, organizational behavior, and generic management studies. Finally, most prior research on appointee-careerist relations has tended to focus early on in an administration, thus deemphasizing the uniqueness of the second term of any presidency.

This book examines the complex nature of relationships between career executives and political appointees within varying organizational settings and the connection between trust and the development of an organization's intellectual capital. I offer and test models that incorporate observations regarding the second George W. Bush administration from interviews and qualitative analysis of open-ended survey items as well as large-N, quantitative survey analysis. The analysis reveals the relative centrality of trust to organizational relationships and how it pertains to any president's strategic use of politicization as a means to leverage bureaucratic power toward his or her intended policy ends.

The importance of this book is the manner in which it spells out the *mechanism* by which efforts at political control can harm agency performance.

Figure 1.1. Theoretical propositions of the administrative presidency

While previous work examining the paradox of presidential control efforts has focused on the "treatment" of politicization (e.g., Lewis, 2008) and associated outcomes, no existing work systematically unpacks the "black box" of organizational behavior that facilitates the connection between politicization and performance. Or, the examination of appointee-careerist relations has not systematically tested the premise that trust is critical to achieving performance.

For instance, as figure 1.1 outlines, both positivist and normative theories of the administrative presidency (e.g., Moe, 1989, 1993; Moe & Howell, 1999; Nathan, 1983) propose that the presidential tools of centralization and politicization will facilitate the advancement of a president's policy goals. However, neither adequately accounts for the interaction of these tools with careerist behavior. Rather, they present fairly deterministic accounts that rely heavily on the assumption of careerist compliance in policy implementation. Likewise (although with contradictory conclusions), later empirical tests of these theories link the treatment of either appointee (careerist) leadership of a given program or the level of politicization in a given agency to purportedly objective measures of performance (e.g., Gilmour & Lewis, 2006b; Lewis, 2008; see also figure 1.2).

Thus, theoretical and empirical handlings of the effects of appointed leadership and politicization on performance and the achievement of presidential policy goals from these perspectives assume that appointed leadership and politicization lead to an emphasis of responsive competence within a respective organization, which leads to mixed results regarding performance and a positive relationship (generally) with advancing a president's policy goals (see figure 1.3). Conversely, these works assume that careerist leadership and diminished politicization lead to an emphasis on neutral competence within a respective organization, which subsequently leads to mixed

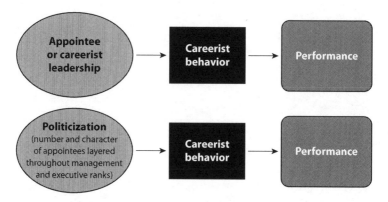

Figure 1.2. Theoretical paths from appointments to performance

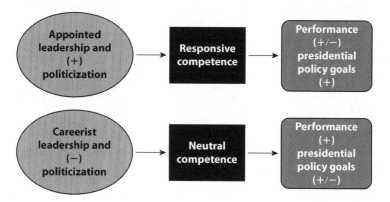

Figure 1.3. Theoretical and empirical paths from appointments to performance

results regarding a president's policy goals and increased objective performance (generally).

However, these treatments of the administrative presidency provide scant empirical evidence supporting, negating, or refining the proposition that these tactics will actually strengthen the modern presidency. These approaches do not sufficiently explain the constraints and incentives that presidents have in advancing their presidential goals administratively, especially a Bush administration that sought to wield bureaucratic power toward the end of an activist agenda. As S. Hess (2002) convincingly noted, "Even an overblown White House staff is simply too inadequate a fulcrum for mov-

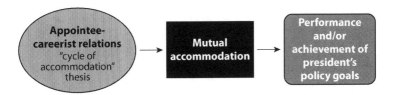

Figure 1.4. The cycle of accommodation thesis

ing the weight of the executive branch, which employs nearly 5 million people and spends over 2 trillion dollars annually" (p. 6).

Indeed, when careerists are called on to take active steps toward realizing a president's policy agenda, providing a network of communication, institutional memory, and professional or technical expertise is a matter of neither neutral nor responsive competence; it is a matter of building a more holistic notion of intellectual capital within the organization that integrates "competence" constructs with an appreciation for an organization's mission, a president's ambitions, and the political and organizational transaction costs inherent to implementation choices.

Treatments of the administrative presidency that more explicitly unpack this "black box" of appointee-careerist relations (e.g., Durant, 1992; Heclo, 1977; Pfiffner, 1987) than the aforementioned work touch on the importance of trust in these relationships (see figure 1.4). But they neither measure the construct nor test the relationship between trust and performance (or the achievement of a president's policy goals) in any systematic fashion. Moreover, some using this approach also treat this relationship as rather deterministic—coming to fruition merely through the unfolding of time—without adequate recognition of other environmental factors that moderate the impact of appointee-careerist relations on organizational outcomes.

My argument advances this scholarship with the simple—but important—contention that presidents (and, by proxy, their appointees) commonly start from the premise of distrust when they attempt to control agencies. In doing so, these control efforts communicate distrust to the career bureaucracy, further diminishing trust throughout the hierarchy. Like trust, distrust is reciprocated. Thus, the decline in trust reduces information sharing between careerists and appointees and hurts agency performance—in terms of both "objective" performance and the president's ability to see through his policy prerogatives administratively. Importantly, I theorize and model the *moderating* effects of politicization and other organizational-level factors on appointee-careerist trust that more accurately capture the contingent nature of these relationships.

Therefore, the role of trust in appointee-careerist relations becomes a critical subject for analysis in studies of presidential control of the bureaucracy. In other words, it is unlikely that information is shared that would be helpful to all participants in a low-trust environment. Information is necessary for presidents to translate their policy goals into outcomes and prevent harmful agency failure. Understanding the link from politicization to trust, trust to information sharing, and, subsequently, information sharing to performance is important to scholarship in political science, public administration, and management. Additionally, evidence is discerned of the need to reconsider if Bush's use of these strategies actually reflected a more contingency-based approach than previously thought and of the utility and importance of incorporating previously untapped research in related fields when studying the administrative presidency. It also indicates several promising areas of future testing, elaborating, and extending of the model into other presidencies, policy areas, and different time periods in any administration.

The Administrative Presidency and George W. Bush

In 2004, writing on the George W. Bush administration's management style leading into its second term, Ron Suskind described the fundamental nature of the "prenuptial agreement" into which all incoming and incumbent appointees were entering with the administration: "All policies come from the White House. Read the script with ardor and good cheer." The president's mission in exercising this decidedly top-down managerial style was to "tame the unwieldy federal bureaucracy, not empower it," resulting in an "odd collection of quiet tacticians and loyal friends" by his second term in office.

Such a philosophy stems from the naturally pragmatic consideration that "administration is policy" (Nathan, 1983) and, moreover, that "personnel is policy" (Moffit, 2001). Yet, pathologies are likely to develop when applying these tactics. Loyalty can become an axiomatic condition for the advancement of ideas and access to information (Golden, 2000; Hirschman,

1970). In those organizations where loyalty is deemed to be especially necessary, appointees may be "layered" through the management ranks to ensure complicity with the president's programmatic goals, often disabling information exchange through careerist ranks (Light, 1995, 2008). When expert information is needed, appointees may bypass careerists and depend on privileged contractors and interest groups—exacerbating accountability issues, discounting contrary advice or evidence, and biasing information. Journalistic accounts of the Bush presidency, such as Suskind's, imply that only the information that comported with the president's agenda made it up the hierarchical management chain.

However, much empirical research refutes the assumption that the strategic placement of political appointees based on loyalty to the president can best achieve "effective" policy and program results (Clinton & Lewis, 2008; Gallo & Lewis, 2012; Gilmour & Lewis, 2006b; Lewis, 2007). Other studies question how responsive career bureaucrats actually are to presidential agendas, regardless of strategy, and to which principals even presidential appointees are responsive (e.g., Eisner & Meier, 1990; Waterman, 1989). Under informational constraints to organizational members consistent with the bureaupathologies of centralization, top-down management approaches, and a heavy reliance on hierarchical chain of command, unintended consequences of policy implementation are probable without the information necessary to "backward map" and identify potential obstacles to top-down policy goals (Elmore, 1979).

Conversely, appointees whose experiences largely derive from outside the confines of a given agency can potentially leverage and combine this "political" expertise with the institutional knowledge that careerists possess to reshape policy and organizations. However, this potential can remain relatively untapped under conditions in which a lack of trust inhibits information exchange between these two respective informational resources.

Various research suggests that political appointees are not likely to stay in their positions long enough to engender trust with career employees or obtain enough institutional insight to be optimally effective in their roles (Chang, Lewis, & McCarty, 2001; Dull, Roberts, Keeney, & Choi, 2012; Gilmour & Lewis, 2006a; Lewis, 2007; Mackenzie, 1987; NAPA, 1985; Wood & Marchbanks, 2007). Presidents often choose agency executives for purposes other than their management ability (Weko, 1995). There are several political considerations that "may or may not involve policy considerations" and can interfere or even conflict with the employment of political appointees as an administrative strategy (Wilson, 1989, p. 198).

Nonetheless, there remains significant evidence that the strategic use of appointment powers is an effective technique in obtaining responsiveness from career staff (Dickinson & Rudalevige, 2004; Golden, 2000; Wood & Waterman, 1994), and that presidents' willingness to widen and strengthen its use has endured (Light, 1995, 2008; Mackenzie, 2002). Presidents can presumably achieve more responsive competence in the White House and the federal bureaucracy by negotiating for and attaining increases in the number of appointments (e.g., Moe, 1993; Nathan, 1983).

Of course, career personnel may pursue their own goals and resist a president's agenda. Careerists might exercise "voice" by leaking information detrimental to the president's goals, thereby mobilizing interest groups and members of Congress. And while there is some indication of the "two-way street" in analysis of appointee-careerist relations (Krause, 1999), the overwhelming evidence points to the significant impact that "the tools of the administrative presidency had on the behavior of . . . career civil servants" (Golden, 2000, p. 31). Careerists' responses, in this research, were found to be largely deferential to both the stimulus of strategic appointee placement and the "jigsaw puzzle" management techniques promoted by the Reagan administration, though many theoretical conceits of the administrative presidency from political science continue to focus on the exceptions to the general findings.

Joists or Jigsaws?

An extension of the politicization strategy, the jigsaw puzzle management approach relies on the assumption that career bureaucrats will act to sabotage the popular mandates for presidential action in areas that do not comport with the status quo that careerists are purportedly interested in maintaining (Sanera, 1984). Therefore, the normative prescription is set forth that appointees should subvert these perceived careerist intentions by bypassing career Senior Executive Service (SES) personnel for policy advice, using them to carry out programs "while keeping them in the dark as to the overall strategy being pursued" (Benda & Levine, 1988; Golden, 2000; Ingraham, 1995; Pfiffner, 1985): "Career staff will supply information, but they should never become involved in the formulation of agenda-related policy objectives. . . . [O]nce controversial policy goals are formulated, they should not be released in total to the career staff. Thus, the political executive and his political staff become 'jigsaw puzzle' managers. Other staff see and work on the individual pieces, but never have enough of the pieces to be able to learn the entire picture" (Sanera, 1984).[4]

As Golden (2000) argued, the default reaction of career bureaucrats is to be responsive to political leadership, even in circumstances that may be adverse to their policy and political beliefs. Organizational theory and social psychology scholarship informs us that organizational actors rarely act on their ideological beliefs when those actions are undesirable in the face of organizational incentive structures (Wilson, 1989). Given the flexibility appointees are afforded to sanction and reward career staff through both reorganizational tactics and demotion, we should expect a largely responsive civil service in the career executive ranks based on those premises. Yet, the analysis that supports the effectiveness of the jigsaw approach is almost exclusively culled from the Reagan administration. These findings should not be assumed as generalizable across administrations. While the jigsaw puzzle management approach is based on a fundamental distrust of the career bureaucracy, careerists' reactions to the techniques do vary (Golden, 2000). At the same time, exit, voice, and loyalty may be better thought of as continuums of acquiescent-to-defensive-to-prosocial behaviors (Dyne, Ang, & Botero, 2003). In other words (as anyone who has watched the classic BBC series *Yes, Minister*, will tell you), what *looks like* loyalty might *actually be* passive responsiveness that does not advance an appointee's ability to see through presidential prerogatives.

Therefore, the relations between careerist executives and appointees may have profound impacts on the political and policy successes of an administration and its legacy (Heclo, 1977; Pfiffner, 1991a). And if the Reagan administration's stance toward the federal bureaucracy was to "stop doing what you're doing" (Reagan, 1989), the Bush administration's "big government conservatism" may have driven the strategy of appointee placement as a means of leveraging administrative capacity to see through an activist agenda (Durant, Stazyk, & Resh, 2010a) in some policy areas while attempting to limit administrative capacity in others. Indeed, in chapter 5 of this book, I offer a specific instance in which the explicit intention of the Bush administration was to include career executives in critical decision-making processes across executive branch agencies.

Consequently, when positive action is desired by an administration, the relationships that develop between short-term appointees and career staff become a paramount consideration in determining the responsiveness of career staff. If the placement of political appointees is meant to combine strategically the "expert substantive knowledge" of departments with the "single-minded devotion to the president's interest" (Rudalevige, 2002, p. 11), then it is important to understand under which conditions the appointment strategy can be used to cheaply and effectively advantage the president's access to information (i.e., in order to advance presidential agendas) and how expectations of its usefulness can be shaped under each. In other words, the onus may lay on appointed leadership to build the interlacing "joists" of mutual support within their organization through both horizontal and vertical integration of information sharing. In the argument that follows, I show that appointees' optimistic trust in career agency employees during the George W. Bush administration was a necessary cornerstone to this outcome.

Few studies examining strategic appointments focus on the second term of an administration, thus deemphasizing what most prior research suggests is the exceptionality of the second term of any presidency—where a president's policy goals might be more explicit and better aligned with appointee prerogatives than during the first term. Especially in inaugural terms, appointees are chosen for reasons other than loyalty, even when loyalty is the primary objective in personnel decisions (Pfiffner, 1996; Weko, 1995). Presidents may concentrate on implementation issues and leveraging administrative power more in the second term by relying on thickened layers of politically faithful appointees when agency operations must be a consideration (Aberbach & Rockman, 1988). At the same time, significant turnover in leadership positions from the first to the second term may place substantial transaction costs on implementation of the president's prerogatives when the president and his appointees must depend on career expertise and discretion.

Appointments as Critical Institutional Links

The institutional system of the presidency includes both the formally established organizations and ephemeral structures that are affected by (and affect) the president's ability to marshal resources according to the incentives and constraints of his position in the American separation of powers. Critically centered in this system are the various departments, agencies, governmental corporations, and public-private partnerships that comprise the federal bureaucracy, especially those formally set in the executive branch but collectively known as the "administrative state." This term refers to the collection of expert agencies "tasked with important governing functions through loosely drawn statutes that empower unelected officials to undertake such important matters as preventing 'unfair competition,' granting licenses as 'the public interest, convenience or necessity' will indicate, maintaining a 'fair and orderly market,' and so forth" (Rohr, 1986, p. xi).

An institution in itself, the administrative state might be considered modern America's answer to the inertia and friction inherent to a separation-of-powers system (Rosenbloom, 1983). Despite the accumulation of executive, legislative, and judicial functions, modern public administration doctrine has increasingly focused on "elected and appointed executives to be the primary sources of energy, efficiency, and leadership in managing public agencies." This, in turn, is endogenous to a political culture that "aggrandize[s] the importance of the presidency and presidential powers" (Rosenbloom, 2010, p. 101).

It is argued that Congress and the judiciary have (with notable exceptions) gradually deferred power to the presidency, such that the current Obama presidency has inherited "more constitutional and legal power than any president in U.S. history" (Balkin, 2008). The increased complexity of policy demands has led Congress to delegate substantial discretion to agencies, which allows administrators "ample opportunity to move in a number of different directions in enforcing the law" (Rourke, 1991, p. 125). Therefore, presidents have sought to substitute their policy judgment for that of the Congress, the judiciary, and the career bureaucracy through one or more of the following means: centralizing of administrative decision making and regulatory review, politicizing the bureaucracy through appointment powers, exercising "top-down" budget and policy procedures, reorganizing agencies, altering decision premises and career paths of careerists and SES personnel, and applying the unilateral tools of the executive.

It is the politicization strategy on which the present study is focused. Yet, it is certainly not entirely separable from the centralization strategy or other administrative tools. Centralization and politicization, especially, have been used simultaneously, variously leading to complementary or contradictory outcomes (Hissam, 2007; Newland, 1983). While centralizing policy formulation in the White House may effectively allow a president to circumvent congressional and bureaucratic policy preferences, implementation success of a president's policies depends on the ability of the White House to "monitor, prod, and pressure [the bureaucracy] to carry out policy" (Durant & Resh, 2010, p. 580). Thus, politicization of bureaucratic ranks is thought to be complementary to, and an extension of, centralization. Indeed, if Nathan's (1983) axiom that "personnel is policy" is true, then the centralized selection of personnel by the White House is, in itself, an apt example of the complementary nature of these two strategies.

Modern presidents from Roosevelt through Reagan have attempted to centralize administrative decision-making by expanding the institutional capacity of the inner–White House bureaucracy and politicizing bureaucratic agencies of the executive branch (Moe, 1989). As government has taken a more aggressive role in tackling societal issues, the public has increasingly looked to the president as the generalized leader of government. Indeed, as figure 1.5 indicates, political culture and public opinion has increasingly centered on the presidency—or the executive branch more generally—as the locus of societal solutions or problems.

Mainly, the effect of increased expectations has constrained presidents' respective ability to attain their goals.[5] And with this reality comes a fear that is readily translatable into distrust of the bureaucracy. With a president's reelection and historical reputation overall dependent on the career bureaucracy, what if bureaucrats exercise their inevitable discretion to make and implement policies in ways that, intentionally or inadvertently, do not advance a president's policy agenda?

Therefore, the argument follows that a president maximizes the "structures and resources closest to him" in the pursuit of responsive competence through the resources that offer him the most flexibility in changing institutional structures: centralizing policymaking and the politicization of the bureaucracy through appointment powers (Moe, 1993). The use of both resources is thought to, in the aggregate, accomplish better organizational coherence to presidential prerogatives and increase the White House's organizational aptitude by centralizing the institutional presidency in the White House "through greater size, division of labor, specialization, hierarchic coordination, [and] formal linkages with outside organizations and constituencies" (p. 244).

The second, more flexible, and constitutionally legitimate resource is the increased focus on political appointments. Moe argues that presidents

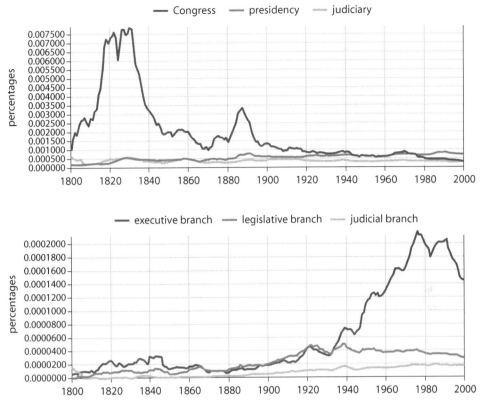

Figure 1.5. Use of the terms "presidency" and "executive branch" in comparison to competing institutions through the Corpus of American English, 1800–2000. *Source.* Google Labs—Books Ngram Viewer (available at http://ngrams.googlelabs.com/).

achieve responsiveness through the selection of appointees based on loyalty, ideological proximity to the president, or identifiable support of the president's policy prerogatives. By negotiating for and attaining increases in the number of appointments, it is believed that presidents can achieve more responsive competence in the White House and the federal bureaucracy (Durant & Resh, 2010). This act of increasing the number and managerial influence of appointees within agencies while simultaneously isolating and centralizing organizational decision-making and its deliberation to a corps of identified loyalists is commonly referred to as "politicization" (Lewis, 2008; Suleiman, 2003).[6] And it is a trend that has gradually increased over fits and pauses since the Civil Service Reform Act of 1978 (CSRA).

Politicization by Gradation: The Early Development of the Administrative Presidency

The transition from the Carter to Reagan administration enabled the Reagan presidency to emphasize the politicization strategy as a feasible means to see through its transformational policy agenda as the catalyst of regime reconstruction. While the Nixon administration is most commonly associated with the advent of the "administrative presidency" (first coined by Richard Nathan in 1976), it is important to recognize that after the downfall of the Nixon presidency and Gerald Ford's subsequently brief and quiet maintenance of an increasingly "imperiled presidency" (Cronin, 1978), Jimmy Carter entered office with a similar distrust of the permanent Washington bureaucracy. Rhetorically, Carter argued that his distrust was based more in the established structure and processes of the federal bureaucracy than in the character of career bureaucrats. Paradoxically, Carter sought to reform the civil service system in a way that (unintentionally or not) might have had more lasting effects on the establishment of the "administrative presidency" as an enduring collective strategy and jeopardizing the role of career bureaucrats than anything Nixon ever put into practice.

Carter argued that the inefficiencies of a system that was made inflexible by red tape and technical complexity necessitated a comprehensive overhaul of the federal bureaucracy. The CSRA was the product of the Carter administration's personnel management project, which sought to "modernize human resource management by streamlining the system through simplification and decentralization, to restructure for better management by replacing the Civil Service Commission, creating the Senior Executive Service (SES), and to address such issues as productivity, job quality, workforce planning, recruiting, training, development, compensation, and performance evaluation" (Brook, 2000, p. 2). While the CSRA ostensibly sought to maintain the principle of merit "while improving the management of the federal personnel system," the SES was founded under the premise of ensuring more responsiveness to the president's agenda in the executive levels of the career civil service (Huddleston & Boyer, 1996). Responsiveness was to be achieved by making career SES members subject to performance bonuses and relocation within a department, and allowing 10% of their ranks to be politically appointed.

The SES was to be primarily a corps of careerists presumably selected for executive positions based on their leadership qualifications rather than their technical expertise. A recent National Academy of Public Administration (NAPA) study argues that SES members provide a key connection between appointees and the remainder of federal employees—managing and overseeing practically every federal government activity. As indicated in the NAPA (2009) report and OPM data, most SES members have long tenures in government, and a majority also possess at least six years of experience within their current organization: "They bring to the table both subject matter expertise and a detailed knowledge of the 'moving parts' and key stakeholders that affect their agency or department."

Yet, such a glowing depiction of SES leadership may be a bit partial, just as employing such terms as "neutral" or "responsive" competence implies that the archaic notion of a politics-administration dichotomy is still very much assumed by advocates of the career bureaucracy. The most frequently cited definition of "neutral competence" is one filled with contradictions and conflicting principles: "Neutral competence is a strange amalgam of loyalty that argues back, partisanship that shifts with the changing partisans, [and] independence that depends on others" (Heclo qtd. in Seidman & Gilmour, 1986, p. 73).

As Aberbach and Rockman (1988) have cogently argued, the notion of "neutral competence" implies that SES personnel are merely empty vessels of organizational knowledge and substantive expertise who willingly provide their political leadership with the information needed to make fully informed policy decisions. Politicization proponents argue that no one can conceivably lack interests and objectives across policy domains, especially those who have such intimate and operational relationships with issue network actors. In this same vein, organization theory has long established that "people seek favorable associational conditions from their viewpoint and tend to gravitate toward organizations that share their personal values and norms and where they can work comfortably with colleagues of the same professional, educational, and social backgrounds" (Seidman, 1998). "Consequently, it follows that if all 'parties' have interests, the concept of 'neutral competence' lacks operational meaning" (Aberbach & Rockman, 1988). Instead, bureaucrats may prioritize their own goals ahead of the president's.

This logic is consistent with the general trend of thought in public administration and political science scholarship: "Whether through self-selection (Brehm & Gates, 1997) or indoctrination to an agency mission (Downs, 1967), one does not have to ascribe pernicious motives to public employees to believe that they have policy interests that may differ from those of the president" (Lowery, 2000, p. 93). Yet, there is little question that institutional memory and continuity is critical to the success of an organization and its leadership (see more about this distinction in chapter 2 on the notion of "institutional competence"). Therefore, the creation of the SES was thought to address the "conflict between the desire for greater political responsiveness and the desire for greater managerial capability and independence" (Ban, 2000, p. 58). Although it is debated whether political responsiveness to the president was indeed its intent,[7] subsequent evaluations of the creation of the SES have identified the CSRA as giving "potent partisan powers to the party that controls the presidency" (Brook, 2000, p. 8). Thus, CSRA and the SES have been called "Carter's gift to Reagan"—facilitating the Reagan administration's ability to politicize the executive branch (Michaels, 1997, p. 164).

Reagan's Reconstruction and the "Republican" Tendency toward Politicization

Much of the scholarship examining the administrative presidency, and especially the politicization strategy, focuses on the Reagan administration for several interconnected reasons. First, the Reagan administration arguably marks the most successful and systematic implementation of the politicization strategy to achieve a president's policy goals (Wood & Waterman, 1994). Second, Reagan's rhetoric represented an acute and overt distrust of the career bureaucracy (Michaels, 1997; Pfiffner, 1985, 1987, 1991b; Reagan, 1989). Third, the "Reagan Revolution" fundamentally redefined the "terms and conditions of legitimate national government" and instituted a new conservative regime that would continue for decades (Skowronek, 2008, p. 96). Finally, Reagan's politicization strategy was implemented in conjunction with an organized managerial approach that served as a model for subsequent presidencies but most markedly for the George W. Bush administration (Moynihan & Roberts, 2010; Warshaw, 2006).

According to Durant (1992), "Upon assuming the presidency, Ronald Reagan relentlessly applied an administrative strategy to the pursuit of his policy goals in a fashion and to an extent unprecedented in terms of its strategic significance, scope, and philosophical zeal." While this is a multipronged approach involving contextual strategies and unilateral tools, there were two foundational elements of Reagan's administrative presidency that relate to the focus of this book:

1. "Appointing 'movement' conservatives, intimate associates, and kindred philosophical spirits to key posts throughout the bureaucracy to direct and control its operations"
2. "Pursuing major intra-departmental reorganizations designed to symbolize and institutionalize the purposes of the president" (p. 4)

Empirical evidence indicates that Reagan appointees' fealty and ideological proximity to presidential prerogatives were, indeed, driving forces behind the placement of many appointees (Durant, 1992; Wood & Waterman, 1994) in order to formulate the bounds of careerist discretion to conform with the president's prerogatives, structure the missions of organizations according to those goals, and shift policy direction through human capital reorganizations (Durant & Resh, 2010) (i.e., "jigsaw" management, Pfiffner, 1985).

Politicization and the execution of jigsaw management during the Reagan presidency involved a micromanaged, top-down personnel selection effort to identify presidential (or "movement") loyalists to place within the 10% of SES ranks who could be politically appointed, as well as the approximately 1,300 Schedule C appointees. The screening process from the White House's Office of Presidential Personnel (OPP) was singularly occupied with the criterion of "loyalty" to the president's ideology and programmatic goals. The Reagan administration instituted a standard practice, since replicated during the George W. Bush presidency, that "the [d]irector of the Office of Presidential Personnel approves each Schedule C appointment" (Pfiffner & Patterson, 2001). The Reagan administration also increased the number of these appointees. In the first six years of the Reagan administration, both noncareer SES and Schedule C appointments increased by 13% (Ingraham, Thompson, & Eisenberg, 1995).

The Reagan administration also politicized the Office of Personnel Management (OPM), which oversees the administration of the civil service system and the SES. This was accompanied by a hierarchical, top-down governance structure in many areas of government (especially regulatory and social welfare agencies) in which the means (deregulation, devolution, and downsizing) and the ends (stopping government action) were well aligned and well supported by political staff. Additionally, the administration (through OPM) took advantage of the CSRA's provisions that allowed the reassignment of career SES members "from one job or geographic location to another" (Salamon & Abramson, 1984, pp. 46–47). With considerable expansion, each of these characteristics (e.g., centralized personnel and policy control, loyalty-focused selection patterns, increased number of lower-level appointments) reveal a good deal of "partisan learning," in which Reagan copied his co-partisan predecessor's (Nixon) staffing patterns (Walcott & Hult, 2005). At the same time, the amalgamation of the CSRA reforms, increases in lower-level appointees, centralized personnel selection, and the Reagan administration's primary goal to "stop" government action in various policy areas essentially sealed "presidential political domination of the federal government's personnel management" (Newland, 1983, p. 15).

This selection of ideological loyalists was not lost on career bureaucrats either. Seventy percent of career executives who responded to one survey "agreed that the first-term Reagan White House 'emphasized ideology in making appointments to [his/her] agency'" (Maranto, 2002, p. 91). While the strategic appointment of loyalists and jigsaw puzzle management techniques are based on an overall distrust and lack of respect for the professional character of careerists, careerists' behavioral reactions to the techniques did vary. Yet, it is argued that careerists' actions and goals were amenable to manipulation through both the stimulus of strategic appointee placement and the "jigsaw" management techniques promoted by the administration (Wood & Waterman, 1994).

The Reagan administration was able to usher in the dominance of a new political regime. Yet, the administration's antibureaucratic stance may have only served as conceptual evidence of its effort to reconstruct the institutional infrastructure of the old liberal regime. Reagan did not as much "[clear] the ground of obstructions to his alternative" as much as he was able to make rhetorical assaults that undermined the legitimacy of liberal government while simultaneously generating lasting norms within the existing institutional arrangements that favored his preferred ends (Aberbach & Rockman, 1995; Skowronek, 2008, pp. 97–98).

When George H. W. Bush entered the White House, there was a general expectation that he would continue to deliver on the Reagan regime's commitments and extend its reign. Yet, Bush entered the forty-first presidency without an ability to exactly define "what these commitments entail, how they are to be adapted to new conditions, [or] what else they can accommodate" (Skowronek, 2008, p. 101). So, Bush introduced a "kinder and gentler" conservative policy agenda that was epitomized in the Clean Air Act Amendments of 1990 and in policies for the disabled. He came from a more centrist and nonpartisan ideological background and "felt at home with a centrist, expert bureaucracy" (Maranto, 2002, p. 97). This meant that his personnel decisions were based on the premise of appointed leaders to provide "stewardship" to agencies rather than any need for radical change from the previous administration's policy agenda. Thus, Bush emphasized personal loyalty but without the ideological baggage of "movement" conservatism that was accompanied by any overt distrust of the career bureaucracy (Maranto, 2002). Bush also highly valued competence in his personnel selections, which entailed a focus on Washington insiders who were professionally oriented with the agencies in which they were placed (Maranto, 2002; Michaels, 1997).

The George H. W. Bush administration did not layer lower-level appointees throughout middle-management ranks of targeted agencies. Rather, the White House used its appointments more to reward supporters who were more centrist and perceived as competent to career government workers (Ingraham et al., 1995; Maranto, 2002; Pfiffner, 1990). This was accompanied by considerable flexibility for cabinet secretaries to select subcabinet appointments. However, the administration did allow for about half of the Schedule C positions to be set aside for "campaign workers and key supporters," which "caused some administrative problems" (Pfiffner, 1990). But, for the most part, Bush was credited by the career civil service as appointing competent and trustworthy people. Fifty percent of respondents to Robert Maranto's (1993) survey of members of the SES indicated "trusting Bush appointees" compared to "37 percent trusting first-term Reagan appointees" (Maranto, 2002, p. 99).

Indeed, the years of the George H. W. Bush administration saw only modest increases in the number of Schedule-C appointments, as opposed to the 17% increase during the first six years of the Reagan administration (Ingraham et al., 1995). Additionally, the number of noncareer SES positions actually decreased during the George H. W. Bush administration. He also came *closer* to implementing the "multiple advocacy" approach to managing the White House—in which the president creates a "basis for structured, balanced debate among policy advocates drawn from different parts of the organization (or, as necessary, from outside the organization)"—than any president since Eisenhower (George, 1972, p. 751).

Although Bush vigorously pursued his preferred policy ends through other strategic tools of the administrative presidency, he pursued a largely nonpartisan management style in respect to personnel selection and placement (Maranto, 2002). Thus, the George H. W. Bush administration serves as counterevidence to the idea that the politicization strategy is inevitably implemented by Republican presidents. But, as reflected in many reports of his son's administrative presidency, and as we see in the following discussion, politicization remains a strategy that has been implemented by subsequent presidents of both political parties.

Initial evidence of a political management strategy during the Clinton administration was lacking, partly due to systematic turnover of appointees from the Bush administration. However, as Ingraham and her associates documented, there emerged "anecdotal evidence [pointing] to a careful and somewhat punitive reexamination of the line between political and career authority" (Ingraham et al., 1995, p. 269). There was a higher rate of turnover within the career SES ranks than in the previous two presidencies, as careerists who were put into political positions by the previous administrations were scuttled to lower-level "career-reserved" positions and others left their agencies or government altogether.

As Lewis (2008) noted, a "frontal assault" technique in which career managers are pressured to leave, transferred to "organizational Siberia," or otherwise isolated from important organizational decision-making is a common political management technique (p. 33). The Clinton administration was reported to have applied this technique in its first year, targeting career SES members in the previous Bush administration who were centrally involved in the implementation of policies adverse to their preferences (Pear, 1992). And as Lewis's (2008) work also demonstrated, party changes tend to lead to increased politicization (p. 109).

Importantly, the Clinton administration's stance toward bureaucratic *action* (rather than stopping things from happening) was one of the most active of any administration since Carter. Like Carter, Clinton used an administrative strategy to advance his policies. Moreover, Clinton sought to implement an active agenda that required bureaucratic expertise in developing regulations, actively pursuing enforcement, and administratively reversing countless Reagan initiatives. Thereby, Clinton sought to leverage administrative power to see through a liberal activist agenda, one that was purportedly more in line with the preferences of the career bureaucracy staffing domestic agencies (which might have made it easier to implement).

The apparent need for the politicization strategy is attenuated if the careerists' ideological and programmatic proclivities align with the president's without the stimuli of appointed loyalists. Administrative actions that Clinton pursued included increasing consumer protection regulations, prioritizing research and development in renewable energy, aggressive enforcement of the National Labor Relations Act and OSHA regulations, and increased oversight within the financial sector, among others (Rothstein, 2002). Each of these areas empowered regulatory agencies and programs created by traditionally Democratic constituencies that had in many ways been prevented from pursuing legislatively mandated means of enforcement under Reagan and Bush. Yet, a broad characterization of the Clinton administration simply "turning the power on" for agencies to pursue regulatory enforcement lacks a nuanced understanding of the varying opportunities that presidents have to influence bureaucratic discretion and action. This also lacks an understanding of Clinton's policy agenda, which he pursued as a "New Democrat" who accommodated many of the Reagan regime's principles that industry groups favored.

It is often argued that the Clinton administration lacked a "clearly defined policy vision" (Greenstein, 2005, p. 227). In many ways, however, Clinton was captured by the liberal wing of the Democratic Party for the first two years of his presidency (a wing he later turned to in his last two years during the Lewinsky controversy and impeachment hearings). Clinton, however, moved decidedly to the center and campaigned on a centrist agenda in response to the Republicans' takeover of the House in 1994.

In many ways, this seeming shift in ideology was consonant with an identifiable centrist strategy from the start of his presidency. For example, with Clinton's election, many thought that centralized regulatory review would be abandoned (Katzen, 2009). However, Clinton issued EO 12866 in 1993 and undoubtedly retained the essential framework of EO 12291, a critical element of Reagan's centralization strategy that created the Office of Information and Regulatory Affairs (OIRA). The technical differences between Clinton's EO and its progenitor were relatively modest. According to West (2005), "EO 12866 was crafted in such a way that it pleased everyone from the Sierra Club to the US Chamber of Commerce" (p. 81), reflecting Clinton's centrist policy agenda. As Shapiro (2004) argued, it "cemented the place of regulatory impact analysis and OIRA's review authority in the regulatory process" while making rather nominal changes to how this review took place (p. 4). Clinton also introduced the use of "prompt letters" in which OIRA would preemptively advise agencies to prioritize and take specific regulatory actions through the suggestion of OIRA's own unsolicited analysis.

In respect to the executive-administrative complex, the Clinton administration's preemptive approach was especially evident in the Clinton-Gore National Performance Review (NPR). NPR seemed to represent an alternative approach to administrative reform that attempted to appeal to "ideologues of all stripes" (Skowronek, 2008, p. 109) by proposing an amalgamation of managerial philosophies that were not that different to preexisting prescriptions from the Reagan era (e.g., the Grace Commission). NPR—borrowing heavily from "management-light" appropriations of "public choice theory's critique of bureaucracy, agency theory's perspective on the contractual relations between principals and their agents, and transaction cost theory's attention to more than production costs"—simultaneously represented a departure from traditional hierarchical control models of presidential dominance while promoting the reduction or elimination of legislative controls on the bureaucracy (Lowery, 2000, p. 81). NPR sought to empower the bureaucracy through calls for increased entrepreneurship in middle management while eliminating "red tape" that presumably emanated from legislative "micromanagement" through procedural mandates (Shipan, 2005). Like Clinton's approach to regulatory oversight, NPR was intended to "facilitate the 'moderately activist government' favored by President Clinton" (Lowery, 2000, p. 87).

Rhetorically, NPR intended to reduce middle-management ranks within the career bureaucracy, eliminating approximately 300,000 career jobs (Shoop, 1994). This would allow for the locus of decision-making to rise higher up along agency hierarchies while simultaneously allowing more room for Schedule C and noncareer SES appointees to operate within that void, expanding their discretion. However, the results of reform were quite the opposite. As Kettl (2000) documented, the rhetoric that drove the federal government's downsizing during the Clinton era actually resulted in the biggest reductions coming in the support positions of frontline workers.

NPR presented yet another stage in the development of the modern administrative presidency in terms of politicization, as the reduction of federal employment had the effect of expanding the proportion of political appointees to career employees. As Light (1995) concluded, over the period of outward expansion and the development of the administrative state, there has been a forceful "thickening" of government, which was "marked by a proliferation of deputy secretaries, undersecretaries, deputy undersecretaries, assistant secretaries, deputy assistant secretaries, associate deputy assistant secretaries, and chiefs of staff" (Seidman, 1998, p. 112). Yet, accompanying the increased layering of appointees at the upper echelons of organizational structures, federal agencies remained only marginally capable of changing their "[overall] structures, budgets, personnel decisions, priorities, and decision rules" to accommodate this outward and upward expansion (Durant & Warber, 2001, p. 222).

George W. Bush, "Big Government Conservatism," and Politicization

President George W. Bush began his transition into the White House by "quietly building the most conservative administration in modern times, surpassing even Ronald Reagan in the ideological commitment of his appointments" (Milbank & Nakashima, 2001). Inheriting eight years of Clinton's administrative mark compelled the Bush administration, like Reagan and Clinton before him, to target strategically those agencies and programs that were presumably opposed to its goals (Lewis, 2008, p. 113). The Bush administration pursued a coordinated personnel selection process that eclipsed even the Reagan administration's in its zeal for comprehensive loyalty to the president (Moynihan & Roberts, 2010).

Clay Johnson, Bush's Yale classmate and chief of staff in Texas, was quickly put in charge of political appointments as assistant to the president and director of presidential personnel (and soon after named deputy director of management at OMB). The Bush transition team assembled perhaps the most sophisticated and comprehensive database of appointee applicants that had ever been created by an incoming administration (Patterson, Pfiffner, & Lewis, 2008). Johnson kept the opinion that one measure of effectiveness was the degree to which the preferences and identity of candidates for appointment were aligned with the administration's (Romano, 2007; Warshaw, 2006).

Johnson proclaimed that his very first question in interviews to potential appointees was "Do you want to work in the White House, or do you want to work in George Bush's White House?" (Romano, 2007). Bush was faced with considerable pressure to appoint campaign workers and members of supportive coalition constituencies to Schedule C appointments. While the definition of loyalty is "not a fixed target," the Bush administration, like Reagan's, saw it as a primary criterion for appointment (Moynihan & Roberts, 2010; Patterson et al., 2008, p. 20). To balance the focus on loyalty with these demands, incoming cabinet secretaries were given their choice of three candidates to subcabinet-level appointments that were preselected by the Office of Presidential Personnel (OPP) and the White House's political affairs office (Warshaw, 2006).

The orthodoxy of the Reagan regime, while resilient, was less than coherent. To win election, Bush attempted to reconstitute the conservative electoral coalition, one that simultaneously absorbed the principles of social and economic conservatism while promoting government activism to reach those objectives. Bush's effort to build a permanent conservative electoral coalition was labeled by both supporters and opponents as "big government conservatism" (Durant, Stazyk, & Resh, 2010, p. 373). As conservative pundit Fred Barnes so aptly described it, "The essence of Bush's big government conservatism is a trade-off. To gain free-market reforms and expand individual choice, he's willing to broaden programs and increase spending" (Barnes, 2003).

Undeniably, the Bush administration oversaw a larger increase in spending on domestic programs than any president since Richard Nixon. And while the War on Terror played an undeniable role in this increase, Bush also oversaw aggressive and increased roles for programs that were traditionally associated with Democratic constituencies. As Karl Rove explained in the concluding passage of his memoir, Bush "went deep into Democratic territory to show how government can use the tools of capitalism to soften its rough justice." When asked if he considered himself a "small-government conservative," however, Bush replied in the negative, qualifying himself as an "efficient government conservative" (Shirley & Devine, 2010). His conception of executive management seemed to emphasize instituting market mechanisms in the public sector through the increased use of outsourcing and "smart regulation" while relying on a decidedly hierarchical, top-down management approach within the confines of executive agencies to implement an activist agenda that expanded the scope of the federal government in several areas pleasing his diverse electoral base (Anrig, 2007; OMB, 2000; Pfiffner, 2007).

The Bush administration increased the pressure to outsource the implementation of federal services through contracting (Cooper, 2011), increasing substantially the Clintonian trend of increasing the number of contract-generated jobs. Light (2008) documented an increase of 2,466,000 contract jobs from 2002 to 2006, relative to a mere 54,000-job increase in the civil service and a 20,000-job decrease in military personnel (p. 197). Meanwhile, the capacity to properly monitor this contracted workforce was suspect, as the federal contract management workforce declined by at least 22% (Cooper, 2011, p. 9). Perhaps as a result of these trends, scandals arose that focused on the increasing use of "pinstripe patronage" schemes—such as no-bid contracts to corporate sponsors of the Bush campaign (Feeney & Kingsley, 2008; Tolchin & Tolchin, 2010), exploitation of small-business contracting set-asides (Resh & Marvel, 2012; Scherer, 2005), revolving door practices established between contractors and political appointees (D. F. Thompson, 2009), and the growth of inherently governmental responsibilities carried out by private contractors (Durant, Girth, & Johnston, 2010; Scahill, 2007).

The Bush administration also continued Clinton's EO 12866 as the guiding instrument of regulatory review procedures. There was every indication that OIRA oversight was associated with appointees who were deferential to OIRA opinions (Hissam, 2007). As John Graham noted in his memoir of his tenure as OIRA director, "In making appointments to regulatory agencies, President Bush looked for candidates who understood the need to approach federal regulation from a benefit-cost perspective" (Bush, 2010, p. 258). Graham also continued the Clinton-era practice of "prompt letters" that were used in a manner sympathetic to industry interests (Dudley, 2005).

Moreover, OIRA targeted regulatory analysis performed by careerists who were asked to do more analysis with fewer resources (leaving appointees more likely to depend on industry to provide potentially biased data), while congressional oversight of the review process was largely absent under unified Republican branches (Katzen, 2009). By 2007, Bush amended EO 12866 with EO 13422, which required each agency to name one appointee as the "regulatory officer" to vet all regulations proposed by their respective agencies and prioritize the issuance of rules that diminished environmental safeguards and additional checks on industry (Hissam, 2007; Katzen, 2009). This action infuriated many public interest and environmental groups, helped justify the policy politicization characterization, and signaled fast-track considerations for regulatory development for several identified policy areas by the incoming Obama administration (OMBWatch, 2009; Savage, 2009). He also sought to have agency "guidance documents" reviewed by OMB, documents with instructions on how to interpret existing laws and regulations (new and old).

In line with the efforts of his predecessors, Bush sought to centralize policymaking in the White House and the EOP to circumvent the collective action problems of Congress and avoid the "shirking, moral hazard, and adverse selection problems with the bureaucracy" (Durant & Resh, 2010, p. 579). And the first six years of the Bush administration were accompanied by an intermittently unified party government that enabled the president to formulate policy within the confines of the White House without a consistent challenge of congressional oversight. Consequently, the Bush administration built an internal White House bureaucracy that replicated agency policymaking capabilities within it to assure a top-down decision structure, in many ways echoing that of the Reagan White House.

The implicit assumption underlying this strategy is that such a path is necessary to achieve desired results for the presidency (Moe, 1993). Yet, the increased centralization of policymaking capacity in the EOP calls for more top-down management that disregards the potential development of the same bureaucratic pathologies that are present in any large, hierarchical organization (i.e., stovepiped responsibilities, lack of integration and communication across hybrid policy domains, lack of "on-the-ground" perspectives and anticipation of implementation problems, and so on) (Durant & Resh, 2010).

The 2006 shift to a Democratic majority in Congress was accompanied by an overt readiness to exercise its inherent oversight powers. As a mirrored dynamic during the last two years of the Obama administration may evidence, this forced President Bush to look inward to the structure he created within the White House, where he identified many of the organizational dilemmas enumerated previously. Reacting more to the grievances of his internal staff, however, Bush sat down with Clay Johnson to review the organizational chart of the White House. What he found was "a tangled mess, with lines of authority crossing and blurred. . . . It started with 'cluster' and ended with four more letters" (Bush, 2010, p. 95). Although this realization led to the replacement of Andrew Card with Josh Bolton as Bush's chief of staff, it is uncertain as to whether the president as clearly recognized another paradox of centralization: especially when a president is trying to make things happen (rather than stop them from happening), "implementation depends on precisely those actors the White House has tried to circumvent through centralization" (Durant & Resh, 2010, p. 580).

If Bush was cognizant of this paradox, the White House's solution was a familiar one: expanded outsourcing, centralized regulatory development and oversight, and the centralization of policymaking in the White House. These efforts were supplemented by a personnel management strategy in which the Bush administration politicized agencies by layering appointees who were antagonistic to the career bureaucracy in "liberal" domestic and regulatory agencies while layering patronage appointments in "friendly" ones (Hedge, 2009; Lewis, 2008; Moynihan & Roberts, 2010; Warshaw, 2006). Much like the Reagan administration, and a sign of the Republican "partisan learning" that Hult and Walcott (2004) predicted across political time, the Bush administration employed a management style "marked by secrecy, speed, and top-down control" (Pfiffner, 2007, p. 6). Even if the Bush administration's objectives were not the same as Reagan's more small-government conservatism, the management approach appeared very similar to Reagan's. Screening appointees for loyalty to the president's agenda was consistent with the Reagan White House, and one element of Reagan's management strategy included a significant increase in the number of non-career SES and Schedule C appointees.

Certainly, the personnel management advice emanating from Washington's most prominent conservative think tank was evocative of the same advice the organization proffered to the Reagan administration two decades earlier. In a document that clearly outlines the hostility the writers held toward the career civil service, Moffit and his colleagues (2001) outlined the following propositions (among others) that resonate with the jigsaw management approach of the Reagan administration:[8]

1. "The new [p]resident must make liberal use of his power of appointment, get a loyal team in place to carry out his agenda, and insist on accountability while maintaining a clear distinction between career and noncareer employees."

2. "Political appointees must be in charge of implementing the [p]resi-
dent's policies and readily available to speak for the [a]dministration."
3. "Political appointees should make key management decisions; such
decisions should not be delegated to the career bureaucracy."
4. "The new [a]dministration should provide a clear rationale for continued reductions in the size of the federal workforce and for management changes; workforce reductions should be well planned and
systematically implemented."

If this strategy were implemented by the Bush administration (and I return
to this question in chapters 3, 4, and 5, offering analysis that qualifies this
judgment), we would expect to see an increase in the number of lower-level,
at-will appointments, especially during the second term when patronage
appointments seem less likely and appointments for the purpose of aligning
agency actions to a president's preferences are more likely. And, indeed, as
reflected in table 1.1, we find that the second term of the Bush administration saw a substantial increase in these at-will presidential appointments in
cabinet departments. From 2003 to 2007, there was over a 13% increase in
the number of Schedule C and noncareer SES appointments, including the
Department of Homeland Security (DHS) (and a 12% increase from the sev-
enth year [1999] of the Clinton administration in non-DHS appointments).[9]

Proponents of politicization strategies for the Bush administration may
have been, on the surface, warranted in the aforementioned reasoning. SES
views were often incongruous to the views of Bush appointees. For instance,
while most SES personnel described themselves as independents, Democrats
still outnumbered Republicans within SES ranks by a ratio of 2:1. Additionally, the concept of a president's popular mandate to change policies in his
preferred direction was not a shared one among appointees and career SES
members: "While almost 70 percent of the George W. Bush appointees
agreed that 'if a president believes that something should be done about
an important national issue, other policy makers should defer to him,' only
43 percent of the SES career civil servants felt this way" (Aberbach & Peterson, 2005). At least anecdotally, evidence from the interviews conducted for
this book indicates that this difference is not isolated to only the Bush
administration.

However, as I noted earlier, there is substantial evidence that bureaucratic shirking of presidential authority has been rare (also see Edwards,

Table 1.1. Change in number of Schedule C/noncareer SES appointees in cabinet departments, 1998–2007

Cabinet departments	9/30/1999		9/30/2003		9/30/2007	
	Schedule C	Noncareer SES	Schedule C	Noncareer SES	Schedule C	Noncareer SES
Agriculture	204	50	164	42	142	96
Commerce	68	49	88	41	181	42
Defense	114	75	101	88	101	42
Education	126	15	131	18	138	17
Energy	98	42	72	34	79	37
Health and Human Services	55	55	54	43	72	48
Homeland Security	NA	NA	62	32	119	59
Housing and Urban Development	65	17	67	16	56	15
Interior	35	39	37	32	39	30
Justice	44	45	83	54	78	51
Labor	65	26	98	24	104	17
State	56	26	105	35	127	36
Transportation	37	27	35	24	37	31
Treasury	39	26	35	22	52	26
Veterans Affairs	14	8	12	11	2	6
Year total	1,020	500	1,144	516	1,327	553
Increase	1,520	NA	1,660	140	1,880	220
Percentage	NA		9.21%		13.25%	

Source: Office of Personnel Management's central personnel data file (available at http://www.fedscope.opm.gov/).
Note: NA = not available.

2001). As Wilson (1989) noted, "What is surprising is not that bureaucrats sometimes can defy the president but that they support his programs as much as they do" (p. 279, as quoted in Edwards, 2001). Consequently, it is important to understand under which conditions the appointment strategy can be used to cheaply and effectively advantage the president's access to information (i.e., in order to advance presidential agendas). It is also important to understand how expectations of its usefulness can be shaped under each. Nonetheless, while a contingent approach to management strategies has been recommended (Durant, 1992; Heclo, 1977), jigsaw puzzle management prescriptions appear to have a far more enduring legacy than a willingness to build joists across institutional and political sources of information within the agencies. But, does this strategy make sense if the intention of a presidential administration is to activate bureaucratic power toward their particular policy ends? Indeed, does the link between the presidency and the administrative state effectively combine competence with the president's prerogatives if there is no inherent incentive for career bureaucrats to effectively share information in an environment of distrust? Exactly what do we mean by "competence" in this context, and how is it developed? It is this black box that we begin to open in the next chapter.

2

Trust, Intellectual Capital, and the Administrative Presidency

Sanctioned acceptance of both principals and agents is also rooted in a form of trust that is beyond the purview of an explicit contracts framework.

—D. Carpenter & G. A. Krause, *Transactional Authority and Bureaucratic Politics* (2015)

A fundamental tenet of the administrative presidency has been that careerists cannot be trusted to be responsive to presidential policy agendas. And while it is typically claimed that applying the tools of the administrative presidency is motivated by distrust of careerists to carry out those agendas faithfully, no research exists on the extent to which applying the tools may foster a reciprocal distrust, or diminished trust, of political appointees among careerists themselves. This reciprocated distrust may, in turn, reduce the ability of the strategy to advance presidential policy goals in more subtle ways than the overt exit or voice of career employees (Golden, 2000).

Both exit and voice may be conceptualized better as multidimensional constructs that fall along a continuum of acquiescent-to-defensive-to-prosocial behaviors (Dyne, Ang, & Botero, 2003). Acquiescent voice, or silence, may equate to routinized and passive responsiveness. This may look like loyalty, but it can effectively limit the ability of a president and his appointees to exploit institutional competence, wield administrative power, and aggressively pursue a positive policy agenda. This is especially true when presidents and their emissaries are trying to make things happen rather than merely stop things from happening, as was the case in many areas of George W. Bush's "big government conservatism" (Barnes, 2003).

As one (self-identified liberal) career Senior Executive Service (SES) member described his relationship with Bush appointees at the Department of Education: "What's my alternative? I know who I work for. I understand that. I'm an adult. And so let's make this as pleasant as we can."[10]

Although some research identifies trust as a critical factor in appointee-careerist relations for facilitating openness and innovation (Heclo, 1977; Michaels, 1997; Pfiffner, 1991a), studies of the administrative presidency often fail to define the concept of trust or systematically examine its connection to organizational outcomes. Nor, more generally in the governance literature in public administration and public management, can one find ways in which this concept has been imported into studies of the administrative presidency. Similarly unhelpful is literature in the generic management scholarship; little exists in the way of studies on trust that examines how the discrete relationships between actors at higher levels in an organization—the common locus of appointee-careerist relations—affect the perceptions, efforts, and performance of actors at lower levels of the organization. While studies exist that examine the different effects that dyadic (i.e., person-to-person) trust between employees and immediate supervisors has on their subordinates' behavioral responses, no one has examined how dyadic trust established between higher-level employees and their supervisors affects *organizational* outcomes (Colquitt et al., 2007).[11] Thus, as yet, no one has examined how the trust (distrust) that develops between career executives and political appointees affects the perceptions and behaviors of lower-level civil servants (i.e., the subordinates of career employees) who are critical to long-term implementation success. Also uncharted are the effects of these factors on organizational outcomes—in the case of the administrative presidency, if presidential goals are advanced or not.

Bureaucracy, the "Control Paradox," and the Role of Trust in Organizations

The topic of trust within interpersonal relations has been one of central importance in the history of philosophy. Indeed, interpersonal power is fundamental to organizational relationships based on economic, social, and informational exchange. Regardless of whether the conclusions of different philosophers were that mankind should or could trust one another (e.g., Hobbes's conclusions on the nature of man versus Rousseau's), the centrality of the construct is undeniable (Hosmer, 1995). As Golembiewski and

McConkie (1975) remarked, "Perhaps there is no single variable which so thoroughly influences interpersonal and group behavior as does trust, on this point ancient and modern observers typically agree" (p. 131; as quoted in Hosmer, 1995, p. 379). Trust is seen as the essential, yet nebulous, basis of social stability (Blau, 1964; Fukuyama, 1995) and the foundation of both social and economic exchange (Hirsch, 1978).

As Weber put forth, the very purpose of structuring organizational life in a rational bureaucratic form was the unreliability of charismatic leadership or the limited effectiveness of tradition as authority (Handel, 2003b, pp. 5–6). In fact, there is perhaps no social structure from which we seek to ensure reliable behavior in social and economic exchanges between individuals than that of hierarchical organization. Organizations are intended to induce "coordinated action among individuals and groups whose preferences, information, interests, or knowledge *differ*" (March & Simon, 1993, p. 2; emphasis added).

Stated more directly, the rational bureaucratic form of organization allows for the establishment of rules and sanctions that recognize that "all people cannot be trusted at all times to live by internalized ethical rules and do their fair share" (Fukuyama, 1995, p. 25). Reaped in the process, it is assumed, is predictable, honest behavior and credible commitments among organizational actors. This reliability is then intended to lead to the efficient maximization of individual talents toward a set of collective goals or, in the case of federal agencies, to ensure that policy implementation adheres to the public interest (Finer, 1940; Friedrich, 1940).

Conversely, we can make some very basic observations about the limitations these rationalized characteristics—and by extension the logic of the administrative presidency—place on developing "norms of reciprocated cooperation and effort" under varying conditions of individual organizational commitment. As Miller (1992) contended, the "constitution" of any hierarchically organized institution is comprised of "the allocation of generally accepted responsibilities, rules of the game, and property rights that provide the long-run incentives for investment in the firm" (p. 217).

In the context of the appointee-careerist nexus, for instance, short-term political appointees may have little interest in maintaining or protecting the rank and job responsibilities (i.e., "property rights") of long-term careerists who they perceive as obstructive of short-term political gains. As one career executive from the Department of Education observed, "[Appointees] probably had been taught, to some degree, that we weren't to be trusted." With this preconception, appointees may choose, therefore, to alter property rights (i.e., redefine the careerist's position and organizational responsibilities) to accord with their goals through internal reorganization strategies that are founded on this distrust (Durant & Resh, 2010; Pfiffner, 1987). This may have the paradoxical converse effect, however, of decreasing the careerists' incentive for investing effort by exacerbating their level of distrust in appointee intentions. Additionally, as Fukuyama (1995; chapter 19) hypothesizes, there may quite often be an inverse relationship between the institution of control mechanisms in organizations and trust among organizational actors. The more mechanisms of control that an organization puts into place, the less employees may trust managers, and vice versa (p. 224).

All this is consistent with a "control paradox" proffered in economic theories of bureaucracy (Miller, 2004). In terms of agency theory, there is simply no way for a principal to "specify in advance all the behaviors that the organization will require from its employees if it is to survive and thrive" (p. 100). And many tasks within public bureaucracies are difficult to monitor and measure without significant resources allocated to oversight (c.f. Wilson's [1989] taxonomy of agency types). Additionally, "most public bureaucracies are organizations in which individual members are unlikely to produce an *individual* outcome that is measurable and rewardable" (Miller, 2004, p. 104; emphasis original). Indeed, while research on performance measurement in the public sector consistently reveals how the impact of management reforms is "frustratingly difficult to observe and analyze in a systematic way," leadership commitment remains a critical factor in "shaping [their] perceived impact" (Dull, 2009, p. 273). Yet, in order to control employees' behavior, hierarchy, monitoring mechanisms, and exceptionally detailed rules are often instituted by political principals to prevent agency loss. Politicization and centralization represent two characteristic strategies from this perspective for the executive.

In this book, I assume that the motivation toward both politicization and centralization strategies is based on an a priori consideration (by a president's administration, generally) of careerist preferences and reactions at, primarily, the locus of appointee-careerist relations—the executive level. Therefore, prescribed precepts of these strategies align with the basic fundamentals of noncooperative game theory, in which decision rules are founded in strategic goals of higher payoffs, and players make choices out of their own self-interest (Turocy & von Stengel, 2001).

However, in this context, I presume that policy preferences are to some degree ambiguous for the purposes of implementation (Rainey, 2003), and, thus, payoffs are based on having the information necessary to properly (and successfully) articulate a president's policy preferences (Kerwin, 2003). As Aberbach and Rockman (1988) pointed out, "Presidents [and, by proxy, appointees], like consumers, make choices with uncertain information. . . . When presidents [and appointees] come to office without having been exposed to career officials, but often only to horror stories told about them, they too may make decisions inconsistent with their interests" (p. 610). Ceteris paribus, being privy to the largest possible universe of alternatives (*alternative generation*), should lead to the optimal selection (*alternative testing*) (Simon, 1964, p. 7).

Entering a decision-making context on the basis of distrust should limit both alternative generation *and* testing when preferences are ill-defined and other "players" can reasonably assume that distrust and thereby reciprocate. Centralizing decision-making and cutting critical communication from the careerist ranks may serve an appointee's strategic interests in the short term. However, if this tendency renders a careerist unable to receive information about the appointee's credibility when career input is necessary for the purposes of feasible implementation, then this strategic move is, to some degree, futile (Dixit & Nalebuff, 2010, p. 224). Likewise, a career executive's ability to align subordinates' individual and program performance with these goals is compromised. Moreover, career executives' willingness to follow through on appointee directives should be motivated by the perception that doing so advances their own self-interest or those of the organization. Without adequate communication, it would be difficult for a career executive to find either incentive or the ability to make that assessment.

There is also considerable evidence in the public administration literature that cross-cutting control efforts among competing principals is typical and leads to (or exacerbates) goal ambiguity or the possibility of goal displacement (Bohte & Meier, 2000; Chun & Rainey, 2005; Merton, 1940; Rainey, 1993). In addition, even when clear goals and tightened control are possible, they may only lead to acquiescent compliance (Dyne et al., 2003). This acquiescence could be manifest in such manners as (1) silent deference to a misinformed or incompletely informed manager, (2) withholding contrary information based on fear of reprisal, (3) "expressing [only] supportive ideas based on resignation" to managerial preferences, or (4) simply agreeing for the sake of agreement (p. 1363). There is empirical substantiation that this can result in "inferior outcomes" (Miller, 2004, p. 117). Therefore, in simple prisoner's dilemma game theory terms, what looks like cooperation on the part of a careerist may be defection.

The point that imposing control mechanisms can exacerbate inferior outcomes or lead to paradoxical effects has had substantial traction since the "human relations" movement of management studies in the 1930s. Barnard (1938, 1968), for example, argued that one of the most important functions of the executive was to cultivate a culture of trust within the organization to act as a supplement to authority, encourage productivity, and promote loyalty. Yet, economic theories of the firm have been less susceptible to the human relations influence than other strands of organization theory (Handel, 2003a). In addition, even in terms of economic theories of the firm, the "contractual incompleteness" (Coase, 1937) of the principal-agent relationship necessitates some form of cooperative leeway given to the agent to see through the interests of the principal. That is, in order for a successful relationship to form between a principal and an agent, there must be a "sanctioned acceptance" of both the principal's authority and the agent's legitimacy to ensure compliance (Carpenter & Krause, 2015). As game theory illustrates, both players (in this case, the political appointee as principal and the careerist as agent) would be better off if each trusted the other to pursue their collective, long-term interests; prior research suggests that perhaps only the establishment of trust through the expectation of reiterative mutual dependence (i.e., foreshadowing the future) leads to that end (Kreps, 1990). I explicate this point further, in terms of game theory, in the following discussion.

In organizational contexts generally, prior research applicable to the administrative presidency suggests that managers might do better to avoid monitoring employees on the basis of ensuring a minimum level of effort. To be clear, this does not negate the effectiveness of monitoring and control. Rather, "it is the credible threat of tightened monitoring that encourages the employee to provide high levels of effort 'voluntarily'" (Miller, 2004, p. 112). Nonetheless, recent work in generic management studies confirms that hierarchy and centralization limit individual creativity and innovation (Hirst, Van Knippenberg, Chin-Hui, & Sacramento, 2011).

Organization theorists remain divided on the extent to which trust plays an important role in interpersonal, intraorganizational relationships. In their own volume of the seminal Russell Sage Series on Trust, the series' principal editors argue that there is not yet sufficient support for the argument that trust relations are a critical factor in inducing credible commitments among organizational actors. Rather, they argue that *"trust relations and trustworthiness are, at best, complements to organizationally induced incentives"* (Cook, Hardin, & Levi, 2005, p. 134; emphasis original). Contractual theories of organization are premised on assumptions of distrust between principals and agents rather than the possibility of establishing trust. Moreover, many studies assert the importance of employee trust in leadership but fail to link it to organizational outcomes. Rather, these studies examine theoretical antecedents of trust within organizations and model trust in (or trustworthiness of) leadership or management as the dependent variable based on the leader's communication style (c.f. Gimbel, 2001), ability to preserve organizational norms (c.f. Woolston, 2001), consistency between rhetoric and actions (c.f. Simons, 1999), and procedural justice (c.f. Flaherty & Pappas, 2000).

Recent empirical studies, however, do offer some evidence that organizational performance improves when trust exists between managers and their subordinates (Brehm & Gates, 2008; Dyer & Chu, 2003) as well as generalized trust in leadership as significantly related to attitudinal, behavioral, and performance outcomes (Cho & Ringquist, 2011; Davis et al., 2000; Dirks & Ferrin, 2002; Simons & Parks, 2002).

Nonetheless, there remains a scarcity of systematic research that examines the potentially important differences in the *referents* of trust at different levels of organizational leadership, depending on the organizational context and the levels of hierarchy in the organization—a point that I test empirically in the succeeding chapters. This can be very important as lower- and middle management carry out more routine activities such as performance management and supervision, whereas "[s]enior executives perform more strategic functions such as setting strategic direction, allocating resources to various projects and departments, communicating to employees the goals of the organization, and so on" (Dirks & Skarlicki, 2004, pp. 30–31).

Because executives may have the authority to make decisions that affect the overall performance of an organization, and lower- and middle managers may have more impact on individuals' job-related outcomes, it may be that there are "differences in the consequences of the different referents of trust in leadership" (p. 31).

Carrying these insights from the private sector further and extending them to federal agencies and appointee-careerist relations, if individual employees are less likely to generate measurable outputs (Miller, 2004; Radin, 2004), then the relational dynamics among career executives and their political superiors in setting strategic direction may have a significant impact on how middle managers assess individual performance. Executive decision-making involves setting an organization's strategic course, defining its mission, and prioritizing its objectives. Therefore, interpersonal relations at the top of the organization's hierarchy may also affect dyadic (i.e., supervisor-subordinate) relations at lower levels of the hierarchy. In other words, the legitimacy of an agency's appointed leadership is accepted by lower-level managers as a result of the legitimacy they witness those appointees grant to the career executives' expertise.

Employees who do not perceive trust established between career executives and political leadership at the top rungs of the organization may depend more heavily on trusting their immediate supervisors in order to obtain the information necessary to do their jobs well, especially when their immediate supervisors are perceived to be aligned more closely with agency culture and careerist outlooks—as opposed to the foreign influence of "in-and-outer" appointees with more short-term political goals (Heclo, 1978; Mackenzie, 1987, 2002). Repeatedly, the career middle managers who were interviewed for this book pointed to their career superiors (all executives) as their referent for trust in leadership. As one person at the Department of Agriculture put it, "I know who I answer to at the end of the day. The appointees hardly acknowledge us. But, she [the career executive] lets us know where we're safe. We follow her lead . . . not that we don't listen to them [the appointees]. But, they're just not as present in our day-to-day."[12] At the same time, executive relations may also impact lower-level employee perceptions of leadership's trustworthiness, procedural fairness, and the extent of political management techniques (e.g., jigsaw puzzle management) employed within their agencies by appointees.

Therefore, while signals of reliability in top organizational leadership may elicit increases in production by frontline employees (Cho & Ringquist, 2011), *direct* (i.e., *immediate*) *supervisors* are more likely to be referents for trust relations (Dirks & Ferrin, 2002). Brehm and Gates (2008) also found that the ability of immediate supervisors to insulate their subordinates from political interference cultivates trust. Following Brehm and Gates, career SES members may have more capacities for influence than what are generally recognized, in that they are able to minimize the effects of organizational ambiguities on subordinates. If discretion cannot be programmed or routinized completely, then the trust established at the executive level of an organization (in the comparatively large, stratified executive branch agencies that are of interest in this book) may be critically important to advancing a president's interests through implementation.

Conceptualizing Interpersonal Trust in the Appointee-Careerist Nexus

As it relates to relationships within workplace organizations, how do the aforementioned studies conceptualize trust, and how applicable are these to the study of the administrative presidency? As Russell Hardin (2006b) lamented of research on trust, generally: "It is a peculiar fact that most of the current research . . . does not use clear accounts of what is being measured. . . . Trust is therefore treated as an atheoretical term. It is, for example, all of the things that survey respondents think it is" (p. 42). To understand their arguments and application to the study of the administrative presidency, it is useful to conceptualize two types of studies assessing trust and trustworthiness in the literature. One type stresses dyadic, superior-subordinate relationships. The other stresses socially embedded notions of trust building. Both consider context, processes, and history but in different ways.

Dyadic Relationships

Conceptualizations of trust at the microlevel are divided between two camps of researchers in cognate fields related to the administrative presidency such as private management, organizational theory, social psychology, and organizational development: those who conceptualize trust as a process of either communal relationships and those who see them as exchange relationships. In practice, this split is roughly analogous to arguments made in the classic Friedrich-Finer debates in the late 1940s on the utility of "inner checks" (conscience, ethical standards, professionalism) versus "outer checks" (rules, regulations, close monitoring). More explicitly in terms of this cognate literature, theorists tend to align the concept of trust with either calculative (exchange) or noncalculative (communal) accounts of human behavior and motivation. Another camp of researchers, however, tends to avoid the distinction between the two by drawing from the work of Mayer, Davis, and Schoorman (1995). They developed a model of trust that concentrates on exchange partners' cognitive evaluations of one another's "trustworthiness" or assessments of the trustee (i.e., the person who is being trusted) as capable, benevolent, and having integrity. Feedback from outcomes in risk-taking relationships as well as the trustor's (i.e., the person who is doing the trusting) perception of signals of "trustworthiness" from the trustee inform the trustor's judgment. They determine his or her "willingness to be vulnerable to the actions of [the trustee] based on the expectation that the [trustee] will perform a particular action important to the trustor, irrespective of the ability to monitor or control [the trustee]" (p. 712).

Stated in terms of the application of the tools of the administrative presidency, for example, this involves a political appointee's (the trustor's) view of the trustworthiness of the careerists (the trustees) who must carry out the president's agenda, and vice versa. But, it is exactly these domain-specific factors that determine the trustor's assessment of trustworthiness, which leads to distinct complications in the Mayer et al. model. For example, appointees vary their judgments based on the context in which they are dealing with careerists—for example, time frames, needs and availability of particular skills to advance a president's agenda, or placid versus turbulent task or political environments in which to pursue those agendas (Mayer et al., 1995; Zand, 1972).

Applying this concept to the administrative presidency, the organizational context in which actors operate defines the manner in which a political appointee perceives a careerist's ability to perform needed tasks—"the group of skills, competencies, and characteristics that enable a party to have influence" (Mayer et al., 1995, p. 717). Indeed, the organizational theory literature indicates that one cannot separate the trustor's assessment of an organizational actor's skills and competencies from the trustor's expectations of that actor's organizational role, because it is by those skills and competencies that they are presumably fit for that position (Katz & Kahn,

1966). Moreover, through the very premise of bureaucratic rationalization, an appointee or careerist's organizational role may be tied to any other organizational actor's goals, regardless of if they share those particular goals. Alternatively, it might be a careerist's *willingness* to carry out an appointee's goals, rather than her superior competence in comparison to other employees, that determines an appointee's trust in a careerist reporting to her (if one is even available). Likewise, a careerist's willingness to respond positively to a political appointee's wishes may be a function of the goal congruence between these actors rather than perceptions of trustworthiness or established trust. And that careerist's willingness to carry out an appointee's goals, and an appointee's ability to condition a careerist's congruence to those goals, may be dependent on the level of trust that the appointee invests in the careerist (i.e., the "control paradox" reviewed earlier).

Still, prior research suggests that we cannot leave the issue there. A trustee's benevolence—that is, "the extent to which a trustee [let's say, a careerist] is believed to want to do good [for] the trustor [i.e., a political appointee], aside from an egocentric profit motive"—is noncalculative by definition (Mayer et al., 1995, p. 718). In noncalculative relationships, "one is expected to give to the other according to what the other needs as soon as those needs become apparent, rather than treat the other as a partner in an exchange relationship" (Darley, 2004, pp. 136–137). Put more colloquially, there is more to compliance than merely carrots and sticks.

Organization theorists posit that noncalculative trust is related to the idea of emotionally based "personal trust"—that is, to "the confident expectations of benign intentions by another agent" (Dunn, 1990, p. 74). Granted, political-appointee relationships are inherently dominated by the need for exchanges specific to that particular context. That is, there is a job that must be done if the president's agenda is to move forward. But aside from this "logic of consequences," a "logic of appropriateness" also frames responses by careerists (March & Olsen, 1976). Thus, for a mutually beneficial relationship between an appointee and a careerist to occur and advance a president's policy or program agenda, what the appointee is asking the careerist to do must not violate established norms, professional values, and agency procedures (Carpenter & Krause, 2015). The same logic of appropriateness applies to career managers' orders to their subordinates. Cueing a potential violation of this assumption was the opinion of one appointee from the Obama administration, for instance, who put it thusly, "They're [careerists] always giving me their interpretation of what's constitutional. We [the administration] write the laws! Let us worry about that." But, this is not an isolated opinion of one appointee. The same sense of compartmentalization of "politics" (i.e., lawmaking) versus "administration" (i.e., implementation) was ostensibly embraced throughout the interviews I conducted with GWB appointees as well:

> So I think that's important. If you're going to have a meeting and talk about a sensitive topic, you know not to invite career staff because it's going to put them in an awkward position. So I think you just have to think about who you're involving and how and at the right time. Because not only are you protecting conversations you might be having that are more political in nature, but you want to protect the career employee from hearing that also. Too many times you can portray to the career employee that they're not part of a discussion. Just don't even get into that. They know when there are political discussions that they don't even want to be a part of, and you should just make that very clear and go on down the road. I think too often you get into this gray area where you're not making that clear to the career employee and having a general understanding that, "You know what? Some things are more political within the department, and we're not going to ask you to engage in that because you shouldn't and you don't need to." [13]

As noted, a major component of appropriateness is goal congruence. To the extent that a political appointee is pursuing a policy that careerists perceive as inconsistent with legislative intent, for example, the latter may find ways to resist (overtly or covertly, actively or passively) or "defect" in terms of game theory. And to the extent that political appointees perceive this, or see real or imagined "bureaucratic drift" from legislative intent (real or contrived), their trust in careerists diminishes (Shepsle, 1992). Complicating this relationship further, of course, is research indicating that one's perception of benevolence (i.e., benevolent intentions) might go beyond congruence of policy goals. A sense of procedural duty or normative perceptions of one's role is important. Thus, perceptions of an appointee's infidelity to the letter and spirit of the Administrative Procedure Act, for example, may provoke resistance from careerists. For instance, in interviews with regulatory analysts at the Department of Agriculture's Animal and Plant Health Inspection Service (APHIS), I found that the analysts' latent acceptance of the administration's interpretation of stakeholder importance was based on their perceptions of the efforts the appointed leadership made to exhaustively identify affected populations of APHIS rulemaking (Resh, 2012). So, too, might normative perceptions of the role of presidents, the proper executive-congressional relationship, and the appropriate role of the career bureaucracy in a democratic republic also matter in careerists' perceptions of an appointee's benevolence. Illustrative is the extensive literature in public administration on public service motivation spawned by Perry and Wise's (1990) seminal work on this topic.

Similarly, subordinates' perceptions of the benevolence of mid-level career managers is likely to depend on the psychological "contract" (Simon, 1997) when they joined the public service. Specifically, friction can ensue if they perceive that anyone's orders to them are beyond their skills, not part of the original job they were hired for, or illegal or immoral. Of course, "outcomes perceived as fair [by supervisors] are not always favorable to the perceiver [i.e., to careerist subordinates]" (Adams, 2005, p. 154). Thus, careerists' perceptions of the likely outcome of presidential or legislative drift playing out in their managers' orders to them may sour trust.

Concomitantly, prior research warns us not to view the appointee-careerist relationship as trustful or distrustful based solely on specific interactions at a particular point in time. For example, perceptions of integrity as an aspect of trustworthiness must be conceptualized as a "broader concept involving issues such as (1) the consistency of the trustee's past actions, (2) belief that the trustee has a strong sense of justice, and (3) the extent to which the trustee's action and words are consistent" (Cho & Ringquist, 2011, p. 56; citing Mayer et al., 1995). The consistency aspects of this argument are consonant with the "folk theorem" of repetitive games in formal decision-making analysis, where "patterns of cooperation can be established as rational behavior when players' fear of [loss] in the future outweighs their gain from defecting today" (Turocy & von Stengel, 2001, p. 10).

Expectations matter—and not just at the individual superior-subordinate level. Public agencies—and careerists—have (or have access to) an institutional memory regarding reputations of "in-and-outer" political appointees based on their prior federal stints in federal agencies. So, too, do appointees have similar expectations about careerists generally, and in particular agencies, based on personal or shared experiences among members of issue networks in any given policy areas (Heclo, 1978).

More explicitly, careerist's expectations of appointee behavior may be premised on what I call "inverse partisan learning." Adapting Walcott and Hult's (1994) concept of "partisan learning" to appointee-careerist relations, over time and across different administrations careerists learn to anticipate the "tendency [for presidents and their appointees] to transmit organizational philosophy along party lines" (Walcott & Hult, 2005, p. 305). Because careerists may base their approximations of an appointee's trustworthiness on past relations with appointees from administrations of the same party, it becomes incumbent upon new appointees to establish their own respective capacity for credible commitment. For instance, in one interview I conducted with a career member of the SES at the Department of Education, the respondent characterized his ability to establish trust in his relations with incoming appointees as dependent upon their partisan orientation, among other factors: "Obviously it depends on the individual and the context. I've found pretty much whoever comes in there's an initial distrust . . . [or] not total confidence in the career staff. [This distrust is] probably a little stronger with Republicans because I think they tend to think, A, they have a probably less positive notion of government to begin with [and], B, they kind of think the Department of Education is probably mostly Democrats here. . . . Sometimes I think that Republicans are a little more suspicious coming in." Another SES interviewee from the Department of Education provided a similar characterization: "Any politicos can be distrustful of career people. My experience is that [that] tends to be truer of Republicans than Democrats." Both of these comments reflect the careerists' own proclivity to assume a tendency for Republican appointees to be distrustful based on their partisan affiliations within the context of a traditionally Democrat-aligned agency.

In addition, any competent presidential transition routinely offers these perspectives to incoming administrations, as do Washington think tanks with ideological moorings to particular presidents. Consider, for example, the Heritage Foundation's Mandate for Leadership series for the incoming Reagan and George W. Bush administrations, the Democratic Leadership Council's efforts for the Clinton administration, and the Center for American Progress for the Obama administration. All are credited in shaping the expectations of political appointees in these administrations and helping to inform their use of the administrative presidency to advance presidential agendas.

Again, I want to emphasize that objective conditions or reasons are not as determinative of evaluations of trustworthiness as are perceptions. For example, prior research from cognate fields shows that students of the administrative presidency should expect that "it is the perceived level of integrity that is important rather than the reasons why the perception is formed" (Mayer et al., 1995, p. 720). Thus, the use of perceptual data in studies of trust are not only commonplace but are critical to assess.

It is also important to understand from prior management research that a one-way relationship seldom exists in which it is simply the trustor's assessment of the trustee that determines the action of trust. In the political appointee-careerist nexus, for example, organizational actors are mutually dependent on one another to attain their respective goals (Heclo, 1977). If the president or his appointees had the means to accomplish their policy prerogatives without the career bureaucracy, they would certainly do so, and vice versa. Such is part of the purpose of contracting previously federal activities to private and nonprofit actors. However, despite the federal government's increasing reliance on such indirect tools of governance (Kelman, 2002), the career bureaucracy is still a predominant force and resource in how governmental power is wielded.

Of course, even if the actors involved in a dyadic relationship perceive competence and benevolence in each other for the purposes of one particular risk-taking exchange, prior research in cognate fields suggests that they may not do so if they do not "see the shadow of the future" (i.e., repeated exchanges over time) or if the risk outweighs the mutual trust involved. The "shadow of the future" may play heavily into a person's calculations. As Axelrod (1984) wrote, "When the interaction is likely to continue for a long time, and the players care enough about their future together, the conditions are ripe for the emergence and maintenance of cooperation" (p. 182).[14]

So, to what extent can career executives expect repeated interaction for sustained periods of time? Over the past three decades, increased partisanship, interbranch competition, and recognition of appointments as an effective tool of presidential power have combined to produce extensive delays in Senate confirmation of presidential appointees, increased rates of turnover in these positions, and extended lengths of vacancy. Despite the frequent public discussions over the problems of confirmation delay and vacancies, little attention has been paid to the actual consequences of these incidents.

There is certainly a valid argument to be made that confirmation delay hamstrings the president's ability to put his preferred leadership into place in federal agencies. There is a significant symbolic value of presidential power at stake based on the president's ability to quickly and successfully put his appointments in place. Moreover, the median tenure of presidential appointees stands at approximately two years (Dull & Roberts, 2009). With the frequency of turnover, accompanied by presidential inattention to a given position, congressionally induced confirmation delay, and the scarcity of qualified individuals available at a given point in time, vacancies can become common. The relative absence of political leadership over time implies weakness or inattention on the part of the president, intensifies expectancy on behalf of career employees of short-term appointee tenure, and risks a diminished capacity to meeting an agency's policy and management goals.

From a strictly human resource management perspective, filling these positions becomes an unwieldy and erratic process, accompanied by the day-to-day necessity of having competent leadership in place to ensure effectual administrative operations. As O'Connell (2008) wrote: "Vacancies, particularly if frequent and lengthy, may have detrimental consequences for the modern administrative state. They contribute to agency inaction, foster confusion among nonpolitical employees, and undermine agency legitimacy" (p. 914).

However, what is more surprising, as O'Connell (2008) observed, "is that vacancies also can have beneficial repercussions for agency performance" (p. 914). The absence of political leadership in place at agencies can have the unobvious consequence of ensuring efficient operations as agencies are led by career SES personnel who have long tenures in government and tend to have established trust within the career ranks of their respective organizations. At the same time, if an appointee enters into an organization from the basis of distrust and imposes control mechanisms out of his fear of agency loss, he or she will not be able to learn from risk-taking exchanges to develop a level of trust that will, in turn, diminish the risk of opportunism. Thus, critical to my arguments in this book, research indicates that limiting oneself to an incomplete range of alternatives means that a manager will also limit her ability to combine or access information that can lead to innovation (Nahapiet & Ghoshal, 1998; Simon, 1964). Each actor will only come to this realization through a process of learning and attempts at cooperation (Hardin, 2006a).

All this is consonant with the theory of social exchange, in which one actor "voluntarily provides a benefit to another, invoking an obligation of the other party to reciprocate by providing some benefit in return." Yet, the benefits "are rarely specified a priori or explicitly negotiated in social exchanges. Thus providing benefits is a voluntary action" (Whitener et al., 1998, p. 515; citing Blau, 1964). Therefore, it goes beyond conventional notions of calculative trust used in most agency theories of principal-agent relationships. That is, there is no assurance that there will be any reciprocation of benefits in a given exchange, nor is there a guarantee for future benefits. But, through the exchange, each actor is able to reveal their credibility to the other for the purpose of future exchanges that will presumably escalate to "higher-value benefits" to both parties (Whitener et al., 1998, p. 515; citing Blau, 1964). Thus, if establishing trust in supervisors or organizational leadership improves organizational outcomes, then it is incumbent upon hierarchical superiors to engage in this behavior to "increase the likelihood that employees will reciprocate and trust them" (Whitener et al., 1998, p. 516). This should especially be the case in government agencies in which average career employee tenure far exceeds the average tenure of presidential appointees.

Two SES interviewees in particular spoke about their efforts to establish trust in their relations with their appointed superiors, and both acknowledged that this would have been easier if the political appointees entered the relationship as, what Russell Hardin would call, "optimistic trusters."[15] In other words, the appointees' inherent distrust in the career executives (1) legitimated the careerists' "inverse partisan learning" and (2) inhibited their own ability to leverage institutional competence.

Building on this point, I separately interviewed one middle manager who directly reported to a career executive.[16] The way she characterized her boss's relationship with Bush appointees indicated that it was less than optimal: "You [appointees] come in and you behave as though you have nothing to learn from the career people. You don't need them. You don't respect or want their input. I mean, that's all trust and respect. They [Bush appointees] did not have people [careerists] at the table. My boss, who has been in [his position] for many years and is well respected, he was not involved in the conversations. It was only until much later that he became involved in the conversations." These are disturbing perceptions if widely shared and point to the importance of cultivating and nurturing trust-based appointee-careerist relations over time.

Trust as Socially Embedded

Premised on such widespread empirical conclusions in the management literature, important implications for the modeling of appointee-careerist relationships arise. Yes, one might try to account for these relationships parsimoniously through the rational choice account of trust, in which there are two central elements: (1) "incentives of the trusted to fulfill the trust" and (2) "knowledge to allow the trust[o]r to trust (or recommend distrust)" (Hardin, 1993, p. 505). However, a more empirically accurate model of trust building would incorporate more heavily the idea of context within which these dyadic relationships marinate. Such a literature does exist and will play a major role in the models I develop in chapters 4 and 5. Presently, I focus on social, political, professional, and structural aspects of this context as they relate to the administrative presidency.

Prior research from cognate fields of study applicable to the administrative presidency indicates that understanding trust in relationships between appointees and careerists is improved if Russell Hardin's (1993, 2006b) conceptualization of trust as "encapsulated interest" is incorporated in modeling exercises. In the encapsulated interest account of trust, "one's trust turns not on one's own interests but on the interests of the trusted" (Hardin, 1993, p. 505).

Much like the notion of cooperation in repeated games, in the encapsulated interest account of trust, trust must be learned like any other generalization. In Hardin's account, "trust is a three-part relation: A trusts B to do X [or in matters Y]" (1993, p. 506). That is, there are third-party effects (X or Y) on the relationship that affect the incentive A or B has to be trustworthy. These may be "reputational effects" (e.g., those I noted earlier regarding the reputations of political appointees and their prior experiences with careerists), "institutional rewards and sanctions," or intrinsic rewards. To be sure, Mayer, Davis, and Schoorman's (1995) character-based assessment model remains applicable. But, prior research indicates that researchers studying trust within the context of the administrative presidency must understand that assessments of trustworthiness are also shaped by the organizational context in which they operate, the personal and policy goals each actor seeks to further through exchange, and the exchange process itself.

No one—appointees, careerists, or researchers—can simply assume the motives or goals of the actors involved within that organizational context. Thus, prior research by students of management suggests how unwise it is likely to be for appointees to go into agencies with a priori "bureauphilic" or "bureauphobic" expectations and strategies (Durant, 1992). As Heclo (1978) put it, only contingently cooperative strategies on the part of appointees (and careerists for that matter) make sense. Thus, a top-down control strategy like jigsaw puzzle management may be self-defeating for political appointees, as might unconditionally sharing all their information with careerists. Understanding the appropriate strategy only comes about through experience, a willingness to be vulnerable to the supportive and orthogonal areas of expertise another offers, working together to interlace these forms of expertise or knowledge into a coherent structure, and finally allowing these complementary forces to settle over time—in other words, to build the necessary joists of institutional structure. Indeed, even Mayer, Davis, and Schoorman (1995) conceded this point: "[T]he trustor's perception and the interpretation of the context of the relationship will affect both the need for trust and the evaluation of trustworthiness. Changes in such factors as the political climate and the perceived volition of the trustee in the situation can cause a reevaluation of trustworthiness. A strong organizational control system could inhibit the development of trust, because a trustee's actions may be interpreted as responses to that control rather than signs of trustworthiness" (p. 727).

The literature also indicates that a key component of how careerists evaluate trust relationships is whether appointees or supervisors respect them as professionals with expertise. When I asked one interviewee to define trust in the context of her working relationships with political appointees, she recounted the attitude she would like to perceive: "I respect that you're a professional, and I respect that you have knowledge. I respect that you are intelligent, and I respect that you have something to offer because of all those things."[17] Thus, professional reputation, in this instance, can supersede (or takes the place of) the need for "personal trust" (i.e., "the confident expectations of benign intentions by another agent") (Dunn, 1990, p. 74). Protections for careerists from arbitrary, partisan political purposes (e.g., the extent of "jigsaw puzzle management techniques") should also determine the extent to which trust is developed. As the interviewee put it, "We [careerists] know who gets to call the tune, and for the most part we're happy to oblige, unless they ask us something totally unethical or illegal."[18]

Finally, organizational structure, too, is an important determinant of how, or if, trust is established, and with whom. Organizational roles, hierarchy, and specialization determine who a careerist or appointee has access to and how they perceive the importance (or incentives) attached to different individuals within the organization. As one interviewee opined: "What affects your life is who your boss is. You could either love or hate the secretary, but that may be mostly irrelevant to you."[19] One SES member I interviewed was in charge of a policy analysis shop within one agency. This was a position that, by statute, enjoyed exceptional insulation from political interference. As she put it, "They [appointees] can trust me as little as they want. Unless they want to tell each of the board members why I was fired, they *have* to listen to what I have to say and the analysis we produce out of this office" (emphasis added).

The relative "looseness" of the broader network in which an organization is a part has also been argued to be a determinant of how trust develops within an organization. Burt (1997) argued that "cohesive contacts—strongly connected to one another—are likely to have similar information and therefore provide redundant information benefits" (p. 340). Burt (1997) and Granovetter (1973) argued that "weak ties" facilitate the ability to absorb nonredundant information benefits if the network actor in question is placed at a central cog of the network schema—what Burt refers to as spanning the network's "structural hole" (p. 317).

Progress in our understanding will also be made if we consider work by Oliver Williamson (1993). He identified the importance of "social embeddedness" in understanding the exercise of individual choices in organizations generally. As Williamson put it, the calculation of self-interest by individuals "varies systematically with the institutional environment within which transactions are located" (p. 476). Thus, claimed Williamson, while the assumptions of opportunism (incentives) and bounded rationality (knowledge) are adequate for some purposes of analysis, the logic of appropriateness also holds that "social approvals and sanctions" have to be accommodated into the behavioral calculus (p. 475).

"Embeddedness attributes" include the broader cultural expectations and traditions that help regulate exchanges (Williamson, 1993, p. 476), the legalistic rules and procedures that are in place to sanction bad behavior and ensure credible commitments (pp. 477–478), "the obligation to fulfill the definition of a role that is especially important for professionals" (p. 478), or the reputational demands of the network in which one operates (p. 478). Within workplace relationships, each of these embeddedness attributes is presumably manifest through the interaction of formal and informal organization (Barnard, 1938, 1968, p. 122), a relationship at the heart of this book.

Connecting Trust to the Development of Intellectual Capital

Fundamental to my thesis is that prescriptions for withholding information from careerists, or "jigsaw-puzzle management" techniques (Sanera, 1984), ignore the fact that to advance presidential agendas successfully, appointees need information and capacity that only careerists can provide. As one interviewee said, "I'm going to share information with you (the appointee), and I'm going to solicit information from you, because I believe you have something to offer and I respect that you do."[20] Therefore, the development of an organization's intellectual capital—the "knowledge and knowing capability of a social collectivity, such as an organization, intellectual community, or professional practice"—becomes pertinent to all organizations (Nahapiet & Ghoshal, 1998, p. 245), and especially to any study of the appointee-careerist nexus.

Personnel develop organizational capacity and the organization's ability to innovate in order to implement policy and react to environmental contingencies. Importantly for assessment of jigsaw puzzlement management techniques built on an inherent distrust of careerists in public agencies, this entails the development of knowledge that only the organization as a whole can possess. It is "not reducible to what any single individual knows, or even to any simple aggregation of the various competencies and capabilities of all the various individuals" (Nelson & Winter, 1982, p. 63; as cited in Nahapiet & Ghoshal, 1998).

This conceptualization of intellectual capital is intimately tied to the idea of "institutional competence," outlined in the succeeding section. Like intellectual capital, it "acknowledges the significance of socially and contextually embedded forms of knowledge and knowing as a source of value differing from the simple aggregation of the knowledge of a set of individuals" (Nahapiet & Ghoshal, 1998, p. 246). In turn, the notion of intellectual capital expands on institutional competence by recognizing how its development increases the capacity of an organization to (re)combine or exchange knowledge to bring about change.

Janine Nahapiet and Sumantra Ghoshal—two private management scholars—offered a framework for understanding these concepts that incorporates two types of knowledge: tacit and explicit. Tacit knowledge is characterized as "knowing" that is intuitive, incommunicable, and intrinsically linked to professional skills and experiential knowledge. Explicit knowledge is knowledge that is available in the form of "facts, concepts, and frameworks that can be stored and retrieved from memory or personal records" (Nahapiet & Ghoshal, 1998). Both are further qualified as conditionally separable, depending on the level of analysis (i.e., collective or individual). Neither level is independent from the other. However, following Spender, "collective knowledge is the most secure and strategically significant kind of organizational knowledge" and therefore is the focus of intellectual capital in Nahapiet and Ghoshal's framework (Spender, 1996, p. 52).

How collective knowledge is capitalized on is dependent on the level of uncertainty to which an organization must adapt. Consonant with the premises of the administrative presidency (and especially jigsaw puzzle management), the logic of the ideal Weberian bureaucracy presupposes that all the "knowledge necessary to the strategizing and organizational design processes is available at the top of the organization and this underpins its authority base" (Spender, 1996, p. 46). But there is no reason to think that this is so. Organizational learning may be *less* likely if a top-down management approach limits employees' ability to know "what and how to invent or observe about their environment" (p. 47). This is especially true if the organization is expected to respond to a wide and complex array of environmental uncertainties (Chandler, 1962), a typical fate for public agencies. In other words, the various functional units of the organization that need to be coordinated to respond to a particular contingency may be "centralized *above* the level at which response" to that contingency should be organized (Stinchcombe, 1990, p. 100; emphasis added).

Still, not all the literature supports this position and cautions a contingency approach. Applying agency theory to the appointee-careerist nexus, prior research in political science has shown that information asymmetries can favor either the agent (career bureaucrats) or the principal (political appointees), because "principals can offset [an agent's] advantage by turning to lower cost political information" (Waterman & Gill, 2005, p. 28). Thus, while policy expertise tends to be cited as advantaging the agent with greater levels of information than principals possess, tools such as appointee layering may *help* the principals shift the focus from policy expertise to political information—"through the articulation of defined incentive structures" (p. 12). Still, this does not guarantee that a president's policy agenda will advance administratively. And the principal-agent relationship advantage for appointees dissipates when the complexity of agency missions is added to the mix; in this situation, goal conflict has the potential to increase based on the actors' tacit or explicit understanding of those goals. Therefore, the ability to see through either party's goals may necessitate the exchange or combination of the particular types of knowledge that each possesses; and centralization at the top of an organization may preclude this from happening (Chandler, 1962).

Regardless, Nahapiet and Ghoshal (1998) argued that trust "facilitates the development of intellectual capital by affecting the conditions necessary for exchange and combination to occur" (p. 254). Trust increases (1) access to knowledge exchange, (2) the anticipated value of that exchange among actors, and (3) individuals' willingness to take risks. Trust also more fully establishes how actors are connected to one another—"who you reach and how you reach them" (p. 255). Additionally, research in the generic management literature suggests that trust increases the ability to cope with complexity (Luhmann, 1979), as well as ambiguity or uncertainty (Boisot, 1995). But while mutual trust can become an asset created and leveraged through relationships, these relationships are conditioned by the policy domain, individuals' formal responsibilities, and the organization's structure, leadership, goals, and culture.

This cognate literature also has additional implications for administrative strategies to advance a president's agenda through reorganization, a common contextual tool of the administrative presidency. In contradistinction to the logic of the administrative presidency, this body of research indicates that the stability of an organization and the relational conditions therein are important to the development of intellectual capital. It takes time to build trust. And the relationship between trust and knowledge exchange is reciprocal, reflexive, and cumulative. That is, each exchange and combination of information and knowledge is a building block of trust. Moreover, if each exchange or combination is reinforced by a perception of value toward the achievement of individual and collective goals (accordant with calculative accounts of trust), then increased "anticipation of value through such exchanges" follows (Nahapiet & Ghoshal, 1998).

Time, as an element critical to trust building, becomes a critical factor in the appointee-careerist nexus, in particular. Over the course of just one presidential term, there can be as many as two appointments necessary for any one position (on average) (Dull & Roberts, 2009). Moreover, there are limitations on the time that any acting official can serve in a given position. According to the Appointee Vacancy Act of 1998, acting officials can serve in a position for no longer than 210 days from the date an office becomes vacant (with few exceptions), unless the vacancy occurs in the first two months of a new presidential administration, at which time the acting official can serve no longer than 300 days (O'Connell, 2009). This implies that extended leadership vacancies, even when staffed by acting officials, are still subject to turnover if a president is unable to put an appointment in place after the allotted time.

Still, Nahapiet and Ghoshal (1998) argued that potential exchange partners within organizations must *expect* that engagement will create value: "They must anticipate that interaction, exchange, and combination will prove worthwhile, even if they remain uncertain of what will be produced or how" (p. 249). This position is consistent with Hardin's (1993) argument, discussed earlier, that the willingness to trust will lead to superior information exchange. It is also consonant with Whitener and her colleagues' (1998) argument that the role of optimistic trustor is incumbent upon hierarchical superiors. They wrote that the exercise of trust through "sharing and delegation of control may be experienced by the subordinate as a social award: it represents a form of approval extended to the subordinate by the manager" (p. 518). Likewise, Williamson's (1993) argument that the embeddedness attributes of the organization regulate these exchanges resonates with Nahapiet and Ghoshal's (1998) other claim that "knowledge and meaning are always embedded in a social context—both created and sustained through ongoing relationships in such collectivities" (p. 253). As such, another dimension of the "control paradox," noted earlier, arises.

In sum, research in cognate fields of study suggest that students of the administrative presidency must anticipate, first, that the structural and relational embeddedness attributes of the organization condition the opportunity to "make the combination or exchange" through accessibility (Nahapiet & Ghoshal, 1998, p. 249). Second, and innately tied to the encapsulated interest that is shared between actors within the organization, they must understand that there must be some shared anticipation of the value in combining and exchanging intellectual capital—that is, appointees, career executives, and their subordinates must perceive willingness by their counterparts to exchange quality information and engage in trusting relationships. Finally, researchers studying politicization strategies must appreciate that even when the three previous conditions are satisfied to some degree, "the capability to combine information or experience must exist" (p. 250). Therefore, structural and cultural embeddedness attributes may diminish or increase the capacity of organizational actors to participate in exchange relationships.

Bringing Trust and Intellectual Capital Together (Theoretically and Empirically)

The previous section illustrates the complex relationship among three important concepts in the literature on management and organizations: trust, embeddedness, and intellectual capital. I suggested that the establishment of trust is incumbent upon hierarchical superiors to engage in trusting relationships with their subordinates. I also found that previous research neither tests this proposition nor identifies how it affects organizational outcomes. Rather, research connecting superior-subordinate trust to organizational outcomes is limited, especially in the public administration literature and in studies of the administrative presidency (Cho & Ringquist, 2011). And, that which exists does not formally test the role that trust plays in developing an organization's intellectual capital as a precondition to success.

To understand how trust is connected to organizational outcomes relevant to using administrative strategies to advance presidential agendas, we must first unpack the construct of trust as a function of managerial initiative and the embeddedness attributes of interpersonal relationships within organizational settings. Only then can we recognize how these concepts interact to produce organizational intellectual capital and test hypotheses derived from a theoretical model capturing these dynamics. Figure 2.1 provides a heuristic model that helps to explain how trust might affect the development of an organization's intellectual capital.

The model posits a reciprocal relationship between knowledge exchange and mutual dyadic trust between principals and agents. The development of intellectual capital provides a feedback effect that encourages participants to sustain or increase trust in dyadic relationships between superiors and subordinates. Trust is conceptualized as both "encapsulated interest" and character-based assessments that can be both calculative and noncalculative in nature. Like Williamson (1993), I am careful not to discount the

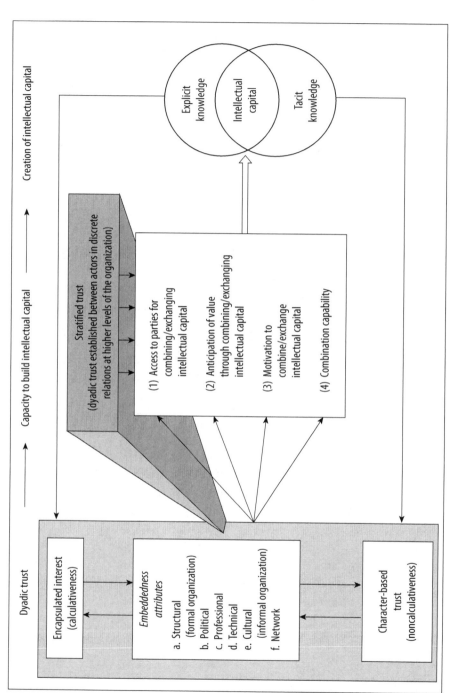

Figure 2.1. A heuristic model of trust and the creation of intellectual capital

importance of noncalculative, personal trust completely. Nonetheless, in the succeeding empirical chapters, I also follow Williamson (1993) and Hardin (1993) in arguing that it is extremely difficult to separate noncalculative trust from the calculative "encapsulated interest" account in the domain of workplace relationships, because such relationships are so innately purpose oriented.

Figure 2.1 also illustrates that the connection between trust and an organization's capacity to build intellectual capital is moderated by the institutional environment in which actors are embedded. Therefore, the conceptualization of "dyadic trust" is the gray box on the left-hand side of the heuristic. Encapsulated interests are informed by character-based assessments and, thereby, interact with different embeddedness attributes of the institutional environment to form the complete construct. This is consistent with my definition of trust as a cumulative and dynamic product of the calculations of the individuals involved, the transaction's elements, and the trading environment of the transaction. In the chapters that follow, I construct measures for several different embeddedness attributes that are common to public organizations.

Additionally, I argue that politicization (i.e., appointee layering) is, in itself, an embeddedness attribute. It is an attempt by presidents to change the structural arrangements of an organization and control careerist discretion. Yet again, I point to West's (1995) argument that the application of the politicization strategy and reorganizing the management structures of agencies "only allows the president to influence the general contours of policy implementation rather than specific actions" (p. 88; what Durant [1992] refers to as "contextual" strategies for the administrative presidency). At the same time, the relative leadership continuity or, conversely, persistence of vacancy in presidentially appointed leadership positions in agencies should also be a critical attribute of the institutional environment. Organizational demands that characterize leadership interregnums include crisis management, disruption, uncertainty, and a search for stability and stewardship (Farquhar, 1995).

The various embeddedness attributes that are defined in the chapters that follow are hypothesized to moderate the impact of trust on intellectual capital capacity in varying degrees and in differing directions in federal agencies. I propose that, namely, politicization negatively affects an organization's capacity to build intellectual capital. Specifically, I propose that lack of trust becomes even more important to knowledge exchange under conditions of politicization and when appointees are trying to make things happen rather than merely stopping things from happening in order to advance a president's policy or program agenda. Politicization diminishes the capacity to build intellectual capital because it signals distrust in careerists, especially career executives.

Therefore, in one set of relationships, politicization diminishes the ability to build trust between career executives and appointees. In a second set of relationships, the trust that is established between career executives and appointees under such conditions becomes even more important to the organization's ability to build intellectual capital. As one career executive put it, "Initially you want to know what the heck's going on with them [appointees] because they not only impact you, they impact everything that's going on—your colleagues and through you, at least, the people under you. . . . [A bad relationship with a political appointee] doesn't just hurt you, it hurts the people who work for you."[21] At the same time, regardless of if the purpose of politicization is to inhibit, exploit, or leverage administrative power, I argue that to accomplish any of these actions requires competent direction and organizational innovation in order to have a lasting, substantive, or intentional effect. As Lewis (2008) argued, no matter what the design of appointee or presidential intentions, one would assume that they want their policy goals achieved competently (p. 62).

Figure 2.1 also illustrates four additional propositions on how the complete construct of trust among political appointees, careerists, and their front-line subordinates, as regulated by its institutional environment, determines the means by which intellectual capital is developed: trust increases (1) the accessibility to organizational actors to combine and exchange information, (2) the anticipated value of these exchanges, (3) individuals' motivation to participate in these exchanges, and (4) the capacity of individuals to participate in exchange.

Each of these relationships, I argue, is also a function of the trust that is established between actors at the top level of the organization. The heuristic offered in figure 2.1 shows the dyadic trust construct projected to a separate conceptualization that I label "stratified trust."[22] Here, I propose that the relationship between trust and intellectual capital for lower-level employees is conditioned by the level of trust that is established between actors in discrete relations at higher levels of the organization.[23]

Thus, I argue that the trust that is established between career executives and political appointees affects the connection between trust and knowledge exchange *throughout* the organization. Most of the literature that unpacks the appointee-careerist nexus focuses on—*and stops at*—the relationships that develop between career executives and appointees. I posit that executives play a distinct role in setting strategic direction for the organization. How relations at this level of the organization play out between appointees and SES personnel should have a significant impact on employees' access to various exchange partners, the value they perceive in knowledge exchange, and their motivation to do so. Specifically, stratified trust (again, the trust developed between actors in discrete relations at the executive level of the hierarchy) should have a significant impact on the trust that is established between middle managers, who must articulate the product of executive relations into definitive expectations of employee performance, and their subordinates.

Building the Joists of Institutional Competence

Terry Moe (1993), who is arguably the most influential theorist of the "explicit contracts paradigm" of bureaucratic control scholarship (Carpenter & Krause, 2015, p. 7), concluded his influential work by criticizing the conventional reliance on "neutral competence" as incompatible with expectations of the modern presidency. However, we should look for empirical support for the proposition that these tactics actually strengthen the modern presidency. To this point, we have scant empirical evidence supporting, negating, or refining this proposition. Moreover, on logical grounds, there is great reason to question this premise (Gailmard & Patty, 2007). For example, the increased politicization within the executive levels of federal agencies might result in increased layers separating the secretary from career bureaucrats who possess the institutional memory and competence necessary to avoid unanticipated consequences of presidential directives (Dickinson, 2005; Light 1995). Furthermore, the scarcity of resources (especially time) should prevent presidents from utilizing both the politicization and centralization strategies at once, when it isn't perceived as necessary (Rudalevige, 2009). Moe and, ostensibly, politicization advocates of the Bush administration seem to see these strategies as simultaneous and complementary.

Although Moe (1993) assembled selective historical evidence from the perspective of past presidents, is this approach sufficient to explain the constraints and incentives that presidents have in advancing their presidential goals administratively, especially a Bush administration that sought to wield bureaucratic power toward the ends of an activist agenda?

Perhaps the greatest shortcoming of Moe's otherwise informative theoretical framework is that he does not account for how events, ideologies, prevalent intellectual tides of management philosophy, and place in political time affect when and where presidents choose to centralize and politicize (Campbell, 2005; Rudalevige, 2009). If the intentions and environmental conditions of the Bush administration differed substantially from the Reagan administration, why should the combined centralization and politicization strategies of the two administrations be so isomorphic and work in the same way? Even the time *within the same administration* may be important as to whether one strategy is emphasized over another, or whether either is employed and to what degree. Politicization advocates seem to prescribe this approach across the board (Moffit, 2001; Moffit et al., 2001; Nathan, 1983; Sanera, 1984), but it would seem that there will never be enough resources to achieve any president's preferred ends, let alone those available to the Bush administration.

As Lewis (2008) argued, pure responsive competence is not adequate, even if the intention of all conservative presidents is to limit the activity of agencies:

> We might think, for example, that conservative presidents want OSHA or the EPA to fail, thinking that a low-competence OSHA or EPA is going to regulate less. Perhaps this is true, but would presidents prefer a low-competence EPA to an EPA that shares the president's conservative ideology and is extremely competent? It is not clear. It is also worth considering whether a low-competence regulatory agency actually regulates less or whether it just regulates erratically. Equally plausible is the case that a low-competence agency produces poorly written regulations that hurt business by increasing uncertainty or by imposing unforeseen political or economic costs. (p. 62)

Yet, limiting the scope of bureaucratic activity was not necessarily the objective in many areas of the Bush administration's policy agenda. OIRA's "smart regulation" standard actively pursued the issuance of regulations that favored industry, much to the chagrin of advocates of neoclassical economics (Dudley, 2005). In several areas of domestic policy, too, the administration attempted to leverage administrative capacity to see through an expanded role of the federal government. The Department of Education, for example, was responsible for the implementation and guidance of Bush's signature domestic policy and legislative victory (No Child Left Behind [NCLB]).

NCLB is an apt illustration of the "big-government conservatism" label that the Bush administration's legacy will most undoubtedly carry. The law profoundly changed, and exponentially increased, the role of the federal government in primary and secondary education, counter to the calls emanating from the Republican Party of the 1990s to "abolish the U.S. Department of Education and roll back the expanse and power of the federal government more generally." Although NCLB "fundamentally altered the role of the Department of Education" from a passive grant-making role to a more forceful oversight role (F. M. Hess & McGuinn, 2009), the nature of cooperative federalism necessitated some acquiescence on the part of the administration to temper some of their more ambitious policy objectives. And there was a critical role for both career executives and managers to play in facilitating negotiations between state and interest group concerns and the administration's aspirations.[24]

Thus, a final reason for avoiding simple dichotomies between "neutral" and "responsive" competence involves the aims of the presidential agenda. Again, and with the notable exception of research studying unilateral tools of the administrative presidency (Howell, 2005; Moe & Howell, 1999), most research on the administrative presidency has focused on presidents trying to stop things from happening (e.g., aggressive regulation) during the first term of their administrations. But as noted with Clinton's prompt letters and Bush's "big government" conservative agenda, there are important instances where presidents are trying to make things happen. In these instances, careerists will be called on to take active steps toward realizing a president's policy agenda. Providing a network of communication, institutional memory, and professional or technical expertise is a matter of neither neutral nor responsive competence; it is a matter of providing "institutional competence."

In line with Seidman (1998), I define institutional competence as an

innate understanding of "an agency's organization and behavior [retrospec-
tively or prospectively], [whereas] one must first know its history, program
patterns, administrative processes, professional hierarchies, constituencies,
and budget structure" (p. 125), and how these characteristics can be employed toward specific actions. This, in turn, requires reciprocal information
sharing between careerists and political appointees, a reciprocity that prior
research suggests depends on trust among parties. And yet politicization
strategies are inherently predicated on distrust. What is more, the politicization strategy itself may render distrust among bureaucrats toward political appointees, thus further diminishing the exchange of information (i.e.,
the capacity for intellectual capital building necessary for success) to develop. Moreover, to merely be responsive to the entreaties of presidents and
their staff risks not only ethical dilemmas but also short-term political gains,
which may come at the expense of longer-range goals and presidential effectiveness if policies are misguided.

As such, advancing an activist agenda requires candid conversations
with presidential emissaries about the institutional capacity to advance
those goals effectively, even if other presidential goals (e.g., budget cuts) fly
in the face of developing capacity. Nor is this conversation helped by placing
additional political appointees within management ranks who do not possess the agency understanding necessary for improved competence. As I
pointed to in the introductory chapter, pathbreaking quantitative analyses
by Gilmour and Lewis (2006a, 2006b) and Lewis (2007, 2008) showed that
"agencies run by appointees or appointee-laden management teams perform
significantly worse than those administered by career managers" (Lewis,
2008, p. 62).[25] However, this work assumes that management effectiveness
is actually the aim of a president's policy agenda rather than diminishing
agency effectives (as Reagan appointees did at the EPA in the 1980s). Regardless, all this leaves us with little understanding of how appointee-
careerist relations can maximize institutional competence in order to advance presidential agendas—even if objective measures of management
effectiveness exist (Durant, 2010). Indeed, the more validly objective the
measures are, the more weakly they may convey a president's actual success
in the policy area that a respective agency is tasked.

As West (1995) argued, application of the politicization strategy and reorganizing the management structures of agencies "only allow the president
to influence the general contours of policy implementation rather than spe-

cific actions" (p. 88). Largely missing from the literature examining appointee-careerist relations is a systematic examination of the factors that enable a president's ability to leverage institutional competence in implementation (Durant & Resh, 2010). Krause and his colleagues (2006) demonstrated that a potential balance can be obtained between career and political managers that may lead to the optimal performance of an agency. Yet, their analysis focused on one particular function (macroeconomic forecasting), within one particular level of government (states), that may not be generalizable to other kinds of agencies (Lewis, 2008, p. 173). This work also does not un-peel the dynamics of the process in which these relationships lead to various outcomes.

In order to understand the effect of appointee layering on organizational effectiveness within executive branch agencies, we must delve further into the institutional dynamics of these agencies to comprehend how everyday transactions between appointees and careerists evolve into the institutional competence necessary for a president's agenda to be effectively implemented. To do so, we must identify the potential areas of conflict between individual careerists and appointees (Maranto, 2005), the varying contexts in which this nexus operates, and how these variables might interact to lead to differing outcomes.

Most of the work that has addressed the causes of conflict between career executives and political appointees concludes by attributing the cause to "the incompetence or extremism" of goal-obsessed political appointees or the intransigence or "shirking" of process-obsessed career bureaucrats. As Maranto (2005) observed, however, much of this conflict actually boils down to a battle for control over the direction of an organization or its policies. These preferences, however, are endogenous to the political and organizational environment in which bureaucrats are embedded (Gailmard & Patty, 2007)—conditions that presidents manipulate through the very application of the administrative presidency. Career bureaucrats have discrete role identities that carry inherent obligations and expertise, and can vary among principals who share or help shape their preferences. Therefore, the gradual appreciation by both appointees and careerists for their separate perspectives can lead to what Pfiffner (1987) referred to as a "cycle of accommodation" between careerists and appointees. Consequently, in order to wield organizational capacity toward a president's goals in implementation entails a process of expanding the careerists' "zone of acceptance" (Simon,

1997) and, possibly, altering the appointed leadership's goals to fit within that zone. This realpolitik notwithstanding, much of the work examining the administrative presidency, and appointee-careerist relations more specifically, points to the trust (or the lack thereof) established between appointees and careerists as inherent (inhibitive) to the process of mutual accommodation (Durant, 1992, 2000; Heclo, 1977; Michaels, 1997; Pfiffner, 1987; Rourke, 1991, 1992).

Prior research in cognate fields not typically incorporated in research on the administrative presidency (e.g., management studies, organization theory, and economic theories of the firm) might help better inform our understanding of trust. I draw from this cognate literature in the following chapters to inform and offer propositions from the model I offer here. Still, a variety of methodological issues (some of which I address empirically) limit a complete understanding of the role of trust and intellectual capital building generally and, hence, in the study of the administrative presidency.

Trust, for example, is conceptualized in varying ways (Hardin, 2006a; Mayer et al., 1995). Other authors identify the trust established between appointees and careerists as critical to success (Michaels, 1997), or they identify distrust as a critical condition of failure in implementation (Rourke, 1992). Yet, the scholarship generally does not succeed in providing an operationalizable (and, hence, commonly accepted and replicable) definition of the construct. Or, the authors simply rely on the term without attempting to define it at all, perhaps assuming a universal definition exists.

Some of the work is less explicit but nonetheless offers obstacles to improving our understanding. For instance, much of the survey analysis of political appointees and career SES personnel addressing appointee-careerist relations asks respondents whether, or the degree to which, they trust their counterparts (Maranto, 1993; Michaels, 1997). Yet, none of this work explicitly connects the level of trust established in these relationships to organizational outcomes or effectiveness.

If appointees must depend on careerists to implement presidential agendas, and build institutional competence to do so, then how appointees build trust with career employees is determined within the areas of potential conflict, such as those Maranto (2005) identified—technical credentials or professional reputation versus incompetence, insularity versus outsiders, ideological differences, and timelines of interaction. At the same time, the conditions and context under which these relationships take place may have an effect on the ability to build trust and, in turn, the effect this trust has on organizational outcomes. One might be keen to question what conditions of trust the layering of appointees throughout an agency's management levels may create.

For example, with the Bush administration's strategy of layering appointees throughout an agency's management levels based on a fundamental distrust of careerists and meant to align agency expertise toward presidential prerogatives, might such a strategy cause distrust of appointees among careerists? And might this distrust disable information exchange within organizations? Paradoxically, this is likely to inhibit the ability of an administration to effectively advantage the president's access to information or to further develop organizational capacity in order to see through his goals. Before assessing these possibilities, however, the link between trust, institutional competence, and organizational performance must be explored more fully.

The chapters that follow employ various empirical techniques to test the theoretical model in figure 2.1. In the process, I hope to explicate the multilevel nature of superior-subordinate relationships embedded within varying organizational settings and the connection between trust and the development of intellectual capital. Ultimately, I hope to reveal the relative centrality of trust to organizational relationships and how it pertains to any president's strategic use of appointments as a means to leverage bureaucratic power toward his intended ends.

3

Connecting Trust to Intellectual Capital through the Multileveled Environment of the Executive Branch

The career staff that I've worked with who are even high level, they have the institutional knowledge. They can say, "This didn't work before." Or, "This is what happened in the past when we tried that." Or, "We tried that 15 years ago under blah-blah-blah, and this is what happened. . . . Terrible idea."

—Anonymous career middle manager at the Department of Education[26]

I think one of the hardest things for new leadership is to involve career staff who have been there, who have been with the programs, with the operations, but to move ahead with your agenda. I know in the Bush administration they were very closed-door for a long time. That loosened up over time, but it was just such an obviously shortsighted technique.

—Anonymous career middle manager at the Department of Education[27]

This chapter focuses on how stratified trust (i.e., the trust established between career executives and political appointees) and politicization (i.e., the number and character of appointees in a given organization) affect an agency's capacity to develop intellectual capital. While trust can become an asset created and leveraged through relationships, these relationships are conditioned by many factors—what Oliver Williamson (1993) referred to as "embeddedness attributes." Transactions between individuals depend not only on the attributes of the individuals involved but on the attributes of the trading environment that shape the transaction. Embeddedness attributes that are particularly important to public organizations include the (1) structural characteristics of the organization (e.g., level of red tape, relative hierarchy, merit protections), (2) political attributes of the organization (e.g., the number of political appointees, the organization's chief policy domain's placement on the president's agenda, the organization's susceptibility to legislative oversight, the continuity of appointed leadership), (3) professional and technical attributes of the organization (e.g., the level of specialized expertise required of its employees), (4) organization's culture (e.g., the informal norms of the organization) (Barnard, 1938, 1968), and (5) relative "looseness" of the organization's network ties (Burt, 1997).

Of course, it takes time to build trust. And the relationship between trust and knowledge exchange is reciprocal. Each exchange or combination of information is presumably spurred by a perception of value toward the achievement of individual and collective goals (accordant with calculative accounts of trust). Increased "anticipation of value through such exchanges" should follow (Nahapiet & Ghoshal, 1998). Therefore, it is difficult to separate the endogeneity inherent to trust and intellectual capital building in dyadic relationships, especially as it concerns calculative accounts of trust. In other words, "I will trust you when I perceive that my interests are encapsulated in your own, and I gain that perception through repeated exchanges of information that advance those interests" (paraphrased in my own terms from Hardin, 2006b).

However, while it is difficult to overcome the endogeneity of trust and intellectual capital building in individual, dyadic relationships between superiors and subordinates, we can more easily distinguish the connection between perceptions of intellectual capital capacity at lower levels of an organization and trust established at higher levels in the organization if we can measure trust established at these levels separately from the individual survey responses of employees at lower levels of the organization. Therefore, in the model developed in this chapter and tested in the subsequent chapter, I do not propose a causal direction for dyadic subordinate-supervisor trust in proximal relationships, though I do expect a positive association. At the same time, I can separate the dyadic trust established among actors at higher levels of the organization as *agency-level* attributes that help define the context in which lower-level employees operate. In particular, the utilization of hierarchical linear modeling techniques provides the most appropriate method of approximating these relationships—a point that I delve into further in this chapter.

Conceptualizing Embeddedness Attributes

I refer to the trust established at executive ranks in discrete, dyadic relationships that are analytically separable from the relationships between superiors and subordinates at lower levels of the organization as "stratified trust." I expect that stratified trust will positively impact perceptions of intellectual capital capacity at lower levels of the organization as well as moderate the importance that lower-level employees attribute to the dyadic trust they have in their own direct superiors. Stratified trust therefore acts as an embeddedness attribute in the sense that this trust will condition the impact on intellectual capital capacity of organizational trust that is established at lower levels of the hierarchy. As Brehm and Gates (2008) argued: "The most conventional view of leadership in political organizations is that leadership trickles down from the top" (p. 144). Therefore, we should expect that career executives who have established trust with their political superiors are able to reduce goal ambiguity, define the bounds of employee behavior in accordance with those goals, and "receive greater latitude in their ability to allocate tasks across subordinates" (p. 145).

Employees who perceive greater latitude attributed to career executives are more likely to trust organizational decision-making processes. In turn, employees' own willingness to exchange knowledge should increase, as they should perceive greater openness to knowledge exchange and anticipate greater rewards for exhibiting a willingness to take part in such exchanges. At the same time, a variety of other embeddedness attributes that regulate organizational hierarchy will condition the relationship between dyadic trust and intellectual capital capacity.

The aforementioned reasoning has several empirical implications for the appointee-careerist nexus in federal agencies. First, and as already emphasized, I expect there to be a direct and positive relationship between the trust in one's superior (dyadic trust) and an organization's ability to develop intellectual capital. This trust is a function of a middle manager's immediate supervisor being prone to (1) giving employees access to important information, (2) permitting employees to exchange information in a way that leads to innovation, and (3) helping employees to align actions to organizational goals.

Second, there will be a direct and positive relationship between the generalized trust one has in his or her organization's leadership and the organization's ability to develop intellectual capital. As Dirks and Skarlicki (2004) posited, "Insofar as individuals make distinctions between their immediate supervisor and the senior executive team, there may be differences in the consequences of the different referents of trust" (p. 31). Dirks and Ferrin (2002) found that dyadic trust is more strongly associated with job-level performance, while trust in leadership (TIL) is more strongly associated with organizational-level variables (Dirks & Skarlicki, 2004).

Third, stratified trust will have a direct and positive relationship on lower-level employees' perceptions of the organization's capacity to build intellectual capital. Career executives' trust in political appointees should be an initial and critical building block for the development of intellectual capital. One of career executives' main responsibilities is to articulate the goals and strategies of their political superiors to their organization's workforce to ensure its implementation. If trust is not established at the very highest strata of the organization, we should expect that lower-level employees' perceptions of intellectual capital capacity will be diminished.

Fourth, stratified trust will impact the relationship between dyadic trust and organizational capacity to build intellectual capital, as well as the relationship between TIL and intellectual capital capacity. Under conditions in which trust is established at the highest strata of an organization's hierarchy, we should expect that this trust (stratified trust) will ease lower-level employees' reliance on their immediate supervisors to assess the capacity to build intellectual capital within the organization. One of the critical roles of executives is to establish organizational culture (Barnard, 1938, 1968). For example, executives who establish trust at the highest ranks of the organization promote a culture of trust by "[placing] a high value on trust and then [communicating] that value to all employees in a way that conveys sincerity and commitment" (Rogers, 1995, p. 15).

Fifth, politicization will serve to inhibit the development of intellectual capital. Politicization of bureaucratic ranks is thought to be complementary to, and an extension of, centralization (e.g., Moe, 1993). The premise of the strategy is to increase the number and managerial influence of appointees within agencies. This is done in order to isolate and centralize organizational decision-making and its deliberation to a corps of identified loyalists.

Sixth, politicization will moderate the relationship between dyadic trust and intellectual capital capacity. It will also moderate the relationship between TIL and intellectual capital capacity.

I also expect that agency ideology will influence intellectual capital capacity as well as the relationship between trust (both dyadic and TIL) and intellectual capital capacity. For example, appointees should be more willing to share information with careerists when they work in agencies with missions that are aligned with their political views. Additionally, relative to the encapsulated interest account of trust, conservative appointees should be more prone to see their interests aligned with the interests of careerists in agencies associated with conservative policy interests. As I outlined in chapter 2, this logic would be consistent with the distrust of careerist intentions that has been the catalyst for politicization strategies over time by various presidencies.

Finally, in examining the outcome of intellectual capital capacity, I am assuming a critical importance of organizational continuity to information exchange. The relative leadership continuity or, conversely, persistence of vacancy in presidentially appointed leadership positions in agencies should also be a critical attribute of the institutional environment. The information that political appointees share with the career bureaucracy is often a reflection of the level of accommodation careerists have gained with political appointees, with mutual trust playing a major role in developing that relationship. If trust is partially a function of the interactions in which trusting actors anticipate quality in both the frequency of exchange and the perceived quality of past interactions, then we can reasonably assume that leadership continuity will enhance that connection, thereby increasing the relative premium one places in TIL and dyadic trust in one's immediate supervisor in order to assess his or her organization's capacity to build intellectual capital.

Over the past three decades, increased partisanship, interbranch competition, and recognition of appointments as an effective tool of presidential power have combined to produce extensive delays in Senate confirmation of presidential appointees, increased rates of turnover in these positions, and extended lengths of vacancy (Dull & Roberts, 2009; Durant & Resh, 2010; Mackenzie, 2002). This may be especially true during the second term of an administration, where the median Senate confirmation time is approximately three months and "the longest-delayed 10 percent of second-term appointees take more than seven months to be confirmed" (Dull, Roberts, Keeney, & Choi, 2012, p. 904). Assuming that a president will choose to allocate his resources (including political capital) strategically (Dickinson, 2005; Rudalevige, 2009), these generalized outcomes in second-term confirmation delay do not include the time that an administration takes to recruit, vet, and nominate a respective appointee.

Therefore, increased congressional scrutiny of the administrative presidency and a president's diminished political capital by the second term deemphasize what most prior research suggests is the exceptionality of the second term of any presidency—where a president's policy goals might be more explicit and better aligned with appointee prerogatives than during the first term (Aberbach & Rockman, 1991). Historically, tools of the "administrative presidency" have been more aggressively used during second terms (Aberbach & Rockman, 2005), when (1) the president's "lame duck" status vis-à-vis Congress is more likely (Rockman, 2012), (2) first-term legislative victories are left to more robust administrative discretion (Luton, 2009), and (3) presidents are more likely to seek to enhance their legacies (Durant & Warber, 2001).

Unlike in inaugural terms, when appointees are chosen for reasons other than loyalty (even when loyalty is the primary objective in personnel decisions [Pfiffner, 1996; Weko, 1995]), presidents may concentrate on implementation issues and leveraging administrative power more in the second term by relying on thickened layers of politically faithful appointees when agency operations must be a consideration (Aberbach & Rockman, 1988). At the same time, significant turnover in leadership positions from the first to the second term may place substantial transaction costs on implementation of the president's prerogatives when the president and his appointees must depend on career expertise and discretion.

Even if the pressures of ensuring successful Senate confirmation were absent, the median tenure of presidential appointees stands at approximately two years. Therefore, over the course of just one presidential term, there can be as many as two appointments necessary for one position (on average) (Dull et al., 2012). There are also limitations on the time that any acting official can serve in a given position. And although there are perfunctory methods available to skirt the Appointee Vacancy Act limits on acting officials' tenure in leadership positions by consistently renewing their temporary appointments (O'Connell, 2009), extended leadership vacancies are still theoretically and practically subject to turnover if a president is unable to put an appointment in place after the allotted time.

From a strictly human resource management perspective, filling these positions becomes an unwieldy and erratic process accompanied by the day-to-day necessity of having competent leadership in place to ensure effectual administrative operations (Lewis, 2008). As Anne Joseph O'Connell (2009) wrote: "Vacancies, particularly if frequent and lengthy, may have detrimental consequences for the modern administrative state. They contribute to agency inaction, foster confusion among nonpolitical employees, and undermine agency legitimacy" (p. 914). Consequently, when action is desired by an administration, the relationships that develop between short-term appointees and career staff should become a paramount consideration in determining the responsiveness of career staff and the subsequent ability of organizations to innovate or change course administratively toward a president's preferred policy direction in a lasting and productive manner.

Organizational trust—the general willingness of both subordinates and superiors to be vulnerable to one another's discretionary actions (without the ability to fully monitor those actions)—may become vital to the ability to advance individual interests within and through the organization (Mishra, 1996). Appointed leadership vacancies, an administration's applied methods of "controlling" bureaucratic output, and the ideological orientation of an agency vis-à-vis the administration may all have moderating impacts on how Pfiffner's (1996) "cycle of accommodation" thesis might be realized. Pfiffner's notion—that, over time, a deeper trust develops between appointees and civil servants—implies that the cycle of accommodation surely should be most felt during a second administration when implementation concerns become increasingly salient.

Moreover, despite the frequent public discussions over the problems of confirmation delay and vacancies, little attention has been paid to the actual consequences of these incidents. There is certainly a valid argument to be made that confirmation delay hamstrings the president's ability to put his preferred leadership into place in federal agencies. There is a significant symbolic value of presidential power at stake based on the president's ability to quickly and successfully put his appointments in place. The frequency of turnover—accompanied by presidential inattention to a given position, congressionally induced confirmation delay, and the scarcity of qualified individuals available at a given point in time—might make vacancies common. The relative absence of political leadership over time implies weakness or inattention on the part of the president and may intensify expectancy on behalf of career employees of short-term appointee tenure while risking a diminished capacity to meeting an agency's policy and management goals.

In the present analysis, I focus on middle managers' perceptions and how they are affected by politicization strategies of the administrative presidency. The idea of the model in this chapter is to illuminate the relationship between trust and intellectual capital capacity as trust develops throughout an organization's hierarchical structure, as well as the accompanying impact of politicization (i.e., appointee layering) on the development of intellectual capital capacity within agencies.

Data and Measures

The unit of analysis for the descriptive investigation in this chapter and the inferential model in the following chapter is federal career middle managers. To test my hypotheses, I use data from the 2006 and 2008 waves of the Federal Human Capital Survey (FHCS), a biennial survey of full-time, permanent federal government employees conducted by the Office of Personnel Management (OPM).[28] I limit the analysis sample for this study to respondents who self-report as managers directly below Senior Executive Service (SES) personnel. As I explained in chapter 2, little to no research exists that measures the effect that executive relations have on the organization as a whole (Dirks & Skarlicki, 2004). As this specifically relates to the administrative presidency, I am interested in how relational dynamics among career executives and their political superiors in setting strategic direction may have a significant impact on the dyadic supervisor-subordinate relations at those lower levels of the hierarchy and on employee perceptions of the trustworthiness of the organization's generalized leadership. This sample of middle managers yielded 38,427 respondents from 36 agencies across the two waves of the survey, a sample that is representative of the full-time, permanent workforce classified at these levels.

The FHCS has been used frequently in public management scholarship (e.g., Fernandez & Moldogaziev, 2011; Fernandez et al. 2015; S.-Y. Lee & Whitford, 2008; Pitts, 2009; Rubin, 2007). It is useful in this study because it allows me to identify respondents who work as middle managers in their agencies. I focus on these employees because my concern is with how politicization and appointee-careerist relations at the highest organizational strata affect policy implementation. A generally accepted premise in studies of organizations is that senior executives perform more strategic functions, such as setting strategic direction, allocating resources, and communicating organizational goals (Dirks & Skarlicki, 2004, p. 31). Middle managers, meanwhile, may have more of an impact on individuals' job-related outcomes. Collectively, they make decisions that directly affect the overall performance of the organization.

Middle managers are also interesting because they work at a critical organizational juncture in the federal hierarchy. Much of what we know about superior-subordinate trust comes from the generic management literature, which tends to focus on either dyadic trust between subordinates and their immediate supervisors or the trust frontline employees have in the generalized leadership of the organization (Dirks & Skarlicki, 2004). As I noted in chapter 2, what seems to be missing from these accounts is how trust established in dyadic relationships that are hierarchically separate and above the relationships established at lower levels of a hierarchy affect the perceptions and performance of lower-level employees. Brehm and Gates (2008) found that trust established between subordinates and middle managers is important, indeed crucial, to street-level performance. Whereas they focus on relatively flat hierarchies, I argue that trust is much the same two-way street for career senior executives, since they must establish trust with subordinate managers as well as with their appointed superiors for optimal knowledge exchange.

Intellectual Capital Capacity

The dependent variable in my model is "intellectual capital capacity," which I occasionally simplify to "intellectual capital" for brevity. Grounded in the literature I reviewed in chapter 2, I measure intellectual capital by asking respondents to identify their level of agreement or satisfaction with eight statements about intellectual capital capacity in their agency. These are: (1) the adequacy of information possession, (2) the adequacy of workforce knowledge possession, (3) the clarity of goals and their prioritization, (4) top-down knowledge accessibility, (5) horizontal knowledge accessibility, (6) the extent of horizontal knowledge exchange, (7) the extent of bottom-up knowledge exchange, and (8) the extent of top-down knowledge exchange. Response options to the first six dimensions include Likert-scale levels of agreement (e.g., 1 = strongly disagree; 5 = strongly agree), while response options to the latter two dimensions include Likert-scale levels of satisfaction (1 = very dissatisfied; 5 = very satisfied).

I sum responses to all eight questions, creating a scale that ranges from 8 (low) to 40 (high). The scale has a high degree of reliability (Cronbach's

Table 3.1. Descriptive statistics

Variable	Obs	Mean	SD	Min	Max
Intellectual capital capacity	38,427	31.26	5.37	8.00	40.00
Dyadic trust	38,427	15.76	3.58	4.00	20.00
Trust in leadership	38,427	13.95	4.18	4.00	20.00
Procedural justice	38,427	28.11	6.30	8.00	40.00
Empowerment	38,427	27.06	5.20	7.00	35.00
Apolitical management	38,427	11.92	2.70	3.00	15.00
Stratified trust	74	16.23	0.47	14.00	18.60
Politicization	74	0.36	0.32	0.00	1.99
Vacancy index	74	5.45	3.89	0	9.55
Agency ideology	74	0.59	1.09	−1.58	2.40
Commission/ind.	74	0.27	0.45	0	1
Budget	74	15.97	2.9	6.91	20.71
Sex (male)	38,427	0.37	0.27	0.00	1.00
Hispanic	38,427	0.02	0.11	0.00	1.00
Age	38,427	3.64	0.78	1.00	5.00
Tenure in government	38,427	5.41	0.75	2.00	7.00
Tenure in organization	38,427	5.24	0.52	2.00	6.00
GS 1–6	38,427	0.00	0.06	0.00	1.00
GS 7–12	38,427	0.16	0.36	0.00	1.00
GS 13–15	38,427	0.73	0.44	0.00	1.00
SES pay	38,427	0.00	0.06	0.00	1.00
SLST pay	38,427	0.00	0.07	0.00	1.00
Other pay	38,427	0.07	0.25	0.00	1.00
HQ	38,418	0.34	0.47	0.00	1.00
Race: White	38,427	0.42	0.49	0.00	1.00
Race: African American	38,427	0.07	0.25	0.00	1.00
Race: Native Hawaiian	38,427	0.08	0.27	0.00	1.00
Race: American Indian	38,427	0.02	0.13	0.00	1.00
Race: More than two races	38,427	0.39	0.49	0.00	1.00
Leaving-1	38,427	0.10	0.29	0.00	1.00
Leaving-2	38,427	0.13	0.33	0.00	1.00
Leaving-3	38,427	0.03	0.18	0.00	1.00
Leaving-4	38,427	0.03	0.17	0.00	1.00
Retiring-1	38,427	0.06	0.24	0.00	1.00
Retiring-2	38,427	0.16	0.37	0.00	1.00
Retiring-3	38,427	0.17	0.38	0.00	1.00

Note: GS = general schedule; SES = Senior Executive Service; SLST = senior-level scientific or professional; HQ = headquarters.

alpha = 0.88), and all items load onto a single factor when analyzed using principal components factor analysis (see table 3.2). On average, managers perceive moderate levels of intellectual capital capacity—the mean value is 31.26 with a standard deviation of 5.37 and responses at both extremes of the scale. Table 3.1 provides all descriptive statistics.

Table 3.2 presents the results of the principal components factor analysis

Table 3.2. Factor analysis: Intellectual capital capacity

Dimension	Survey indicator
Information possession	I have enough information to do my job well.
Workforce knowledge	The workforce has the job-relevant knowledge and skills necessary to accomplish organizational goals.
Goal/priority clarity	I know how my work relates to the agency's goals and priorities.
Top-down knowledge accessibility	Managers communicate the goals and priorities of the organization.
Horizontal knowledge accessibility	Managers promote communication among different work units.
Horizontal knowledge exchange	Employees in my work unit share job knowledge with one another.
Bottom-up knowledge exchange	How satisfied are you with your involvement in decisions that affect your work?
Top-down knowledge exchange	How satisfied are you with the information you receive from management on what's going on in your organization?

Cronbach's alpha test, scale reliability coefficient = 0.88
Eigenvalue(Factor 1) = 4.28
Proportion = 0.54

for the dependent variable (intellectual capital capacity) and summed scales of some of the independent variables in this chapter's analytic model. Table 3.2 reveals a Cronbach's alpha of 0.88, indicating high reliability and that the eigenvalue of the first factor occupies 54% of the total factor space. Additionally, the eigenvalue of the first factor is noticeably greater than any others in the analysis, which suggests a single central construct. Despite the factor analysis' apparent confirmation, I further test the reliability of the construct by examining whether the Cronbach alpha would increase with the omission of any particular item. It appears that the exclusion of any given item actually decreases the overall reliability of the measurement.[29]

Let us now reexamine the individual dimensions to understand their conformity to, and the validity of, the intellectual capital capacity construct. The first dimension represents "information possession" (i.e., the adequacy of the information respondents receive in order to perform). This dimension represents the perceived results of explicit knowledge exchanges in which the respondent is engaged. If the respondent does not possess adequate knowledge or information to do his or her job well, then it is likely that the respondent does not have access to potential exchanges or the ability to engage in exchange, or does not perceive value in engaging in potential exchanges.

As I argued in chapter 2, referencing Nahapiet and Ghoshal (1998), trust is a decisive factor in how an employee perceives the value in engaging in knowledge exchange. Perceptions of value, in turn, lead to the development of intellectual capital within the organization. The second dimension of my measure for intellectual capital capacity, "workforce knowledge," speaks directly to the value of knowledge exchange. If the respondent perceives the workforce in his or her organization as having job-relevant knowledge, then he or she will more likely see the value in such exchanges.

The third dimension of the intellectual capital capacity construct is "goal/priority clarity." Chun and Rainey (2005) defined "goal ambiguity" as "the extent to which an organizational goal or set of goals allows leeway for interpretation, when the organizational goal represents the desired future state of the organization" (p. 531). Two of the dimensions of goal ambiguity used by Chun and Rainey are prone to be determined by internal management processes: (1) leeway in how goals are evaluated as performance is assessed and (2) ambiguity in setting priorities among multiple goals. For instance, organizational leaders may have a direct role in the creation of performance metrics, identifying relative goal attainment (Moynihan, 2008; Radin, 2006). Likewise, employees may be incentivized to trade off secondary or tertiary goals for the goals that leadership deems to be a priority (Hall, 2007). If respondents lack the knowledge of how their individual work relates to the agency's goals, then it is likely that lack of access or opportunity to knowledge exchange was determined by the vertical relationships that preceded this perception.

There is considerable evidence in the public administration literature that control efforts by political principals will lead to goal ambiguity and the possibility of goal displacement (Bohte & Meier, 2000; Chun & Rainey, 2005; Merton, 1940; Rainey, 1993). This dimension is particularly important in determining intellectual capital capacity at the middle-management level. While middle management may carry out more routine activities such as performance management and supervision, their collective performance will be based on the senior executives' ability to set strategic direction, know where and how to allocate resources properly across programs, and communicate to employees the goals of the organization (Dirks & Skarlicki, 2004, pp. 30–31).

Therefore, the "goal clarity" dimension is intimately related to the fourth dimension of the intellectual capital capacity construct—"top-down knowledge accessibility," or the degree to which "managers communicate the goals and priorities of the organization." As I alluded to in chapter 2, Krause (2009) also argued that failing to account for organizational complexity "overstates the capacity of presidential control over executive administration" (p. 74). One central element of organizational complexity in Krause's framework is "vertical coordination," or "the extent to which hierarchical relationships between actors across different levels of an organization share both a common goal and a method for achieving that goal" (p. 75). Vertical coordination is also innately connected to horizontal coordination, here captured as the item "horizontal knowledge accessibility." As Krause (2009) posited, if "the principal issues vague directives allowing for varied interpretations across agents, then horizontal coordination problems will ensue" (p. 78).

Finally, the "accessibility" items primarily measure the access and opportunity that respondents perceive for knowledge exchange within their organization. The last three items in the scale measure the degree to which these exchanges actually take place. This is, as I define in chapter 2 (and labeled in the heuristic of figure 2.1), the "motivation to combine/exchange intellectual capital."

Dyadic Trust

Also grounded in the literature summarized in chapter 2, a primary independent variable of interest is the respondent's trust in his or her immediate supervisor. As in the literature, I refer to this variable as "dyadic trust" because the items direct respondents to the trust they hold in their immediate supervisor as opposed to the general leadership of the organization. To advance a psychometric assessment of trust in studies of career bureaucrats and the administrative presidency, generally it would be best to use existing validated measures that fit with the definition as found in the theoretical literature. Unfortunately, a downside of employing secondary data such as the FHCS requires an approximate measure using what is on hand. Fortunately, the measures here closely follow established scales such as that of Mayer, Davis, and Schoorman (1995), and others. Moreover, FHCS offers the ability to construct two separate instruments that are applicable to the two referents of trust that are of most interest in this study (i.e., dyadic trust and generalized TIL).

I follow Brehm and Gates (2008) in identifying a direct question on the amount of trust one has in his or her immediate supervisor while also capturing ideas of trust that are consonant with character-based conceptualizations of the construct (Mayer, Davis, & Schoorman, 1995). I measure this variable by asking respondents to indicate their level of agreement or satisfaction with four statements related to supervisor trust: (1) the trust or confidence one has in his or her immediate supervisor, (2) the perceived competence of his or her immediate supervisor, (3) the perceived honesty and accessibility of one's immediate supervisor, and (4) the perceived benevolence of one's immediate supervisor. Response options to the first three indicators include Likert-scale levels of agreement (e.g., 1 = strongly disagree; 5 = strongly agree), while response options to the fourth item include levels of satisfaction (e.g., 1 = very dissatisfied; 5 = very satisfied). By adding the responses to all four questions, a scale that ranges from 4 (low) to 20 (high) is created. As indicated in table 3.3, the measure is highly reliable, the factor loadings are strong, and the eigenvalue of the first factor is noticeably greater than any others in the analysis. On average, managers perceive moderately high levels of dyadic trust—the mean value is 15.76 with a standard deviation of 3.58 and responses at both extremes of the scale.

Controlling for other variables identified in the literature reviewed in

Table 3.3. Factor analysis: Dyadic trust in immediate supervisor

Dimension	Survey indicator
Trust/confidence	I have trust and confidence in my supervisor.
Competence	Overall, how good a job do you feel is being done by your immediate supervisor?
Benevolence	My supervisor supports my need to balance work and other life issues.
Honesty and accessibility	Discussions with my supervisor about my performance are worthwhile.

Cronbach's alpha test, scale reliability coefficient = 0.88
Eigenvalue(Factor 1) = 3.0
Proportion = 0.75

chapters 1 and 2, and consonant with the theory that trust leads to the facilitation of information exchange, I generate the following hypothesis:

H_1: Dyadic trust will be directly and positively associated with perceptions of intellectual capital capacity.

Generalized Trust in Leadership

While dyadic trust measures the impact of trust on perceptions of intellectual capital capacity in discrete hierarchical relationships at the individual level, I construct a measure of the generalized trust that respondents hold for the comprehensive leadership of the organization (see table 3.4).

I rely on four indicators that capture dimensions of trust that are highlighted by both Mayer, Davis, and Schoorman's (1995) character-based account of trust and Hardin's (2006a) "encapsulated interest" conceptualization of trust (both of which are explained in more detail in chapter 2). For the former, respondents are asked to rate their level of agreement with statements that reflect positively on the integrity and credibility of their organization's respective leadership. The indicators measure the following: (1) the level of respect for the organization's leadership, (2) the leadership's ability to generate motivation and commitment, and (3) the honesty and integrity of the organization's leaders. In respect to the latter (i.e., encapsulated interest), respondents are asked to rate their level of satisfaction with the policies and practices of the organization's leadership.

Table 3.4. Factor analysis: Generalized trust in leadership (TIL)

Dimension	Survey indicator
Integrity (1)	I have a high level of respect for my organization's senior leaders.
Credible commitment	In my organization, leaders generate high levels of motivation and commitment in the workforce.
Integrity (2)	My organization's leaders maintain high standards of honesty and integrity.
Encapsulated interest	How satisfied are you with the policies and practices of your senior leaders?

Cronbach's alpha test, scale reliability coefficient = 0.90
Eigenvalue(Factor 1) = 3.05
Total Factor Space = 4
Proportion = 1.07

I argue that this is consistent with Hardin's theory that trust is a function of the extent to which a trustor's interests are encapsulated by the actions and interests of the trustee. Recall from chapter 2 that in Hardin's account, trust is a purposive, goal-oriented action in which one trusts because that trustor sees the trustee's goals tied to his own. Satisfaction with the policies and practices of one's organizational leaders implies that one's self-interest is fulfilled through the actions of the leadership.

On average, analysis indicates that managers have rather modest levels of trust in organizational leadership—the mean value of the generalized TIL index for the sample of 38,427 middle managers is 13.95, indicating that respondents score a little above the middle value (3) across the four indicators. The minimum sample value for the index is 4 and the maximum is 20; the standard deviation is 4.18. I expect that the generalized trust one has in his or her organization's leadership will be positively associated with their perceptions of the organization's capacity to develop intellectual capital.

H_2: Trust in the generalized leadership of an organization will have a direct and positive association with perceptions of intellectual capital capacity.

I include several other individual-level control variables in the model. These controls include procedural justice (i.e., the extent to which employees perceive organizational procedures as just and fair [Rubin, 2007]), apolitical management (i.e., the relative lack of partisan management techniques that are based on arbitrary decision-making criteria, illegal applications of personnel management, and coercion [Bowman & West, 2009]), and employee empowerment (i.e., the notion that processes are in place that enable an employee to exercise discretion [Fernandez & Moldogaziev, 2011]).[30] A dummy variable for headquarters (HQ = 1; Field = 0) was used to capture whether the respondent had physical proximity to senior leadership in the organization. Dummy variables are also included to control for other individual-level factors such as age, race, ethnicity, sex, government tenure, and agency tenure.

Stratified Trust

Because the FHCS identifies each respondent's supervisory authority, a differentiation can be made between the trust that middle managers (the unit of analysis for the present study) have in their supervisors (career executives) and the trust that senior executives have in their supervisors (appointees). Stratified trust was measured by averaging SES members' responses for each agency on the dyadic trust index, which captures the general trust established among career executives and their immediate supervisors (political appointees). This produces 72 agency-level observations (36 agencies from the 2006 and 2008 waves of the survey). Because stratified trust is based on the same index as dyadic trust, the theoretical range of values is from 4 to 20, but taking the agency-level average narrows the range to a minimum of 14 and maximum of 18.6 in this data set. The mean value is 16.23, indicating a moderately high level of stratified trust across agencies, and the standard deviation is 0.467.

I expect that the trust career executives have in political appointees will positively impact an organization's intellectual capital capacity and that the importance of TIL and dyadic trust to perceptions of intellectual capital capacity will diminish under conditions of increased stratified trust. That is, respondents will rely less heavily on trust as a method to access avenues of knowledge exchange and methods of combining knowledge within the organization if a culture of trust is established at the executive ranks of the organization.

H_3: Stratified trust will have a positive impact on respondents' perceptions of intellectual capital capacity at lower levels in an organization's hierarchy.

H_4: Stratified trust will diminish the importance of dyadic trust on middle manager's perceptions of intellectual capital capacity.

H_5: Stratified trust will diminish the importance of TIL on middle managers' perceptions of intellectual capital capacity.

Politicization

I rely on CPDF records to measure agency politicization. I divide the total number of Schedule C appointees (SchedC), noncareer SES (NCSES) personnel, and limited-term appointments to SES (LtdSES) by the total number of career SES personnel in each agency to obtain this measure (*politicization*$_{jt}$ = [SchedC$_{jt}$ + NCSES$_{jt}$ + LtdSES$_{jt}$]/CareerSES$_j$). This measure is adapted from Dull and Roberts's (2009) measure of "appointee penetration" and Lewis's (2008) measure as an indicator of agency politicization.

Much of the literature on politicization strategies of the administrative presidency indicates that presidents rely on the flexibility of Schedule C appointments to "layer" loyalists at the top hierarchical echelons of agencies in order to direct policy toward presidential prerogatives (Light, 1995). The data on politicization for this study include 36 agencies over two years, which produces 72 agency-level observations. The values range from 0 to 1.99, with a mean of 0.361 and standard deviation of 0.315. I expect that as politicization increases, it is less likely that respondents will perceive an organization to have the capacity necessary for building intellectual capital. I also expect that TIL and dyadic trust will become more important to the perception of intellectual capital capacity under conditions of increased politicization.

H_6: Politicization will have a negative impact on respondents' perceptions of intellectual capital capacity.

H_7: Politicization will increase the importance of dyadic trust on respondents' perceptions of intellectual capital capacity.

H_8: Politicization will increase the importance of TIL on respondents' perceptions of intellectual capital capacity.

Appointee Vacancies

To capture the construct of "persistent appointee leadership vacancies," I utilize a detailed longitudinal roster of presidential appointment positions and the officials who occupy them. This data collection examines appointments to full-time, civilian PAS positions in all departments, single-headed independent agencies, and Executive Office of the President organizations. Data were collected through formal requests to the Office of Personnel Management and Government Accountability Office and were verified against (or further collected through) published sources, including the Senate nominations database available through Thomas.gov, Congressional Research Service reports, contemporary news coverage accessed by LexisNexis, and online resources such as the GAO's Federal Vacancies Act Resources website (available at http://www.gao.gov/legal/fedvac/vacancies.html). Several PAS positions are omitted, including US attorney and US marshal positions in the Department of Justice; Foreign Service and diplomatic positions in the Department of State; officer corps positions in the civilian uniformed services of the National Oceanic and Atmospheric Administration in the Department of Commerce, and of the Public Health Service in the Department of Health and Human Services; and the officer corps in the military services. Following Dull and Roberts (2009), this data collection effort did not count service in an "acting" position because the study is focused on whether a position is filled with someone who holds the full authority of the office (p. 436, fn. 10).

To account for the differential power of a given appointee position, I derive a vacancy index that standardizes vacancies both within and across organizations using the following equation. D = department or agency (i = 1 ... 32), vd = total vacancy days by appointees (A) at level (k), and ES = executive schedule pay. The equation normalizes the distribution of vacancies across agencies by simultaneously using executive schedule level as a proxy to account for the differential of power of appointees and the number of appointees at each level.

$$Vacancy\ Index_{D_i} = \ln\left(\sum\left(\frac{vd_{A_k}}{A_k} * \ln(ES)\right)\right)$$

In examining the outcome of intellectual capital capacity, I am assuming a critical importance of organizational continuity to information exchange and that "collective knowledge is the most secure and strategically significant kind of organizational knowledge" (Spender, 1996, p. 52). The relative leadership continuity or, conversely, persistence of vacancy in presidentially appointed leadership positions in agencies should also be a critical attribute of the institutional environment. Organizational demands that characterize leadership interregnums include crisis management, disruption, uncertainty, and a search for stability and stewardship (Farquhar, 1995). The information that political appointees share with the career bureaucracy is often a reflection of the level of accommodation careerists have gained with political appointees, with mutual trust playing a major role in developing that relationship. If trust is partially a function of the interactions in which trusting actors anticipate quality in both the frequency of exchange and the perceived quality of past interactions, then we can reasonably assume that leadership continuity will enhance that connection, thereby diminishing the relative premium one places in TIL in order to assess his or her organization's capacity to build intellectual capital. Therefore, as with other agency-level embeddedness attributes, I allow this individual-level coefficient's effect to vary randomly based on the appointee vacancy index.

H_9: Appointee vacancies have a negative association (on average) on respondents' perceptions of intellectual capital capacity.

H_{10}: Appointee vacancies increase the importance of TIL on a middle manager's perceptions of intellectual capital capacity.

H_{11}: Appointee vacancies increase the importance of dyadic trust on a middle manager's perceptions of intellectual capital capacity.

Agency Ideology

I include a measure of "agency ideology" that reflects estimates obtained by Clinton and Lewis's (2008) survey of experts regarding federal agency political ideology. Negative values indicate that agencies are generally considered more liberal, while positive values indicate more conservative agencies. Some of the more conservative agencies include: the Department of Homeland Security (0.88), the Small Business Administration (1.17), the Army (2.04), and the Department of Defense (2.21). Some of the more liberal agencies include: the Department of Education (–1.22), the Department of Health and Human Services (–1.32), and the Equal Employment and Opportunity Commission (–1.58).

Lewis (2008) argued that the "extent to which presidents and their appointees confront career personnel in management positions that do not share their ideology or priorities" is a major factor in influencing the "number and penetration of appointees" in specific agencies (p. 30). Accordingly, proponents of politicization and jigsaw management techniques assume that career bureaucrats who disagree with a president's ideology or policy preferences will act to sabotage presidential action (Sanera, 1984).

Given the consensus that the George W. Bush administration was "the most conservative administration in modern times, surpassing even Ronald Reagan in the ideological commitment of his appointments" (Milbank & Nakashima, 2001), I expect that jigsaw management techniques were less prominent in conservative agencies. As demonstrated in other scholarship, a modified, targeted, or contingent type of jigsaw management technique may be implemented, rather than a broadcloth approach. Consequently, the premium of trust and the referents of that trust should vary by the relative ideological congruence between the agency and the administration. Therefore, I expect that respondents in an agency with a more conservative ideological orientation will more likely perceive their organization as having the capacity to build intellectual capital, because these workers will more likely perceive access, opportunity, and ability to exchange pertinent knowledge within the organization.

H_{12}: An agency's conservatism will be positively associated with respondents' perceptions of intellectual capital capacity.

H_{13}: An agency's conservatism will increase the importance of dyadic trust on respondents' perceptions of intellectual capital capacity.

H_{14}: An agency's conservatism will increase the importance of dyadic trust on respondents' perceptions of intellectual capital capacity.

Other Embeddedness Traits

I include level-2 controls for embeddedness attributes that might influence a respondent's perception of intellectual capital capacity. For example, independent agencies or commissions are more likely to be insulated from presidential interference than executive branch agencies (Moe, 1989). Therefore, a dummy variable is included to account for independent agencies. In addition, a control for "agency size" is constructed by taking the natural log of the agency's total annual budget ($size_{jt} = \ln[budget_{jt}]$).

Descriptive Results and Discussion

In this study, the responses of interest involve a respondent's perception of his or her organization's capacity to build intellectual capital. Table 3.5 provides summary statistics of perceptions of intellectual capital capacity by both the individual-level independent variables of interest (dyadic trust and TIL) and by three relative embeddedness traits of agencies—stratified trust, agency ideology, and politicization. Though there are other key embeddedness traits that are examined in the inferential models of the subsequent chapters (e.g., appointee vacancies), I use these three as explicit examples in this descriptive exercise because their measures are more practically accessible for the purpose of this discussion. The first three columns indicate when dyadic trust is held at low (<P25), moderate (P25↔P75), and high (>P75) levels for each of the level-2 embeddedness traits of theoretical interest held at the same percentiles across rows, respectively. The latter three columns indicates the same for TIL.

There are a few preliminary observations that we can make based on the information in table 3.5. First, we see that perceptions of intellectual capital capacity increase as both dyadic trust and TIL move from low to high values across the sample population, when holding the various embeddedness traits at varying levels. High levels of dyadic trust and TIL are associated with a higher capacity for intellectual capital. This relationship is strength-

Table 3.5. Mean values of intellectual capital capacity under varying individual-level and agency-level conditions

	Dyadic trust (low)	Dyadic trust (moderate)	Dyadic trust (high)	Trust in leadership (low)	Trust in leadership (moderate)	Trust in leadership (high)
Stratified trust						
Low	24.51	31.41	35.07	24.41	30.72	35.72
Moderate	25.17	31.13	35.75	24.80	30.89	36.08
High	25.84	31.32	35.93	24.97	30.96	36.10
Politicization						
Low	25.85	31.41	36.06	25.04	30.92	36.09
Moderate	24.85	30.95	35.41	24.96	30.97	35.99
High	24.92	30.83	35.48	24.21	30.72	35.95
Ideology						
Liberal	24.34	30.94	35.24	24.48	30.96	35.98
Moderate	25.23	31.02	35.61	24.73	30.89	36.01
Conservative	25.48	31.19	35.93	24.86	30.81	36.05

ened, however incrementally, as stratified trust moves from low to higher levels. For example, when dyadic trust is held at a low level, a 1.3-unit increase is associated with a shift from low (<P25) to high (>P75) levels of stratified trust. Conversely, the positive relationships between intellectual capital capacity and either dyadic trust or TIL are usually weakened as the level of politicization increases from low to high values. Finally, we find an unexpected relationship between intellectual capital capacity and agency ideology. Although most of the relationships are strengthened as agency conservatism increases, table 3.5 indicates that conservatism actually weakens the impact of TIL on intellectual capital capacity when TIL is held at a moderate level (although the decrease is small).

While table 3.5 shows bivariate relationships between the dependent variable and the independent variables of interest, table 3.6 shows the direct, bivariate relationships between the individual-level independent variables of interest and the agency-level independent variables of interest. Here, the table indicates that stratified trust has a direct, positive relationship with both dyadic trust and TIL.

As stratified trust increases, there is an associated increase in both dyadic trust and TIL. Table 3.6 also indicates that there is a direct and negative relationship between politicization and the two individual-level variables of interest. As politicization increases from low to high levels, there is an associated decrease in dyadic trust. However, a more severe decrease in TIL is associated with an increase in politicization from low to moderate levels.

Table 3.6. Mean values of dyadic trust and trust in leadership under varying agency-level embeddedness attributes

	Dyadic trust	Trust in leadership
Stratified trust		
Low	15.56	13.30
Moderate	15.69	13.92
High	16.02	14.47
Politicization		
Low	15.97	14.59
Moderate	15.70	13.52
High	15.60	13.70
Ideology		
Liberal	15.78	13.52
Moderate	15.71	13.82
Conservative	15.84	14.32

TIL nominally increases as politicization increases from moderate to high levels. Finally, there is no evident relationship, based on table 3.6, between dyadic trust and ideology, though, the importance of TIL does increase with an agency's relative conservatism.

Figures 3.1 and 3.2 provide a more precise idea of how these conceptualizations of trust are conditioned by different embeddedness attributes through two-dimensional kernel density plots. Following Brehm and Gates's (2008) bivariate method of analysis, "this method produces a nonparametric estimate of the joint probability density, and can be thought of as a smoothed histogram" (p. 123). This method allows us to look at the full range of variance for each trust measure when constrained by the embeddedness attributes of theoretical interest in this study.

Figure 3.1 shows the two-dimensional kernel density plots for dyadic trust as a function of three embeddedness attributes: politicization, agency ideology, and stratified trust. Theoretically, one expects the distribution peaks to be close to the bottom corner for the first graph. In other words, one expects that there are higher levels of trust in agencies with lower levels of politicization.

The first graph confirms this expectation: the graph is populated by peaks toward the "high dyadic trust–low politicization" corner. In the second and third graphs of figure 3.1, dyadic trust is plotted as a function of agency ideology and stratified trust, respectively. Here, I expect that each graph will be populated by peaks toward the right corner, indicating that as agency ideology becomes more conservative, dyadic trust will increase. Additionally, as stratified trust increases, one expects that dyadic trust will

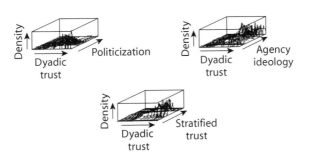

Figure 3.1. Two-dimensional kernel density plots: Dyadic trust versus embeddedness traits

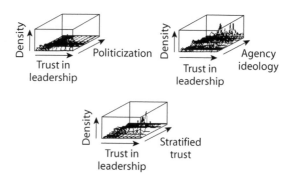

Figure 3.2. Two-dimensional kernel density plots: Trust in leadership versus embeddedness traits

increase (i.e., trust at levels discretely separate from the executive relationships captured by the stratified trust measurement). Indeed, as the two graphs indicate, the distribution of dyadic trust peaks toward the right corners for both.

Figure 3.2 demonstrates the relationships between TIL and the three embeddedness attributes of interest. Here, the first graph implies an expected relationship between politicization and TIL. There are higher levels of TIL in agencies with lower levels of politicization: the graph is populated by peaks toward the "high TIL–low politicization" corner. At the same time, while TIL trends to the right corner in relationship to agency ideology, I find no discernible relationships in the other two graphs in figure 3.2.

As the aforementioned descriptive analysis indicates, we should expect that embeddedness traits will influence the relationship between an individual's trust in the organization's general leadership and his or her perception of intellectual capital capacity. The purpose of the multilevel model in the analysis that follows in chapter 4 is to identify the influence that these embeddedness traits have not only on the agency's capacity for intellectual capital building but also the influence they have on the relationship between an individual's trust in his or her direct superior (dyadic trust) and his or her perception of intellectual capital capacity as well.

4

Appointee-Careerist Relations and Trickle-Down Trust

The Joist-Building Power of Stratified Trust on the Federal Workforce

[Appointees] not only impact you, they impact everything that's going on—your colleagues and through you, at least, the people under you. [A bad relationship with a political appointee] doesn't just hurt you; it hurts the people who work for you.

—Anonymous senior career executive

To measure the impact of trust on intellectual capital capacity across a variety of organizational contexts, an intercept-and-slopes-as-outcomes model that conceptualizes the indirect influence of organizational embeddedness traits on individual perceptions and behaviors is used. An intercept-and-slopes-as-outcomes model enables us to see how the relationship between conceptions of trust and intellectual capital on an individual level is moderated by key contextual-level variables, while intellectual capital as an organizational-level construct is directly impacted by these attributes of the context in which the organization also operates. Trust is a highly context-specific construct, and thus to properly model its relative importance across organizational contexts, it is important to accommodate the differences in key embeddedness traits across a multiplicity of organizations in order to adequately enable replication of the individual-level measurement of the trust constructs (Gillespie, 2012, p. 180). Multilevel modeling accounts for the sensitivity of the measure across unique contexts by accounting for the nested nature of individuals within organizations by controlling for these agency-level differences (i.e., by isolating those traits to which the trust variables might be most sensitive). As the following figures help clarify, dashed lines indicate direct relationships between contextual-level vari-

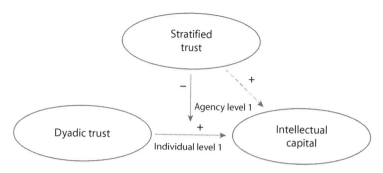

Figure 4.1. Direct and moderating impacts of stratified trust

ables and average perceptions of capacity across the respective organization (i.e., the varying intercept in a respective analytical model), while solid lines indicate direct or directly moderating effects at the individual level.

For example, the figure 4.1 shows a reduced and isolated relationship from figure 2.1. This provides a simple explanation of a hypothesis that is explicitly tested in this chapter's empirical analysis. This heuristic simply states that stratified trust (i.e., the dyadic trust established between career executives and political appointees) will (1) moderate the impact of dyadic trust at lower levels of the organization on individual perceptions of intellectual capital and (2) directly and positively impact intellectual capital at the organizational level. Likewise, figures 4.2–4.4, respectively, state that politicization, agency ideology (on a continuous descending scale from conservative to liberal), and appointee vacancies have a negative impact on intellectual capital at the organizational level while simultaneously increasing the premium that dyadic trust has on respondents' perceptions of organizational capacity.

I include these heuristics to help those readers unfamiliar with hierarchical modeling to better understand the how I test the theory presented in the previous chapter in simpler terms by isolating the larger argument to particular relationships. At the same time, it is critical for the reader to understand the utility of the multilevel approach to statistical modeling in testing the theory outlined in chapter 2. Importantly, I use multilevel regression to account for the fact that respondents are nested in larger agencies. As Heinrich and Hill (2010) argued, it is "challenging to think of a governmental context in which a multilevel conceptualization would not be appropriate,

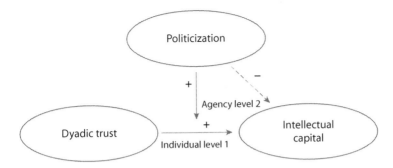

Figure 4.2. Direct and moderating impacts of politicization

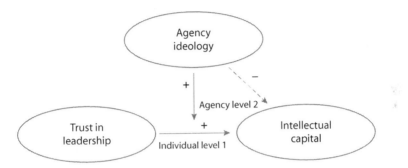

Figure 4.3. Direct and moderating impacts of agency ideology (scale = conservative > liberal)

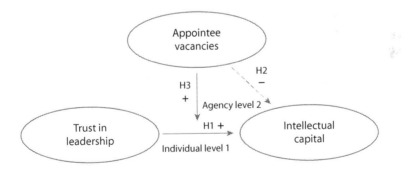

Figure 4.4. Direct and moderating impacts of appointee vacancies

even if the relevant data were not available to explore the multilevel relationships empirically" (p. 836). In this chapter's analysis, for instance, I test
perceptual survey data of respondents across 72 agency-level units of analysis. Thus, I have the advantage of variation among the different agencies'
embeddedness attributes that allow me to test the impact these various
attributes have on individual perceptions and behaviors. Additionally, the
construction of my model as individuals nested within various agency settings allows me to learn how the effects of different individual-level predictors of theoretical interest vary across these settings, based on agency characteristics (i.e., embeddedness).

In statistical analysis, "inference should include the factors used in the
design of data collection." Using traditional cross-sectional designs, such as
a "pooled" ordinary least squares (OLS) regression, ignores the different
sources from which observations are pulled (or at least identifiable dimensions that define the differences between sources). As Gelman and Hill
(2007) pointed out, one solution to overcoming the differences among
sources is "to run a classical regression with predictors at each level." In the
present case, this means that I would impute the agency-level value as a
variable for each unit of analysis. For example, the 72 agency-level observations for "stratified trust" in my data would be imputed across the 38,427
units of analysis. One problem with this approach is that "this does not
correct for differences between [level-2 observations] beyond what is included in the predictors." If, instead, we were to estimate the model with
indicators (dummy variables) for each of the agencies, it is then not possible
to include the agency-level predictors, because the predictors would become collinear with the dummy agency indicators (p. 7). Multilevel models
overcome these limitations by simultaneously fitting both individual- and
group-level models such that the between-agency random variation that is
not explained by the level-2 predictors is captured by the random agency-
level error term.

Model and Method

I estimate the following model of intellectual capital capacity:

LEVEL-1 MODEL

$$Y_{ij} = \beta_{0j} + \beta_{1j}{}^{*}(D_{ij}) + \beta_{2j}{}^{*}(L_{ij}) + Z^{*}(\Lambda) + r_{ij}$$

LEVEL-2 MODEL

$$\beta_{0j} = \gamma_{00} + \gamma_{01}{}^*(S_j) + \gamma_{02}{}^*(P_j) + \gamma_{03}{}^*(V_j) + \gamma_{04}{}^*(I_j) + W^*(\Upsilon) + u_{0j}$$
$$\beta_{1j} = \gamma_{10} + \gamma_{11}{}^*(S_j) + \gamma_{12}{}^*(P_j) + \gamma_{13}{}^*(V_j) + \gamma_{14}{}^*(I_j) + W^*(\Upsilon) + u_{11j}$$
$$\beta_{2j} = \gamma_{20} + \gamma_{21}{}^*(S_j) + \gamma_{22}{}^*(P_j) + \gamma_{23}{}^*(V_j) + \gamma_{24}{}^*(I_j) + W^*(\Upsilon) + u_{12j}$$
$$\Lambda = \gamma_{30} \ldots \gamma_k$$

Y_{ij} is a middle manager's (i) perception of intellectual capital capacity in agency j

L_{ij} is the extent of trust that respondent i has in the generalized leadership of agency j

D_{ij} is the dyadic trust that respondent i has in his or her direct supervisor at agency j

S_j is the extent that trust is established within the executive ranks (stratified trust) at agency j

V_j is the normalized index for appointed leadership vacancies (vacancy index) at agency j in the Congress leading to the day before each wave of the survey was implemented

P_j is the extent to which agency j is politicized

I_j is agency j's ideological association

Z is a vector of level-1 controls

W is a vector of level-2 controls

Λ is a level-1 coefficient vector

Υ is a level-2 coefficient vector

r_{ij} is a random individual-level error term representing the random variation in perceptions of intellectual capital capacity within agencies

u_j is a random agency-level error term representing random variation in the average intellectual capital capacity among (between) agencies.

In the following section, I present the results of the model and discuss their implications.

Results and Discussion

In this study, the responses of interest involve a respondent's perception of his or her organization's capacity to build intellectual capital. The purpose of the multilevel model in my analysis is to identify the influence that embeddedness traits have not only on the agency's capacity for intellectual capital building but also the influence they have on the relationship between an individual's trust in his or her direct superior (dyadic trust) and his or her perception of intellectual capital capacity. I expect that embeddedness traits will influence the relationship between an individual's trust in the organization's general leadership and his or her perception of intellectual capital capacity. To measure these impacts on intellectual capital capacity, I run an intercept-and-slopes-as-outcomes model that conceptualizes the indirect influence of organizational embeddedness traits on individual perceptions and behaviors. Table 4.1 presents the results of this analysis.

First, a one-way ANOVA is run to see how much of the variance is explained by level-2 dynamics (where $INTELCAP_{ij} = \gamma_{00} + u_{0j} + r_{ij}$). By computing the intraclass correlation coefficient, I find that ~5% of the variance in my dependent variable is between agencies.

$$\hat{\rho} = \hat{\tau}_{00}/(\hat{\tau}_{00} + \hat{\sigma}^2) = 1.41115/(1.41115 + 28.146329) = 0.0477$$

However, there is the distinct possibility that agency-level characteristics counterbalance one another across agencies. So, the between-agency variance attributable to the ANOVA model should be interpreted with some caution. When adding the varying slopes of dyadic trust and trust in leadership (TIL), the variance component for level-1 has been reduced from 28.143 to 6.446. This suggests that the proportion of variance explained by between- and within-agency effects for the varying intercept and slopes is 77.1% (28.143 – 6.446)/28.143 = 0.7709). As Gelman (2006) pointed out, however, "one intriguing feature of multilevel models is their ability to separately estimate the predictive effects of an individual predictor and its group-level mean" (p. 434). Therefore, regardless of how much the proportion of variance is explained by the entire model, the justification for using this model is to provide evidence to the "contextual" effects of the predictors of interest (Gelman & Pardoe, 2006).[31]

Both the dyadic trust and TIL variables are statistically significant and have positive associations with intellectual capital capacity. Neither of these findings is surprising. For instance, trust in the generalized leadership of an organization having a direct and positive association with perceptions of intellectual capital capacity (H_2) is consistent with Cho and Ringquist's (2011) findings that the trustworthiness of leadership is an antecedent to agency performance, which is a precept that has been argued since (at the least) Chester Barnard (1938). The hypotheses of particular interest in this study focus on how agency-level characteristics regulate this relationship and, moreover, directly impact perceptions of intellectual capital capacity on average across agencies. Because I have modeled the TIL and dyadic trust slopes and the intercept to vary based on various agency-level attributes such as stratified trust and appointed leadership vacancies, I provide graphs to display the relationship between the outcome and the predictors based on the final analytic results (figures 4.6 and 4.7). By providing the model's results in graphical form, I hope to better explicate the contingent effects of individual-level predictors under varying conditions of embeddedness.

In this analysis, I have modeled variance in the intercept and the slope for TIL to vary based on agency-level characteristics. This allows me to interpret the direct impact that agency-level attributes have on individuals' perceptions of intellectual capital capacity, on average, within their agency. It also allows me to interpret the indirect effects these agency-level characteristics have on the relationship between TIL and intellectual capital capacity. Figure 4.5 shows the regression lines for a random selection of 25% (19) of the 74 agencies, predicting intellectual capital capacity from TIL (Panel A) and dyadic trust (Panel B). While perceptions of intellectual capital capacity increase as TIL increases across all agencies, figure 4.5 shows that (1) intercepts differ by group, with some agencies scoring higher than other agencies at all levels of TIL, and (2) slopes differ by group, with the steepness of the regression lines showing that within some agencies, intellectual capital is more related to TIL than for other agencies (Garson, 2013, p. 92). The variance of intercepts and slopes across agencies for dyadic trust is even more pronounced.

For the direct impacts that agency-level characteristics have on individual perceptions of intellectual capital in their respective agencies, I turn to the level-2 coefficients for the varying intercept. For instance, table 4.1 indicates that stratified trust has a direct, statistically significant association with perceptions of intellectual capital capacity, and the relationship is in the hypothesized, positive direction as well as the largest effect of the level-2 variables. In other words, the model indicates that as stratified trust increases, so, too, do perceptions of intellectual capital capacity among respondents at lower levels of an organization.

However, counter to H_9, the model indicates that as the vacancy index increases, so, too, do average perceptions of intellectual capital capacity among respondents. Despite O'Connell's (2008) observation on the potential, negative impact of appointee vacancies on organizational performance,

Table 4.1. Multilevel regression models predicting intellectual capital capacity (standardized coefficients)

	Model 1		Model 2		Model 3	
	Coef.	SE	Coef.	SE	Coef.	SE
For intercept (1), β_0						
Intercept (2), γ_{00}	0.119***	0.021	0.125***	0.034	0.125***	0.033
Vacancy index, γ_{01}			0.071*	0.040	0.071*	0.040
Stratified trust, γ_{02}			0.092**	0.046	0.092**	0.046
Politicization, γ_{03}			−0.087***	0.028	−0.087***	0.028
Ideology, γ_{04}			−0.040**	0.019	−0.040**	0.019
Agency size (ln(budget)), γ_{05}			−0.074	0.048	−0.075	0.048
Ind./comm., γ_{06}			−0.032	0.046	−0.031	0.046
For trust-in-leadership slope, β_1						
Intercept, γ_{10}	0.262***	0.004	0.339***	0.009	0.267***	0.009
Vacancy index, γ_{11}					−0.027**	0.014
Stratified trust, γ_{12}					−0.0001	0.009
Politicization, γ_{13}					0.009	0.009
Ideology, γ_{14}					0.003	0.006
Agency size (ln(budget)), γ_{15}					−0.015	0.012
Ind./comm., γ_{16}					−0.033*	0.018

For dyadic trust slope, β2

	Coef.	SE	Coef.	SE	Coef.	SE
Intercept, γ_{20}	0.050***	0.004	0.080***	0.007	0.047***	0.006
Vacancy index, γ_{21}					0.015**	0.006
Stratified trust, γ_{22}					−0.013**	0.006
Politicization, γ_{22}					0.002	0.006
Ideology, γ_{23}					0.0001	0.003
Agency size (ln(budget)), γ_{24}					−0.004	0.007
Ind./comm., γ_{25}					0.002	0.010
Individual-level controls						
Procedural fairness, γ_{30}	0.012***	0.001	0.012***	0.001	0.012***	0.001
Empowerment, γ_{40}	0.096***	0.001	0.096***	0.001	0.096***	0.001
Apolitical management, γ_{50}	0.030***	0.001	0.030***	0.001	0.030***	0.001
Age, γ_{60}	0.005***	0.004	0.005***	0.004	0.005***	0.004
Federal tenure, γ_{70}	0.049	0.013	0.049	0.013	0.049	0.013
Agency tenure, γ_{80}	0.037***	0.018	0.037***	0.018	0.037***	0.018
Leaving, γ_{90}	0.060*	0.032	0.060*	0.032	0.060*	0.032
HQ, γ_{100}	−0.054***	0.059	−0.054***	0.059	−0.054***	0.059
Sex, γ_{110}	−0.032	0.010	−0.032	0.010	−0.032	0.010
White, γ_{120}	−0.096**	0.044	−0.096**	0.044	−0.096**	0.044
Hispanic, γ_{130}	0.015	0.023	0.015	0.023	0.015	0.023

Note: Ind./comm. = independent agency or commission; HQ = headquarters; Coef. = coefficient; SE = standard error.
*** $p < .01$; ** $p < .05$; * $p < .1$ (two-tailed)

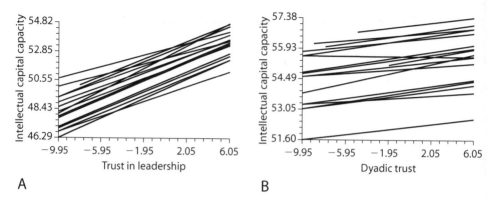

Figure 4.5. **Varying slope of intellectual capital capacity regressed on trust in leadership and dyadic trust**

she posits that "vacancies also can have beneficial repercussions for agency performance." The absence of political leadership at agencies can have the unobvious consequence of ensuring efficient operations as agencies are led by career SES personnel who have long tenures in government and tend to possess at least six years of experience within their current organization. O'Connell's latter observation is consistent with Gilmour and Lewis's (2006b) findings, for example, which raise an important question as to whether many political appointees have the institutional competence necessary to be responsive to the president, manage an agency effectively, and see through agency goals in accordance with the president's preferences.

I also find evidence that politicization has a negative and statistically significant relationship with intellectual capital capacity (H_6). On average, politicization serves to inhibit the development of intellectual capital across agencies. Politicization of bureaucratic ranks is thought to be complementary to, and an extension of, centralization (e.g., Moe, 1993). The premise of the strategy is to increase the number and managerial influence of appointees within agencies. This is done in order to isolate and centralize organizational decision-making and its deliberation to a corps of identified loyalists. Accordingly, proponents of politicization assume that career bureaucrats who disagree with a president's ideology or policy preferences will act to sabotage presidential action (Sanera, 1984). Therefore, the prescription is set forth that appointees should subvert these perceived careerist intentions by bypassing career SES personnel for policy advice, using them to carry out programs "while keeping them in the dark as to the overall strategy being pursued" (Benda & Levine, 1988; Golden, 2000; Ingraham, 1995; Pfiffner, 1985). Here, the evidence suggests that politicization directly limits the development of intellectual capital. This supports prior contentions (e.g., Lewis, 2008) and provides further evidence that politicization hampers the development of institutional competence. Indeed, the increased politicization within the executive levels of federal agencies might result in increased layers separating the secretary from career bureaucrats who possess the institutional memory and competence necessary to avoid unanticipated consequences of presidential directives (Dickinson, 2005; Light, 1995; Moynihan & Roberts, 2010) and thereby inhibit vertical coordination (Krause, 2009).

I predicted that agency ideology would have a positive association with average perceptions of intellectual capital capacity in an organization (H_{12}). I reasoned that appointees in organizations with more conservative orientations would be more likely to improve employee perceptions of access, opportunity, and ability to exchange pertinent knowledge within that organization. Yet, table 4.1 indicates otherwise. The coefficient for ideology on the varying intercept for intellectual capital capacity is negative but indicates that the relative conservatism of agencies has no statistically significant association with managers' perceptions of intellectual capital capacity.

The coefficient for stratified trust on the dyadic trust slope is negative and statistically significant. This provides some confirmatory evidence for H_4. Specifically, this indicates that when a higher level of trust is established among career executives and political appointees, dyadic trust between middle managers and career executives is less important to the middle managers' perceptions of intellectual capital capacity. Recall the theoretical premise for this conclusion, as I explained in chapter 3: most of the literature that unpacks the appointee-career nexus focuses on the relationships that develop between career executives and appointees, and the importance of trust being established within these relationships (e.g., Heclo, 1977; Michaels, 1997; Pfiffner, 1987, 1991a). Therefore, as this is the common locus of appointee-careerist relations, these relations will presumably have a significant impact on the organization, generally. Executives play a distinct role within organizations in setting strategic direction for the organization (Dirks & Skarlicki, 2004). How relations at this level of the organization play out should have a significant impact on employees' access to various ex-

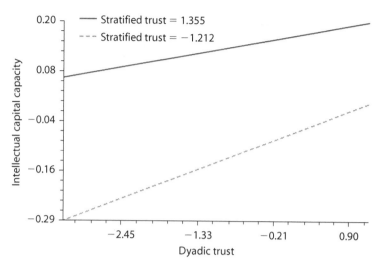

Figure 4.6. Intellectual capital regressed on dyadic trust: Holding stratified trust at the average value of lower and upper quartiles (holding all other variables at their respective means; coefficients are standardized)

change partners, the value they perceive in exchanging knowledge exchange, and their motivation to do so. Specifically, stratified trust (the trust developed between actors in relations at the executive level of the hierarchy) should have a significant impact on the trust that is established between middle managers, who must articulate the product of executive relations into definitive expectations of employee performance, and their subordinates. At the same time, the model shows that stratified trust does not moderate the relationship between TIL and intellectual capital.

To get a clearer idea of the moderating effect of stratified trust on dyadic trust and intellectual capital, compare the black line with the gray regression line in figure 4.6. This shows that when stratified trust is held at a high value (black line), perceptions are that (1) there are higher levels of intellectual capital generally, (2) there is a positive relationship between dyadic trust and intellectual capital, and (3) the slope is less sharp in these relationships than when stratified trust is held at a low level. This indicates that stratified trust has a significant impact on both the level of intellectual capital capacity in an organization and the premium that middle managers will place on dyadic trust in their immediate supervisor to search for access, opportunity,

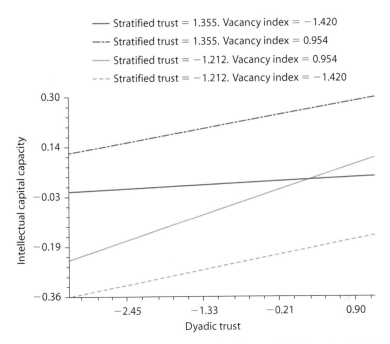

Figure 4.7. Intellectual capital regressed on dyadic trust: Holding stratified trust and the appointee vacancy index at their average value of lower and upper quartiles, respectively (holding all other variables at their respective means; coefficients are standardized)

or ability to engage in knowledge exchange within the organization. In other words, under conditions in which trust is established between career executives and political appointees, middle managers will be less likely to need trust in their direct superiors in order to perceive the organization's capacity to build intellectual capital.

The coefficients for politicization and ideology on both the dyadic trust and TIL slopes are statistically nonsignificant. Interestingly, table 4.1 indicates that the coefficient for the vacancy index on the dyadic trust slope is positive and statistically significant while negative and statistically significant on the TIL slope. This finding implies that appointed leadership vacancies decrease the importance of TIL, but, simultaneously, dyadic trust between middle managers and career executives will be more valued by middle managers seeking access, opportunity, or ability to engage in knowledge exchange. The combined impact of appointee vacancies and stratified trust tell an interesting story. When the vacancy index is held to the average of its highest quartile and stratified trust at its lowest, we see in figure 4.6 that the slope of dyadic trust between managers and their direct superiors is notably pronounced. Moreover, the intercepts (or the average perceptions of intellectual capital capacity) are markedly higher when stratified trust is higher within an organization.

This finding gives some evidence to the notion that there are important "differences in the consequences of the different referents of trust in leadership" (Dirks & Skarlicki, 2004, p. 31), depending on the organizational context and the levels of hierarchy in the organization. If we assume that empirical and journalistic accounts that decision-making in federal agencies was centralized to the appointed executive ranks during the second term of the Bush administration, then the opposing moderating effects of appointee vacancies on different referents of trust in the organization make some sense. Employees who do not perceive the interference inherent to the actual presence of appointed leadership (i.e., when those positions are empty or entrusted to "acting" career officials) may depend less heavily on trusting leadership, while, simultaneously, the trust in their immediate supervisors comes at a higher premium due to the uncertainty presented during times of leadership interregnum in order to obtain the information necessary to do their jobs well.

Conclusion

In this chapter, I provided evidence that the trust established at the highest levels of the organization between career executives and political appointees (i.e., "stratified trust") can have a trickle-down effect on the perception of intellectual capital capacity within agencies. Respondents' perception of the capacity to exchange and combine distinct forms of knowledge between superiors and subordinates throughout organizational hierarchies is in some measure dependent on the level of trust established at the highest rungs of the organizational ladder. When stratified trust is diminished, middle managers appear to put more of a premium on trusting their immediate supervisors (i.e., career executives) in order to assess the organization's intellectual capital capacity.

I also found that an organization's embeddedness attributes are important to the consideration of relationships between appointees and careerists. Namely, the evidence suggests that politicization directly limits the development of intellectual capital across an organization. This supports prior contentions and provides further evidence that politicization hampers the development of institutional competence. By politicizing bureaucratic ranks with lower-level appointees and centralizing decision-making through decidedly top-down arrangements, presidents face the possibility of inhibiting a president's (and, by proxy, his appointees') capacity to develop the institutional competence necessary to successfully implement his policy agenda. This chapter's findings, in regard to middle managers' perceptions, support the supposition that trust between career executives and political appointees matters in federal agencies' development of organizational intellectual capital. I showed that the trust that develops between career SES members and political appointees has effects *throughout* the organization. Middle managers are more likely to perceive the capacity to build intellectual capital in their agencies as trust is established between career executives and political appointees.

Thus, while the administrative presidency scholarship indicates that trust between SES personnel and appointees is important, this chapter's study expands on this notion to show that this connection does not exclusively affect the executive ranks. Rather, the trust (or lack thereof) established at the executive ranks affects the development of intellectual capital in the organization as a whole, thereby affecting individual actors with markedly different roles and responsibilities. Importantly, the moderating impacts that both stratified trust and structural attempts at politicization have on individual perceptions give evidence that politicization is also a cognitive construct related to the perceived motivations underlying the president's administrative strategies. Structural politicization does not present as substantial a direct, or moderating, impact on intellectual capital capacity, as does stratified trust. This finding is consistent with West's (1995) contention that application of the politicization strategy and reorganizing the management structures of agencies "only allows the president to influence the general contours of policy implementation rather than specific actions" (p. 88). Thus, if a president seeks change in agency outputs, regardless of the structural tactics of reorganization, politicization, and centralization, the agency must have the capacity to connect tasks to control mechanisms as most federal agency fields of action—such as economic and research development, intelligence gathering, fiscal policies, and regulations—require horizontal integration under vertically oriented accountability systems

(Bounfour & Edvisson, 2005). These foundational "joists" of organizational capacity are developed through the "black box" of appropriate and logical integration (Krause, 2009; Simon, 1997), which I argue is primarily a product of the trust that is established in organizational leadership—a long-argued, central function of executives (Barnard, 1938). The present chapter provides evidence that helps validate the conceptual premises of the framework I presented in chapter 2. And while I do not have data to test the relationship between intellectual capital and success in advancing Bush's policy agenda, I showed how likely that is based on prior research in the cognate research areas I noted previously and test this notion more directly in the following chapter. In the final chapter of this book, I further discuss the implications of the findings from this chapter, as well as the contribution the book makes to the study of the administrative presidency.

5

Encapsulated Interest and Explicit

Knowledge Exchange

A Case Study of Presidential Transition

How can people trust the harvest until they see it sown?

—Mary Renault, *The King Must Die* (1958)

In chapter 1, I reviewed the literature that put forth the argument that presidents achieve responsiveness to their executive authority through the strategic use of appointment powers and increases in the number of appointments (especially non-Senate confirmed appointments) while simultaneously centralizing policymaking to a cadre of identified loyalists. I also documented how these tactics were aggressively implemented in the G. W. Bush administration. I identified a management technique that extends from this strategy, known commonly in the administrative presidency literature as "jigsaw management" (Ban & Ingraham, 1990; Benda & Levine, 1988; Pfiffner, 1987), which is based on a fundamental distrust of the career bureaucracy. In chapter 2, I reviewed the literature that explores the importance of interpersonal trust in organizations, especially at the executive ranks. I unpacked the idea of trust from cognate literatures, showed its previously unexplored implications for advancing presidential agendas administratively, and offered a model of trust building and its role in advancing those agendas.

In this chapter, I test some of the propositions I put forth in the theoretical framework offered in chapter 2. I focus here on a very narrow piece of the heuristic model previously presented as figure 2.1: the "encapsulated interest" account of trust and its connection to explicit knowledge exchange between appointees and career executives. As discussed in chapter 2, mutual trust can be understood as the areas of interaction in which two or more actors find continuing value in both the exchange and content of information. I have referred to this conceptualization of mutual trust as the "encapsulated interest," or "calculative" account of trust. As previously defined, encapsulated interest refers to the idea that the benefit that one receives from any particular exchange in which one is trusted is a function of "the potential benefit from continuing the series of interactions" (Hardin, 2006b, p. 22).

Moreover, as I argued in chapter 2, encapsulated interest represents only one dimension of trust. It excludes the character-based (Mayer, Davis, & Schoorman, 1995) and emotional (Dunn, 1990) dimensions of the construct, as well as how social norms and obligations may regulate purely calculative exchanges between individuals (i.e., "embeddedness attributes" of an organizational setting) (Williamson, 1993). Therefore, the focus of this chapter provides a narrow, but more parsimonious, conceptualization of trust as "encapsulated interest." Additionally, the dependent variable in this chapter is just one dimension of intellectual capital: explicit knowledge. Here, I am specifically interested in how the establishment of encapsulated interest between career executives and political appointees is associated with explicit knowledge exchange.

I study this question in a policy area that provides a practical focus for analysis because it is one that was simultaneously implemented across agencies, in a largely universal manner, and intended to be carried out according to a centralized presidential mandate from the White House to political appointees. The policy I examine is the Bush administration's preparations for the presidential transition of 2008–2009. Importantly, the mandate from the White House explicitly directs Bush appointees to work *with* career executives in formulating implementation plans and carrying out implementation.

Studying the implementation of a centrally mandated policy from the White House calling for career involvement to make for a smooth transition allows us to indirectly assess the effects of prior appointee-careerist relations in the Bush years. If we find empirically that a jigsaw puzzle management technique was used to implement a policy requiring careerist involvement more broadly, a curious paradox is identified, one that may indicate why knowledge of transition activities was limited (as discussed in greater detail in the following section). If we do not find it, or we find some modified or more nuanced version of jigsaw puzzle management, we will have some evidence that conventional wisdom may have to be rethought and alterative metaphors considered that better fit the data from these surveys.

To test the question of how much careerist input and participation was valued by the Bush administration as input to facilitating the transition, this chapter uses a survey of members of the SES administered by the National Academy of Public Administration (NAPA) in October 2008. This survey addresses SES members' involvement in the 2008–2009 transition, as well as their general perceptions of presidential transitions. The respondents' general perceptions of presidential transitions help inform what factors between appointees and careerists are commonly inhibitive to good appointee-careerist relations.

The unit of analysis for this chapter is a career member of the SES. Data were collected from an electronic survey conducted by NAPA from September 29 to October 24, 2008. The population was based on a census of all career SES personnel working at the time of the survey. According to September 8, 2008, administrative data provided by the US Office of Personnel Management (OPM), the population of filled career SES positions in the United States federal government was 6,481. To protect anonymity, the online survey was available to all agencies with at least three career SES positions filled. The original sampling frame, therefore, was composed of 6,456 people occupying SES positions in 51 departments, agencies, boards, and commissions. The survey was distributed to approximately 4,799 potential respondents and was returned by 1,116, a 23% response rate. The sample appears to be representative of the broader population on key dimensions, but certainly caution is warranted with this response rate.

At the time the survey was implemented, the 2008 presidential election was yet to be decided. By then, the Bush administration had begun extensive activities in preparation for the upcoming transition (Kamensky, 2008; Pear, 2008). As noted in chapter 1, a memo was issued on July 18, 2008, to members of the Presidential Management Council by Clay Johnson, deputy director of the Office of Management and Budget (OMB). The memo directed agency political leaders to (1) name a career executive as the transition coordinator at each agency, (2) name a career executive "to serve in place of departing political officials in each major bureau," (3) develop a briefing book identifying each agency's organization, performance goals, and key personnel, and (4) "identify 'hot' issues that need the attention of the new administration" (Johnson, 2008; Kamensky, 2008). As I also observed in that chapter, Johnson encouraged appointees to "do transition planning with (not to) career officials" (Kamensky, 2008; emphasis added). Therefore, NAPA's October 2008 survey presented an opportunity to gain an insightful look at the activity involved with the Bush administration's transition management plan.

As I also discussed in the first chapter, the general perception of presidency scholars and journalists prior to that memo was that the Bush administration replicated the jigsaw puzzle management practices of the Reagan administration in many ways. The White House had (1) centralized WHO approval for each Schedule C appointment (Pfiffner & Patterson, 2001; Warshaw, 2006), (2) developed a hierarchical, top-down governance structure in many areas of government (Suskind, 2004), (3) emphasized ideological loyalty as appointee selection criteria (Romano, 2007; Warshaw, 2006), and (4) exercised a general rejection of the career bureaucracy's involvement in day-to-day implementation and policymaking decisions (Hedge, 2009; Lewis, 2008; Moynihan & Roberts, 2010; Warshaw, 2006).

Thus, in many ways this chapter offers a critical case analysis; if anything, we should see evidence of faithful implementation given the White House's explicit call for appointees to cooperate with careerists. Moreover, the analysis allows us to examine how the administration's general management approach *prior* to transition activities might affect how the administration made use of career SES members in an area for which the creation and existence of the SES is particularly suitable. That is, as noted, the SES was ostensibly created to establish a cadre of top-level career officials who could provide both continuity of institutional purpose and responsiveness to political officials (Ingraham, 2005). The question is whether managerial tactics that were prevalent within the Bush administration inhibited the ability for the administration to later leverage the institutional competence of the SES to facilitate the transfer of political leadership. In other words, how did management activities prior to the transition affect the involvement of career SES personnel during the transition?

In the following sections, I provide a brief introduction considering the nature of presidential transitions generally and some career SES members' introductory perceptions of how the Bush administration approached its transition planning. I present a model to test the influence that on-hand heuristics of agency settings may have on SES members' perceptions of general impediments to successful appointed leadership transitions. The findings speak directly to relations between career SES members and political appointees in practice, and help inform this study's main inferential model. The evidence provided by the respondents indicates that distrust and jigsaw management techniques prevent the utilization of the institutional knowledge and experience that SES personnel presumably provide while also inhibiting success during leadership transitions.

In the main inferential model, I use multilevel logistic regression to model the manner in which a president's administrative strategies and an agency's political environment moderate a career executive's propensity to have explicit awareness of important policy decisions. I find evidence of careerists being "kept in the dark" in a manner that is, in part, consistent with evidence of jigsaw puzzle management. At the same time, explicit policy knowledge varied among respondents based on the degree to which their interests were encapsulated in the appointees' own—indicating that a conditional cooperation strategy was being employed by Bush appointees. Moreover, I find that cooperation was moderated by the degree to which the agency had been subject to persistent appointee vacancies leading up to transition preparations and the relative ideological orientation of the agency. The importance of appointee trust in career executives is more robust in liberal agencies. And, the likelihood of awareness is diminished, on average, in agencies that have had appointees in place on a more consistent basis leading up to the transition. Thus, cooperation was contingent on organizational, political, and interpersonal conditions that regulated the degree to which career executives were explicitly aware of these preparations. The major irony that I focus on is the degree to which appointees inhibited the president's ability to have an expressed implementation preference followed through.

Presidential Transitions, Jigsaw Puzzle Management, and the Bush Administration

Presidential transitions have been characterized as a time that brings about "scramble, discomfiture, reshuffling, [and] adjustment" within issue networks and the agencies with which they interact (Neustadt, 1990, p. 257). Therefore, this changeover, especially accompanied by a change in the partisan identification of the administration, presents a particularly interesting time at which to study how the outgoing administration's administrative strategies affect an incoming administration's ability to "hit the ground running" (Pfiffner, 1996). Despite great advancements in the study of presidential transitions over the last twenty years (e.g., Burke, 2002; Kumar, Edwards, Pfiffner, & Sullivan, 2000; Pfiffner, 2009), this research tends to focus on preparations by incoming administrations. Little work examines the preparations that outgoing administrations make to facilitate the transfer of power (see Kumar, 2009, for a notable exception). There is a particular lacuna in research that examines these preparations from the perspective of the career service that is, arguably, most central to maintaining continuity between administrations.

Presidential Transitions

It is commonly understood that the turnover of executive power presents a great challenge in the United States' system of governance. It is probably, in many ways, amazing to observers outside of the United States to believe that we can maintain relative continuity between administrations, given the institutionalized advantages a parliamentary system has over our separation of powers. In most parliamentary systems, only the top cabinet offices change hands between governments, the transitions are completed quickly, and cabinet members are usually experienced members of the legislature with substantive expertise in their assigned areas and anticipated assignment to these chairs once their party is in power (i.e., members of the "shadow government") (Pfiffner, 1996).

In the United States, however, the transfer of executive power is more complex. Indeed, new presidents face the personnel challenges I alluded to in chapter 1—including more than 4,000 appointments throughout different layers of the bureaucracy and appointments often made with political considerations outside of substantive or institutional expertise. They also must take place amid considerable albeit unrealistic public expectations that delay is an indication of an administration in disarray, as well as a need to take advantage of a limited window of time to leverage popularity, to see through a general policy platform consistent with campaign promises, one that can be framed as a public "mandate" (Aberbach & Rockman, 1988; Beckmann & Godfrey, 2007).

Contributing to this problem, delays in Senate confirmation of political appointees compound the difficulties modern presidents face in seeing through their electoral agendas (Light, 1995; Mackenzie, 1987; O'Connell, 2009). A report by the Center for American Progress noted that the average number of days it took to fill a Senate-confirmed agency position for the first time for the last four presidencies ranged from 193.69 days (Reagan) to 267.39 days (Clinton) (O'Connell, 2009). In fact, 100 days after President Obama's inauguration, a total of just 12.8% (66) of Senate-confirmed appointee (PAS) positions had been filled, an additional 20.8% (107) had been nominated, and another 7% (36) announced, leaving 300 PAS jobs vacant in both name and practice by April 27, 2009.

Yet the modern lexicon of presidential politics places an unrealistic or misplaced emphasis on the "honeymoon" period of the first 100 days in office, with appointment delays indicating that something is amiss with a new administration by not "hitting the ground running." The implication is that the absence of appointed leadership hands agencies' policymaking powers to the careerists in place at the time of initial transition (Kingdon, 2003; Kumar, 2002). In the eyes of some, this is not a problem. As a report by the National Academy of Public Administration (NAPA) states: "It is not unusual for SES members to serve as the interim agency leadership, temporarily taking on roles normally reserved for appointees. They are the stewards of their agency, responsible for 'making the trains run on time' and maintaining routine business during a time of leadership transition" (NAPA, 2009). However, as O'Connell (2009) wrote, these officials "generally lack sufficient authority to direct career civil servants" and may be reluctant to initiate action, which may result in careerists regressing to inertia in reaction to an environment of uncertainty and out of fear of future reprisal for decisions antithetical to future appointees' preferences.

Arguably, however, scholars should think of transitions in broader terms than the period following inauguration day. Transition activity also takes place prior to election and in the eleven-week period between election and inauguration. These activities have been institutionalized through budget appropriations and practice since the Truman presidency (Pfiffner, 1996). Prior research suggests that significant support is provided to incoming presidents and their appointees by the outgoing administration, "good government" organizations (e.g., the White House Transition Project, NAPA), and think tanks (e.g., the Presidential Appointee Initiative of the Brookings Institution) (Burke, 2002; Felzenberg, 2000; Kumar, 2002; Kumar et al., 2000; Pfiffner, 1996).

Thus, without question, a great deal of information is exchanged between administrations during the periods preceding inauguration, most of which is communicated through the channels of the federal bureaucracy.

How complete, accurate, and timely that this information is, and how prior appointee-careerist relations affect this transfer of information, has not been systematically explored in prior research. To be successful in ensuring that ongoing government operations are maintained (and substantive policy emphases in a transition to an administration of the same party), political appointees must convey to careerists the importance of information sharing, careerists must have the information to convey, and they must be predisposed toward sharing that information. I would contend that if any one of these factors is missing, a policy of cooperation will be less than successful. And a prerequisite to realizing these factors is the way information, appointee-careerist relations, and trust of careerists has materialized in previous years.

The Bush Transition and Jigsaw Puzzlement Management

As noted, the transfer of leadership between administrations provides an opportunity for officials to make the most of institutional and substantive expertise as central values. As Chang et al. (2001) exhibited, the end of an administration's term is a time in which political appointees are more likely to resign before the term has ended. Therefore, the Bush administration's preparation for the transition was timely, and its reliance on selecting career officials who were knowledgeable and predisposed to help was particularly necessary. Moreover, the 2008–2009 transfer of presidential administrations presented only the fourth time since the passage of the Twenty-Second Amendment (1947) that Americans and the career bureaucracy knew that "they could anticipate a fresh face in the next presidency" (Kumar, 2002, p. 7)—as neither party's nominees were incumbent or former vice presidents or presidents.

Descriptive evidence from the 2008 NAPA survey of SES members suggests that—despite Bush's announced aim to have appointees "do transition planning with (not to) career officials"—transition activities in the Bush administration were not thoroughly coordinated throughout the career executive levels. In fact, there is evidence that SES members were "left in the dark" on critical transition decisions, characteristics consonant with "jigsaw puzzle management." For example, over 70 days after the Johnson memorandum was issued, 21.5% of the SES respondents indicated that they had "no knowledge of transition activities" in their agencies (see table 5.1), despite indications of activity awareness by at least some respondents within

Table 5.1. Explicit activity awareness

Which of the following activities is your organization currently doing, or planning to do in the next few months, to prepare for the next transition? (Select all that apply.)	Yes	No
Preparing information describing the mandate of the agency and any scheduled reauthorizations	751 (67%)	365 (33%)
Examining the agency's programs strategically in relation to the new president's agenda	401 (36%)	715 (64%)
Scheduling briefings on key programs/initiatives within the agency	577 (52%)	539 (48%)
Arranging briefings on who does what in the agency, including areas of staff expertise and existing gap areas	529 (47%)	587 (53%)
Preparing information about budget, funding issues, and, if applicable, continuing resolutions within the agency	775 (69%)	341 (31%)
Describing relationships with relevant congressional committees and members	422 (38%)	694 (62%)
Outlining relationships and initiatives with other federal agencies, including involvement on interagency councils	414 (37%)	702 (63%)
Developing descriptions of key external stakeholders and the status of their relationship with the agency	466 (42%)	650 (58%)
Developing a list of predecessors and other subject matter experts who might advise the new leadership on targeted issues	152 (14%)	964 (86%)
Assessing sensitive issues that pose a threat to the agency and the administration	550 (49%)	566 (51%)
Cannot answer; I have no knowledge of transition activities in this agency	240 (22%)	876 (78%)

Source: NAPA, Presidential Transition Survey of the SES (Question 13).

each agency. Moreover, shortly after the data were collected and a preliminary analysis was conducted, NAPA hosted a panel during its annual meeting that reviewed the results publicly. One panelist made clear how surprising and normatively problematic it was that so many SES members were unaware of any transition activities: "I'm a charter member of the SES, and the response of 20 percent of existing senior executives who said they could not answer the question of the transition activities under way at their agencies—that's deplorable. . . . The whole premise of the Senior Executive Service is that you have the management skills and the leadership skills to step up to the plate."

Therefore, a centrally mandated policy from the White House calling for career involvement in transition planning had major gaps in implementation that varied across respondents. Indeed, these responses imply that some form of jigsaw management was occurring, at least to some extent. But further evidence is needed to confirm this. NAPA survey data allow me to address, first, what career executive respondents think impedes transitions generally, then whether they perceive that these largely jigsaw puzzle management impediments were occurring during the Bush transition. As evidence of the potential obstacles jigsaw management presents to effective transition, I employ a rank-ordered logistic regression model to evaluate the likelihood that respondents will choose elements of jigsaw management strategies as impediments toward a successful presidential transition. Having established the relative prominence of these factors as impediments, generally, I then model the likelihood that careerists will have explicit knowledge of transition preparations based on the trust they have established with Bush appointees, as well as the conditions in which trust comes at a higher premium toward the likelihood of policy knowledge.

SES Perceptions of Transition Impediments

The NAPA survey asked career SES respondents to identify what they perceived to be the impediments to a successful presidential transition generally (NAPA, 2009). The survey instrument provided a list of thirteen potential impediments to a successful presidential transition (including "other"). The respondents were asked to rank the top three impediments. As one might imagine, delay in Senate confirmations of appointed agency leaders was ranked as having the biggest impact on slowing transition.

However, there were several other impediments that ranked highly and speak directly to relations between career SES members and political appointees in practice. The evidence provided by the respondents indicates that an undervaluation of the institutional knowledge and experience that SES personnel presumably provide, as well as a general distrust in the careerist ranks, will present significant impediments to leadership transitions. Of the thirteen potential impediments, over 25% of respondents ranked at least one of the following as a significant impediment:

- Delays in confirmation of Senate-confirmed appointees (58%)
- Reticence to identify and leverage career staff expertise (38%)
- Appointees' eagerness to change organizational structure (35%)
- Distrust (34%)

- Appointees' eagerness to change policy (28%)
- Lack of preparation by the appointee (25%)

While both delays and lack of preparation are commonly identified as obstacles to transition (Gilmour & Lewis, 2006a; Lewis, 2007; Mackenzie, 1987, 2002), both speak more to the procedural impediments preceding confirmation that fall outside the direct interaction between careerists and appointees (Mackenzie, 2002). After weighting the responses according to the ranks the respondents assigned to each, I found that "appointees' eagerness to change organizational structure," "distrust," and "reticence to identify and leverage career staff expertise" become the second, third, and fourth biggest potential impediments to successful transitions, respectively (see table 5.2).

These perceptions suggest that jigsaw management techniques are prevalent in appointee practice generally—distrust of careerists, leaving them "in the dark" on important policy decisions, and the reorganization of human capital within an agency. To provide some insight as to how these perceptions might emerge, I test a series of hypotheses using a rank-ordered logit model that assumes responses based on availability heuristics (Tversky & Kahneman, 1973). In other words, I posit that respondents will most likely rank specific impediments above the most commonly identified impediment (i.e., "confirmation delay"), given characteristics of the organizational environment in which they are embedded at the time of the survey. To do so, I derive four characteristics that are most prominently associated with appointee-careerist relations: trust, agency ideology, politicization, and appointed leadership vacancies.

Appointee-SES Relations

The first variable of interest is drawn from the respondents' perceptions of their relationships with Bush administration appointees. As previously discussed, "distrust" was selected by a sizable proportion of the respondents (33.78%) as an important impediment to a successful 2008–2009 transition. Some have posited that trust can be seen as an individual's calculation of the expected value of future informational interactions with another individual to achieve individual and collective action goals (Coleman, 1990; Lundin, 2007; Olson, 1965; Ostrom, 2000). By this account, mutual trust can be understood as the areas of interaction in which two or more actors find continuing value in both the exchange and content of informa-

Table 5.2. Common impediments to successful transitions

"Which of the following challenges have the biggest impact on slowing the transition?"	Unweighted sum	Rank	First rank	Second rank	Third rank	Weighted sum	Weighted rank
Delays in confirmation of Senate-confirmed appointees	644	1	1395	198	80	1673	1
Appointees' eagerness to change organizational structure	385	3	468	266	96	830	2
Distrust	377	4	408	256	113	777	3
Reticence to identify and leverage career staff expertise	425	2	246	290	198	734	4
Appointees' eagerness to change policy	313	5	324	206	102	632	5
Lack of preparation by the appointee	282	6	249	232	83	564	6
High number of appointees throughout multiple levels in the agency	177	7	99	130	79	308	7
Partisanship	163	9	102	146	56	304	8
Role confusion of the appointee	171	8	87	140	72	299	9
Role confusion among staff resulting from change	160	10	57	108	87	252	10
Level of planning within the agency	131	11	81	110	49	240	11
Level of SES receptivity to new ideas and directions	94	12	27	74	48	149	12
Other	75	13	75	38	31	144	13

Source: NAPA, Presidential Transition Survey of the SES (Question 11).

tion. I refer to this conceptualization of mutual trust as the "encapsulated interest," or the benefit that one receives from any particular exchange in which one is trusted is a function of "the potential benefit from continuing the series of interactions" (Hardin, 2006b, p. 22).

The presumed benefit for career executives is involvement in policymaking and explicit possession of knowledge critical to policy implementation. In my interviews with both career SES members and political appointees, a common refrain from career SES members was succinctly summarized by one career senior executive: "I like being at the table. I like being part of the decisions. And, my job is to demonstrate loyalty and value to politicals so I can do that."[32] Accordingly, I operationalize trust as a function of both frequency of exchange and the perceived quality of information shared among actors (Ostrom, 1998).[33]

The NAPA survey offers four indicators of the relationship between political appointees and SES members that capture the "encapsulated interest" established over the span of the administration. Survey respondents were first asked how often they interact with PAS and then how often they interact with non-Senate-confirmed presidential appointees (PA), on a five-point scale from "very frequently (at least weekly)" to "not at all." Subsequent to these two questions, respondents were asked to rate the overall influence of their interactions with both PAS and PA, respectively, on another five-point scale ranging from "great influence" to "no influence." If the data conform to the construct of encapsulated interest between SES members and appointees, responses to the individual questions should be highly correlated and a linear function of the underlying construct (i.e., encapsulated interest) (Langbein & Felbinger, 2006). Using iterated principal factor analysis, I find support that these indicators do converge to a common latent construct. This is supported in these data by a Cronbach's alpha of 0.85 and factor analysis coefficients that are positive and account for the overwhelming proportion of factor space (table 5.3).

In the following discussion, I refer to the factor score for this construct as the appointee trust index, as it represents the trust that a respondent has established collectively with appointees in his or her organization. In the rank-ordered logistic model that follows, I hypothesize that the probability that distrust is selected above the reference category is positively correlated with a respondent's appointee trust index (H_{15}). In other words, assuming that availability heuristics are employed, those respondents who have estab-

Table 5.3. Factor analysis: Appointee trust index

Construct: Appointee-SES mutual trust

Variable	Factor loading
Interact w/ PAS	0.779
Interact w/ PA	0.827
Influence w/ PAS	0.734
Influence w/ PA	0.847
Eigenvalue	2.547
Factor space	4.000

Note: PAS = Senate-confirmed political appointees; PA = non-Senate-confirmed political appointees; SES = Senior Executive Service.

lished trust with appointees at the time of the survey are more likely to se-lect distrust as an impediment to successful transitions, generally, because of the trust they have established with current appointees. Conversely, those respondents who have not are less likely to rank highly distrust as a general impediment, because future distrust will be consistent with the sta-tus quo (if availability heuristics are being employed in responses).

Appointee Vacancies

Realistically, there may be few, if any, appointees in place to facilitate or intervene in communications between the White House and the career bureaucracy in preparation for a transition, as appointees are more likely to resign before the second term has ended (Chang et al., 2001). As Pfiffner (2009) posited, transitions are "affected by the anticipation of a possible change of administration by both political appointees and members of the career services" (p. 85). I argue that SES members in agencies will be more likely to be aware of transition activities if their agencies are subject to per-sistent appointed leadership vacancies. To capture the construct of "persis-tent appointee leadership vacancies," I utilize a detailed longitudinal roster of presidential appointment positions and the officials who occupy them. That is, I look at the number of days that various PAS were not filled within agencies over the 110th Congress, leading to the implementation of the NAPA survey (i.e., January 3, 2007–September 29, 2008).

To account for the differential power of a given appointee position, I derive the same vacancy index from the equation in chapter 3, which standardizes vacancies both within and across organizations. Consistent with the findings from chapter 4, we should expect that respondents in agencies subject to persistent appointee vacancies will more likely rank various jigsaw management techniques higher than confirmation delay as important impediments to successful transitions (H_{16}).

I account for both the relative ideology of the agency and the level of unilateral appointments the president has brought to bear on the agency by using the same Clinton and Lewis (2008) agency ideology estimates and OPM CPDF records for lower-level appointments (i.e., politicization) that I employed in the previous chapter. Lewis (2008) argued that the "extent to which presidents and their appointees confront career personnel in management positions that do not share their ideology or priorities" is a major factor in influencing the application of strategic appointments based on a presumption of distrust in the career bureaucracy (p. 30). Accordingly, I expect that liberal agencies will be more likely to rank distrust higher than other potential impediments (H_{17}). Moreover, I expect that respondents in more politicized agencies will rely on this heuristic to rank distrust above other potential transition impediments (H_{18}).

Table 5.4 provides the rank-ordered logit results for the individual coefficients and the overall model fit. In this type of model, we are interested in whether given alternatives are ranked above a baseline expectation. If the logit coefficient for a particular alternative is negative, this means that the predicted probability of the alternative being ranked above our baseline

Table 5.4 Rank-ordered logit analysis

Rank	b(SE)	Group variable: Agency
Eagerness to change policy	−0.757***	No. of observations = 6414
	(0.196)	No. of groups = 32
Eagerness to change organizational structure	−1.616***	Base comparison category: "Confirmation delay"
	(0.222)	Observations per group:
Distrust	−1.215***	minimum = 6
	(0.196)	average = 200.44
Lack of appointee preparation	−0.875***	maximum = 1218
	(0.205)	Log likelihood = −6256.507
Reticence to leverage SES experience	−1.232***	LR chi2(95) = 547.44
	(0.191)	Prob > chi2 = 0.000

Note: SE = standard error; SES = Senior Executive Service.
*** $p < .01$; ** $p < .05$; * $p < .1$ (two-tailed)

expectation is null. In this model, I chose "delay in Senate confirmation" as the base category, eliminating nonjigsaw alternatives from the analysis, all of which (on average) ranked lower across the survey than the alternatives listed here in the table. The baseline expectation of confirmation delay was the highest-ranked impediment to successful transition, making the likelihood that any of these alternatives would be ranked above that baseline unlikely. The negative coefficients and their statistical significance confirm this likelihood.

More interestingly, table 5.5 provides the coefficients of agency and individual characteristics, measuring the likelihood that any given alternative will be ranked above the baseline comparison (confirmation delay), given that characteristic (and holding all others constant). For example, we see in the first row of table 5.5 that distrust is more likely to be ranked above the

Table 5.5. Rank-ordered logit analysis

Change policy X . . .			
Vacancy index	Trust index	Politicization	Agency ideology
b	b	b	b
(SE)	(SE)	(SE)	(SE)
0.004	−0.180***	−0.095	−0.073
(0.022)	(0.067)	(0.200)	(0.089)
Change structure X . . .			
Vacancy index	Trust index	Politicization	Agency ideology
0.062*	0.028	−0.106	−0.084
(0.024)	(0.071)	(0.200)	(0.091)
Distrust X . . .			
Vacancy index	Trust index	Politicization	Agency ideology
0.017	**0.121***	0.004	**−0.187***
(0.021)	(0.064)	(0.180)	(0.084)
Lack of preparation X . . .			
Vacancy index	Trust index	Politicization	Agency ideology
0.016	−0.284***	−0.051	**0.225***
(0.022)	(0.070)	(0.216)	(0.093)
Not leveraging SES X . . .			
Vacancy index	Trust index	Politicization	Agency ideology
0.041*	**0.134***	−0.146	−0.064
(0.020)	(0.059)	(0.177)	(0.081)

Note: Bold type represents significant findings; SE = standard error.
*** p < .01; ** p < .05; * p < .1 (two-tailed)

baseline category if the respondent has a high amount of trust established with current appointees, or if the respondent is in a liberal agency. Those who have established trust in current appointees are more likely to value the importance of that trust (or lack thereof) than those who have not. Moreover, we see throughout table 5.5 that most of my expectations are confirmed based on the assumption of availability heuristics—with the exception of politicization, which has no statistically significant effect on rankings at all. Notably, respondents in agencies with more persistent appointee vacancies, where SES members are more likely to have "acting" leadership roles, are more likely to rank "reticence to leverage SES expertise" and an appointee's "eagerness to change organizational structure" as more important impediments than confirmation delay. Collectively, the findings tell us that on-hand heuristics could be at work in identifying generalized impediments to successful transition.

Nonetheless, we can only use the results of tables 5.4 and 5.5 in a descriptive sense, as the assumption of availability is too tenuous to conclusively attribute these generalized impediments to appointee-careerist relations at the time of the survey. I employ this rank-ordered logistic analysis as indirect substantiation to the claim that jigsaw management and distrust are prevalent among organizations, generally, and likely over the course of the Bush administration (assuming that availability, in part, drives response). I argue that the analysis bears out a more contingent approach, dependent upon both the agency environment and the personal relationships that develop within those environments.

In the analysis that follows, I use other survey indicators for the main inferential model to measure how the establishment of trust between career executives and political appointees is associated with knowledge exchange. This exchange is not only a key to carrying out the Johnson memo. If it was not present in carrying out a procedural or management agenda like what the White House was proposing, it is unlikely that policy initiatives pursued administratively would fare any better in terms of needed sharing of information (and most likely worse).

Therefore, in the following analysis, I employ a varying-intercept-and-slope multilevel logistic regression to model the likelihood that a respondent is aware of any transition activity within their organization. Consonant with Pfiffner's "cycle of accommodation" thesis, I argue that transition activity awareness is a function of the trust that respondents have established with appointees within their organization (trust index). However, I argue that the premium that trust has on this likelihood is a function of the political and organizational characteristics of the agency in which these relationships are embedded. Thus, I allow both the intercept and the trust index slope to vary, focusing on the moderating influence of the agency-level variables vacancy index, politicization, and agency ideology.

In doing so, I juxtapose the "jigsaw puzzle" syndrome with Pfiffner's notion that, over time, a deeper trust develops between appointees and civil servants, implying that the cycle of accommodation surely should be most felt at the end of an administration. Because there is evidence that such cooperation was incomplete, I argue that this cycle is not institutionalized. Nor, does it come about as a result of a presidential edict, since personal relationships come and go fairly quickly given the brevity with which political appointees stay in their jobs and are regulated by the prior administrative strategies and political considerations that an administration has put in place.

Awareness of Planned or Ongoing Transition Activities

The dependent variable is a dichotomous variable indicating whether the respondent is aware of any transition activity within his or her organization during the Bush transition period. Data for this measure were collected via a survey item asking respondents to identify whether their agencies were involved in any number of 11 different activities in preparation for the upcoming transition (see table 5.1).

While a variable could have been constructed that counted the number of activities of which the respondents were aware, I am more interested in capturing why such a large proportion of the respondents are *completely unaware* of transition activities in their respective organizations. In addition, the organizational and policy dynamics of the different agencies may be more of a determinant of the types of activities that are taking place than anything else. Therefore, a dichotomous variable of whether they are aware of any activity (activity awareness = 1; no activity awareness = 0) is all that is necessary to capture the construct of "explicit activity awareness." The dichotomous variable was scored as a "1" if any of the activities were checked by the respondent and as a "0" if the respondent checked "Cannot answer; I have no knowledge of transition activities in this agency."

In examining the outcome of explicit knowledge exchange, I am assuming a critical importance of this exchange to organizational continuity and effectiveness, and that "collective knowledge is the most secure and strategically significant kind of organizational knowledge" (Spender, 1996, p. 52). As Neustadt (1990) described presidential transitions, the ability to cope with its inherent uncertainty depends on the operational capacity of the standing presidency: "Can a president keep the presidency going, turn out the work that keeps government going, and hand both on, reasonably intact, to his successor?" (p. 232).

The information that political appointees share with members of the SES is often a reflection of the level of personal involvement that SES members have with political appointees, with mutual trust playing a major role in developing that relationship. If trust is partially a function of the interactions in which trusting actors anticipate quality in both the frequency of exchange and the perceived quality of past interactions, then we can reasonably assume some connection between the identification of policy goals and trust—as has been evidenced in policy implementation studies (e.g., Lundin, 2007).

Controls

I include a series of fixed controls that might explain the likelihood that SES members are aware of ongoing transition preparation activities. The survey provides respondents with the opportunity to indicate which actors are potentially involved in the preparation for transition in their organization. In reality, the participation of different actors should lead to different outcomes, if appointees are indeed practicing jigsaw management techniques or using parallel institutions (e.g., contractors or think tanks) to carry out the president's agenda. The respondent's own participation is dropped from the model due to potential endogeneity. Even so, the correlation between whether the respondent is personally involved in transition preparations and activity awareness is a moderate 0.41. This indicates that appointees might name SES personnel as nominally involved with transition preparation, while appointees carried out the preparations (if at all) through other means.[34]

I also include measures of career tenure because career senior executives are typically more likely to have experience in the area of leadership change. As evidenced in previous studies, the average tenure of political appointees tends to be rather short in comparison to the tenure of career executives

(Chang, Lewis, & McCarty, 2001; Wood & Marchbanks, 2007). Therefore, members of the SES who have experienced the turnover of previous appointees may be less likely to develop a trusting relationship with new appointees, given the expectation of another impending turnover.

The NAPA survey includes indicators of tenure in the SES, in government, and in the respondent's current organization. NAPA researchers used the same ordinal scale that is employed in OPM surveys, such as the Federal Human Capital Survey, instead of asking the respondent to state an exact number of years. Two other indicators serve as rough proxy indicators of transition experience, asking the number of appointee transitions that the respondent has experienced during his or her tenure and the number of presidential transitions during his or her tenure.

A range of other circumstances may determine whether members of the SES are aware of important decisions and activities within their respective agency. One survey item asked the respondent to identify his or her location as "headquarters" or "field." A dummy variable for headquarters (headquarters = 1; field = 0) was used to capture whether the respondent had physical proximity to his or her political principals. A dummy variable is included if the respondent has had previous training/orientation for working with political appointees. Additionally, there are dummy variables included for whether the respondent identifies his or her position as housed in a "department, agency/bureau, or commission/board." Dummy variables are also included to determine whether the respondent reports to an appointee or careerist. Table 5.6 provides summary statistics for each of the aforementioned measures.

I construct a multilevel logistic regression model with the binary outcome of whether the respondent is aware of transition activities within his or her organization ($\Pr(\text{AWARE}_{ij} = 1 \mid \beta_j) = \phi_{ij}$; $\log[\phi_{ij}/(1 - \phi_{ij})] = \eta_{ij}$):

LEVEL-1 MODEL

$$\text{AWARE}_{ij} = \beta_{0j} + \beta_{1j}{}^{*}(T_{ij}) + Z^{*}(\Lambda) + r_{ij}$$

LEVEL-2 MODEL

$$\beta_{0j} = \gamma_{00} + \gamma_{01}{}^{*}(V_j) + \gamma_{02}{}^{*}(P_j) + \gamma_{03}{}^{*}(I_j) + u_{0j}$$
$$\beta_{1j} = \gamma_{10} + \gamma_{11}{}^{*}(V_j) + \gamma_{12}{}^{*}(P_j) + \gamma_{13}{}^{*}(I_j) + u_{11j}$$
$$\Lambda = \gamma_{30} \ldots \gamma_k$$

Table 5.6. Summary statistics

Variable	N	Mean	SD	Min	Max
Activity awareness	1116	0.785	0.411	0	1
Trust index	1116	1.945	0.880	0	3.187
Vacancy index	32	3.811	4.105	0	9.593
Agency ideology	32	0.141	0.972	−1.58	2.21
Politicization	32	0.559	0.496	0.033	2
Department	1116	0.402	0.491	0	1
Agency/bureau	1116	0.473	0.500	0	1
Board/commission	1116	0.077	0.267	0	1
SES experience	1115	3.078	1.414	1	6
Government experience	940	5.243	1.219	1	6
Agency experience	969	4.025	1.740	1	6
Transition experience	1116	3.039	4.303	0	22
Presidential transition experience	1116	1.699	2.382	0	9
Training	1116	0.281	0.848	0	9
PA involvement	1116	0.581	0.494	0	1
Other SES involvement	1116	0.841	0.366	0	1
Staff involvement	1116	0.645	0.479	0	1
External agency involvement	1116	0.093	0.291	0	1
Contractor involvement	1116	0.103	0.304	0	1
Good government involvement	1116	0.047	0.211	0	1
Program expert involvement	1116	0.412	0.492	0	1
HQ	1116	0.726	0.155	0	1
PAS report	1116	0.237	0.426	0	1
PA report	1116	0.092	0.290	0	1
NCSES report	1116	0.057	0.233	0	1

Note: PAS = Senate-confirmed political appointees; PA = non-Senate-confirmed political appointees; NCSES = noncareer Senior Executive Service; SES = Senior Executive Service; HQ = headquarters.

T_{ij} is the trust that respondent i has established with appointees (trust index) at agency j (variable is centered at the group mean)

V_j is the extent that appointee positions have been vacant over the 110th Congress (vacancy index) at agency j (variable is centered at the grand mean)

P_j is the extent to which unilateral appointments are layered through executive and upper-management ranks of agency j (politicization) (variable is centered at the grand mean)

I_j is agency j's ideological association (agency ideology) (variable is centered at the grand mean)

Z is a vector of level-1 controls

Λ is a level-1 coefficient vector

Υ is a level-2 coefficient vector

r_{ij} is a random individual-level error term

u_j is a random agency-level error term

Results

Table 5.7 reports the results of the multilevel logistic regression for transition activity awareness of SES members.[35] Similar to the model employed in the previous chapter, the purpose of the multilevel model in the present analysis is to identify the influence that specific organizational-level traits have not only on the likelihood that respondents have explicit awareness of transition activities but also the influence these organizational-level characteristics have on the relationship between the trust that an individual has established with political appointees in his or her organization (trust index) and his or her awareness of transition activities as well. I expect that these organizational-level traits will influence the relationship between the trust index and a respondent's likelihood of transition awareness.

Table 5.7 provides evidence of both the direct and indirect relationships between various agency-level attributes and transition activity awareness. Trust index is statistically significant and has a positive association with transition activity awareness, indicating (as expected) that respondents with more established trust with appointees are more likely to be aware of ongoing transition activities within their respective agencies. This is not surprising, and it is consistent with Pfiffner's "cycle of accommodation" thesis. What may be surprising, however, is that the appointee vacancy index has a positive and statistically significant impact on the intercept, indicating that respondents in agencies subject to persistent appointee vacancies in the time leading up to the survey are (on average) more likely to be aware of ongoing transition activities than respondents in agencies that are not. In other words, the longer consistently appointed leadership has been in place, the less likely those appointees are to inform careerists of transition preparations (which is antithetical to the Bush mandate but perhaps in line with the administration's general management approach prior to the transition). This is consistent with the findings on general intellectual capital capacity discussed in chapter 4. However, in this context, we see how this translates to a specific policy area common to all agencies. Additionally, the coefficient for agency ideology is negatively associated with the slope for

Table 5.7. Varying-intercept-and-slope multilevel logistic regression analysis

	Coefficient	Robust(SE)
For intercept(1), $\beta 0$		
Intercept, $\gamma 00$	−0.668***	(0.193)
Vacancy index, $\gamma 01$	0.110*	(0.059)
Agency ideology, $\gamma 02$	0.384	(0.306)
Politicization, $\gamma 03$	0.522	(0.406)
For trust index, $\beta 1$		
Intercept, $\gamma 10$	1.002***	(0.159)
Vacancy index, $\gamma 11$	−0.035	(0.041)
Agency ideology, $\gamma 12$	−0.281**	(0.137)
Politicization, $\gamma 13$	0.033	(0.345)
Department, $\beta 2$	−0.666	(0.571)
Agency/bureau, $\beta 3$	−0.085	(0.582)
Board/commission, $\beta 4$	−0.342	(0.765)
SES tenure, $\beta 5$	−0.074	(0.074)
Government tenure, $\beta 6$	−0.197**	(0.109)
Agency tenure, $\beta 7$	0.057	(0.085)
Transition experience, $\beta 8$	0.028	(0.034)
Presidential transition experience, $\beta 9$	−0.013	(0.050)
Training, $\beta 10$	0.336	(0.230)
PA involvement, $\beta 11$	0.168	(0.208)
Other SES, $\beta 12$	1.064***	(0.275)
Staff involvement, $\beta 13$	0.412**	(0.198)
External agency involvement, $\beta 14$	0.380	(0.393)
Contractor involvement, $\beta 15$	−0.095	(0.522)
Good government involvement, $\beta 16$	−0.143	(0.823)
Expert involvement, $\beta 17$	0.457*	(0.268)
HQ, $\beta 18$	0.467	(0.000)
PAS report, $\beta 19$	0.367	(0.316)
PA report, $\beta 20$	0.224	(0.318)
NCSES report, $\beta 21$	−0.381	(0.562)

Note: Agency-level observations = 32; individual-level observations = 940; PAS = Senate-confirmed political appointees; PA = non-Senate-confirmed political appointees; NCSES = noncareer Senior Executive Service; SES = Senior Executive Service; HQ = headquarters; SE = standard error.

*** $p < .01$; ** $p < .05$; * $p < .1$ (two-tailed)

trust index on transition activity awareness, indicating that the slope for trust is more robustly positive in agencies that have liberal ideological orientations.

Because I have allowed the slope and the intercept to vary based on the indirect influence of various agency-level attributes, I provide graphs to better explicate the contingent effects of individual-level predictors under varying conditions of embeddedness. In this model, I have allowed the intercept to vary based on agency-level characteristics. This allows me to interpret the direct impact that agency-level attributes have on individuals' likelihood to be aware of transition activities, on average, within their agency. One can think of these relationships as the starting point of the relationship between individual-level variables and the dependent variable. Table 5.7 indicates that the appointee vacancy index has a direct, statistically significant association with the likelihood that respondents are aware of transition activities, and the relationship is in the hypothesized positive direction. In other words, as the appointee vacancy index increases, so, too, does the average likelihood of activity awareness among respondents within each agency. We find no evidence that politicization or agency ideology have any impact on the intercept.

Next, I turn to the hypotheses that predict how different agency-level attributes will moderate the slope of the trust index on transition activity awareness. Figure 5.1 shows the slopes of trust index across the sample of agencies. The figure indicates that there is indeed variation in the slope. In other words, the relationship between trust index and activity awareness changes based on the organizational environment in which respondents operate.

We see in table 5.7 that only the agency ideology coefficient is significant. Figure 5.2 shows how these relationships vary based on that particular agency-level attribute. By holding agency ideology at its upper (conservative) and lower (liberal) quartile averages, we see that trust has a higher premium in liberally oriented agencies (i.e., a more robustly positive relationship). This indicates that trust is a more precious commodity for the purposes of explicit knowledge exchange in agencies that are more liberally oriented. In conservative agencies, trust matters less to the likelihood that career respondents are aware of transition preparations.

These findings support the notion that appointee trust is critical to explicit knowledge exchange in organizations. First, the relationship between trust and explicit activity awareness implies that trust "turns not on one's own interests but on the interests of the trusted" (Hardin, 2006b, p. 22). Career SES members who have established the trust of appointees are more likely to be aware of transition activities in their organization. More importantly, however, my findings imply that trust is conditioned by the ideological orientation of the agency. Therefore, the benefit that a career executive receives in being trusted is more marked in agencies that do not presumably

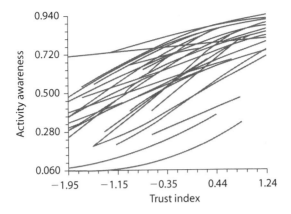

Figure 5.1. Varying intercepts and slopes across agency population

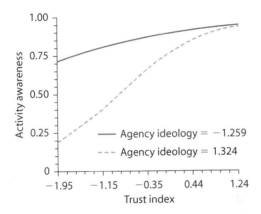

Figure 5.2. Moderating influence of agency ideology on trust index slope

share the ideological preferences of those appointed by a conservative administration.

The findings are telling in respect to the potential practice of jigsaw management techniques. If, indeed, Bush administration appointees were generally exercising such techniques (leaving careerists in the dark to important policy decisions), the pattern indicated in the findings should emerge. The pattern indicates that when appointees are occupying leadership ranks, career executives in those agencies are less likely to be aware of ongoing transition activities. Thus, I argue that these findings collectively provide evidence that reveals an insightful irony in common strategies of the administrative presidency. When the Bush administration sought the involvement of careerist input, the administration's emissaries potentially interfered in the unilateral directive to do so. If the inability to establish trust is, indeed, a result of jigsaw management practices across the Bush administration, such a strategy contradicts some of the articulated reasons for the existence of the SES. While the evidence I present here does not directly test the presumption that jigsaw management practices were in fact prevalent, the pictures that emerge from both the rank-ordered logit analysis and the main inferential model are consonant with those accounts.

Conclusion

The evidence presented in this research offers an indirect challenge to Pfiffner's "cycle of accommodation" between appointees and careerists. As one interviewee opined, "I think one of the hardest things for [political appointees] is to involve career staff who've been there, who have been with the programs, with the operations, and move ahead with your agenda. I think a lot of times. . . . I know in the Bush administration, they were very closed-door for a long time. That *may have* loosened up over time, but it was just such an obviously short-sighted technique."[36] The fact that the likelihood of careerists' awareness is neither zero nor unity attests to the "cycle of accommodation" thesis proffered by Pfiffner. Indeed, as another executive put it, "In the end, you usually develop a very good relationship. The way you do it is you're loyal to whoever's [sic] here, and you work hard for them. If they're any good, they discover quickly that you're quite an asset to them."[37] Thus, the thrust of this analysis is to test the extent to which that cycle completes itself and *the conditions under which* this cycle is more or less likely to come to fruition. The evidence points to a modified or contingent approach to jigsaw management (or, conversely, accommodation) in which both agency-level and individual-level characteristics influence that approach.

There is evidence that appointees inhibited information sharing with careerists despite the administration's unilateral orders to work closely with careerists. I find evidence of careerists being "kept in the dark" in a manner that is, in part, consistent with evidence of jigsaw puzzle management. Moreover, I find that cooperation was moderated by the degree to which the agency had been subject to persistent appointee vacancies leading up to transition preparations and the relative ideological orientation of the agency. The importance of appointee trust in career executives is more robust in liberal agencies. And, the likelihood of awareness is diminished, on average, in agencies that have had appointees in place on a more consistent basis leading up to the transition. Thus, cooperation was contingent on organizational, political, and interpersonal conditions that regulated the degree to which career executives were explicitly aware of these preparations. The major irony that I focus on is the degree to which appointees inhibited the president's ability to have an expressed implementation preference followed through.

The more consistently that appointed leadership had been in place in a given agency, the less likely those appointees were to inform careerists of transition preparations. Thus, while institutional powers are important, they do not give our president complete dominion over the executive branch through unilateral powers. Here, we find a presidential directive to cooperate with careerists' founder because of previous management choices (i.e., jigsaw management). It is uncertain as to what the discount factor might be among appointees for ignoring OMB directives to involve career executives. We are also not able to discern the extent to which appointees will act as free agents depending on where they might fall on the president's policy agenda at a given time.

Yet, institutional arguments of presidential power have long prevailed in much of the presidency scholarship, such as the notion that selective recruitment and ideological identification can make self-executing commands implicit within the executive branch (e.g., Howell, 2005; Sperlich, 1969). Indeed, the same is ostensibly presumed by both advocates and opponents of the modern administrative presidency. I find that, especially at the end of an administration, Neustadt's (1990) characterization of the presidency as a weak institutional position may still hold, and that transactional leadership (even with supposedly "loyalist" appointees) may be a better source of that individual's power. However, this is supposition, as the data allow me to examine only appointee-careerist relations and not how the president's administration interacts with appointees beyond the issuance of an executive memorandum.

Nonetheless, in liberally oriented agencies especially, the pathologies that developed as a result of the Bush administration's strategic use of the president's appointment powers did not align with the intent of his unilateral order, implying that ideology was a more powerful determinant than loyalty in this context. Even so, the success of that order was dependent upon the conditional trust that a selection of careerists had previously established with appointees, as well as the relative continuity of appointee positions being filled over time. In many ways, the analysis here indicates that the cycle of accommodation thesis—at least in a second term—is incomplete or, more accurately, conditional. Moreover, any presidential administration must recognize that an edict to advance its agenda through appointee-careerist cooperation will not be self-executing.

6

Rethinking the Administrative Presidency

You may be deceived if you trust too much, but you will live in torment if you do not trust enough.

—Frank Crane, quoted in *Business Education World*, Vol. 15 (1935), p. 172

The "politicization of organizational life" is increasingly becoming the reality of the modern administrative state (Heclo, 1978; Kerwin, West, & Furlong, 2010). Political appointees now take up over 25% of the "management layers between the top and bottom of most departments and agencies."[38] As noted throughout this book, the appointment powers of the United States' president have been argued to be a valuable method for advancing, and making career civil servants responsive to, presidential agendas (Durant, 1992; Golden, 2000; Wood & Waterman, 1994). Yet, applying this central tool of the administrative presidency is motivated by distrust of careerists to faithfully carry out those agendas (e.g., Ban & Ingraham, 1990; Moynihan & Roberts, 2010; Pfiffner, 1991a). And while researchers have contended that trust is a critical factor in appointees' relative capacity to wield administrative power toward a president's intended goals (Durant, 1992, 2000; Heclo, 1977; Michaels, 1997; Pfiffner, 1987; Rourke, 1991, 1992), this research has not been applied with any degree of sophistication as presidents try to advance their policy agendas administratively. Consequently, I offered an integrated model of these relationships employing precepts from cognate fields such as private management studies, organization theory, and game theory.

However, findings from the extant work examining the connection between interpersonal trust and organizational outcomes have been mixed. It has not yet been established whether interpersonal trust is anything more than complementary to institutional incentives and monitoring mechanisms. For example, some have suggested that trust is critical to advancing organizational effectiveness (Brehm & Gates, 2008), while other theorists argue that sufficient support for the argument that trust relations are anything but "complements to organizationally induced incentives" is lacking (Cook, Hardin, & Levi, 2005, p. 134). An important reason for this insufficiency may be that trust is such a context-dependent construct, and that it is difficult to model its relative importance across varying organizational contexts (Gillespie, 2012). By accommodating differences in key organizational-level traits, however, I was able to adequately enable replication of the individual-level measurement of trust across a multiplicity of executive branch agencies.

This book establishes a critical link between appointee-careerist trust and institutional competence by accounting for the varying political, structural, professional, and relational conditions under which "encapsulated interest" and "personal trust" might exist among appointees and career executives. I examined how different dimensions of trust are connected to the exchange and combination of information within organizational settings (i.e., the development of "intellectual capital").

In the process, I showed that the application of these tools has a paradoxical effect from its intent. By politicizing bureaucratic ranks with lower-level appointees and centralizing decision-making through decidedly top-down arrangements, presidents foster further distrust of political appointees among careerists. This reciprocated distrust, in turn, inhibits a president's (and, by proxy, his appointees') capacity to develop the institutional competence necessary to successfully implement his policy agenda. Rather than successfully advancing a president's agenda through jigsaw management approaches that seek to leverage careerists' "neutral" competence without risking some sort of pushback, obstruction, or subversion, we find that these strategies serve to undermine the potential "joist building" of institutional competence that is fundamental to that intent. Political appointees, as Dilulio (2014) cogently put it, "function for the most part as political appointees, not professional public administrators" (p. 96). The fear of subversion, in other words, is misguided. As one career executive observed, "There's a sense that all federal agencies are information sieves, that if you share information with the career people you might as well be . . . putting it out on the Web. That's not really the case. I think very little leaks. I think what does tend to leak are, frankly, deliberate leaks from the top or occasionally leaks by politicals."[39]

Where We've Been: The Joist-Building of Institutional Competence

This is not to say that the role of political appointees is not critical to the development of an organization's intellectual capital. Presidential appointees define and prioritize the value orientation of the organization. They offer a democratic dimension to leadership as emissaries of the sole elected office in the United States executive branch. Appointments are made for both patronage and policy, and seldom are the constructs wholly separate considerations (Rose, 2005). Presidents use patronage to engender support for their administration in a given policy area and to simultaneously "signal policy" by appointing prominent issue network actors (p. 80). Therefore, appointees may present perspectives that more comprehensively and simultaneously accommodate the value sets representative of the issue networks to which the organization is central (Heclo, 1978).

In this book, I follow Seidman (1998) by defining institutional competence as explicit and implicit knowledge of an organization's "history, program patterns, administrative processes, professional hierarchies, constituencies, and budget structure" (p. 125), and how these characteristics can be employed toward specific actions. I put forth the argument that intellectual capital—"the knowledge and knowing capability of a social collectivity, such as an organization, intellectual community, or professional practice" (Nahapiet & Ghoshal, 1998)—is inately tied to the institutional competence that is necessary to advance presidential agendas administratively (Seidman, 1998). It provides a clear, conceptual link to the concept of human capital, which "reflects the belief that human beings in an organization and their skills and knowledge are the organization's most important assets, more important than other forms of capital such as [physical] and financial assets" (Rainey, 2003). Upon this premise, the argument followed that in order to develop the intellectual capital necessary to advance presidential agendas, presidential appointees must manage in a manner that sufficiently incorporates human capital—that is, the collective and differential assets provided by both political and career personnel—in an agency that possesses the knowledge and capacity to implement this agenda competently.

To do so, I followed a very basic premise of leadership theory—that authority is a cognitive construct that is a function of the trust that a leader engenders. In other words, following Barnard (1938, pp. 163–164), authority "rests upon the acceptance or consent of individuals." It is not a function only of the formal mechanisms of control. Absent the willingness to be vulnerable to the perspectives and expertise of the employees one is expected to lead, there is little hope that any vulnerability will be reciprocated.

I offered a model of these relationships, which was discerned from the administrative presidency literature, but, more importantly, that integrated the findings from a variety of cognate literatures (including private management, organization theory, public management, and social psychology). This proved powerful in accounting for trust and institutional capacity in the analyses that I pursued in the subsequent chapters. Moreover, given its uniqueness and significant explanatory power in this study, it should serve to advance our understanding of an underdeveloped area of research on the executive branch: appointee-careerist relations and how these relations impact the organization.

Simply put, interpersonal trust between career executives and political appointees of the George W. Bush administration had a notable impact on the development of intellectual capital within federal agencies *throughout various hierarchical levels*. This is a critical expansion of the study of the administrative presidency. It confirms previous contentions that trust among careerists and appointees was crucial, but does so by providing systematic evidence that uniquely focuses on how appointee-careerist trust at the highest organizational strata affected organizations as a whole, or how the relative lack of trust could interfere with presidential edicts that demanded cooperation.

My analyses of the perceptions of middle-manager respondents indicate that the trust that is established at the highest levels of the organization between career executives and political appointees (i.e., stratified trust) has a downward effect on the perception of intellectual capital capacity within agencies. In other words, the capacity to both exchange and combine distinct forms of knowledge between superiors and subordinates throughout organizational hierarchies is dependent on the level of trust established at the highest rungs of the organizational ladder. Most importantly, this relationship is moderated by the institutional environment in which appointee-careerist relations are embedded.

These findings show that the trust that develops between career SES members and political appointees has effects *throughout* the organization. Middle managers are more likely to perceive the capacity to build intellectual capital in their agencies as trust is established between career executives and political appointees. So, while chapter 5 indicates that explicit knowledge exchange between SES personnel and appointees increases with trust (measured as encapsulated interest), chapter 4 offers a glimpse into how this connection does not exclusively affect the executive ranks. Rather, the trust (or lack thereof) established at the executive ranks affects the development of intellectual capital in the organization as a whole—the joists that are fundamental to institution building and capacity—and thereby limits the effectiveness of short-term political appointees with markedly different roles and responsibilities.

In chapter 5, I focused exclusively on the relations between appointees and careerists at the executive level of organizations. I narrowed the conceptualization of trust to encapsulated interest—the idea that the benefit that one receives from any particular exchange in which one is trusted is a function of "the potential benefit from continuing the series of interactions" (Hardin, 2006b, p. 22). I identified descriptive evidence that jigsaw management techniques serve as common inhibitors to appointees' ability to leverage institutional competence. After testing to see if respondents perceived these kinds of tactics during the transition, I found that they did and that it varied in terms of the level of encapsulated trust established. As such, my findings indicate that jigsaw management was not as cohesive a strategy as some have claimed or as doable as proponents expected, and that a more ad hoc managerial ideology developed based on interpersonal trust. And, while I found that politicization (measured as a ratio of lower-level political appointees to career SES personnel) inhibits intellectual capital capacity (which supports prior contentions), moderating effects of politicization on the relationship between interpersonal trust and intellectual capital capacity, as well as trust in leadership (TIL) and intellectual capital capacity, do not exist. Rather, cognitive (not structural) politicization (i.e., the relative lack of established stratified trust) had the largest moderating effect and direct effects.

The finding that politicization does not moderate the relationship between trust and perceptions of intellectual capital capacity at lower levels of the organization's hierarchy does *not*, however, suggest that the layering of appointees within executive and management ranks of agencies has *no bearing* on organizational outcomes. Similarly, while there is no evidence in chapter 5 that politicization affects the average policy awareness of executives, these findings (or lack thereof) elevate the importance of interpersonal interactions between appointees and careerists as the focus of analysis, where most of the quantitative empirical explorations of the phenomenon, as well as administrative reform prescriptions, focus on structural aspects of politicization (i.e., the number of appointees in management and executive positions in a given agency).

As Gilmour and Lewis (2006b) implied, political appointees may not have the institutional competence necessary to be responsive to the president and see through agency goals in accordance with the president's preferences. This might explain why, in both chapters 4 and 5, we find that vacancies have a directly positive correlation with careerist assessments of their organization's intellectual capital capacity and career executives' explicit awareness of transition preparations, respectively. This raises an important question as to whether many political appointees actually have the institutional competence necessary to be responsive to the president, manage an agency effectively, and see through agency goals in accordance with the president's preferences. However, we should avoid a whole-cloth characterization of political versus career orientation. Rather, the more accurate takeaway from this book should be that it is the central importance of establishing trust at the executive levels of an agency by signaling and acting on a willingness to incorporate careerists and their relative expertise into a horizontal model of authority, albeit under a vertically oriented accountability system (Bounfour & Edvisson, 2005; Carpenter & Krause, 2015).

The Administrative Presidency and the Importance of Trust

This book is organized into three interconnected parts for the purpose of providing (1) a background to the development of the administrative presidency, (2) a theoretical framework for examining the impact of appointee-careerist relations on organizational outcomes, and (3) empirical examination in which these relations are modeled as determinants of organizational outcomes. Pfiffner (2007, p. 7) observed that George W. Bush's management style was "marked by secrecy, speed, and top-down control" that was most reflective of the Reagan administration and the "partisan learning" that Hult and Walcott (2004) predicted. Yet, as I outlined in chapter 1, while Bush pursued this agenda using these administrative strategies (relying on ideological loyalty, increased appointee layering, and centralized management), they were not necessarily amenable to realizing his goals. This presents the question as to whether the combined centralization and politicization strategies of the two administrations should be so similar. The intentions and environmental conditions of the Bush administration differed substantially from the Reagan administration. I questioned whether the application of such administrative strategies would necessarily advance the interests of a Bush administration (or any administration) that sought to wield administrative power to advance new agendas rather than stop old ones?

These questions lead me to examine the idea of bureaucratic competence as it has been variously defined in the public administration and political science literature. Although I did not explicitly quote James D. Carroll's (1976) basic syllogism in chapter 2, the essence of my argument is similar. Carroll wrote, "Administration is knowledge. Knowledge is power. Administration is power" (p. 578). Indeed, most studies of the US presidency, as well as politics and public management generally, ultimately involve questions about power. From where is the president's power derived? How do political executives exercise power? What are the opportunities and constraints placed on individual presidents by context, public expectations, institutions, and law? Does presidential power derive from the Constitution, the people, his individual ability as a leader, or elsewhere?

My argument is that part of the president's power derives from his ability to harness and develop the institutional competence of the bureaucracy toward his policy agenda—especially when that agenda seeks to wield administrative power rather than inhibit it. While there are multiple constraints on any president's ability to entirely control the executive branch, I posited that politicization and the management techniques that the Bush administration employed may have led to quite the opposite of what it was intended to do. This might especially be the case based on Andrew Rudalevige's (2002) argument that politicization is intended as a means to tactically unite institutional and responsive competence to cheaply and effectively advantage the president's access to information (i.e., in order to advance presidential agendas). In turn, I argued that any given president's access to information is contingent on careerists' ability to exchange and (re)combine knowledge with an administration and its appointees in a way that can successfully make this happen.

I also pointed to the extant literature that examines appointee-careerist relations—as well as to interviews with SES members that I had conducted for this book—to posit that this type of jigsaw puzzle management might not even be necessary. These sources provided evidence that loyalty to presidential prerogatives is, largely, careerists' default response (Edwards, 2001; Golden, 2000; Michaels, 1997; Wilson, 1989; Wood & Waterman, 1994). Additionally, even if a president's primary stance vis-à-vis the bureaucracy is to limit its power, this should not equate to limiting its capacity to develop and maintain institutional competence. A low-competence agency may produce erratic, unendurable, or unforeseen results that do not comport with the president's long-term objectives (Lewis, 2008, p. 62).

Traditional, principal-agent models of organizational behavior that are applied to presidential-bureaucratic relations are premised on assumptions of distrust between principals and agents rather than the possibility of establishing trust (Whitener et al., 1998). Hence, the organization theory that predominates studies of appointee-careerist relations in political science largely ignores evidence from both the human relations and social exchange strains of organization theory, which argue that trust acts as a supplement to authority, encourages productivity, and promotes loyalty (Barnard, 1938, 1968; Blau, 1964; Carpenter & Krause, 2015; Gouldner, 1954). Even without this literature, there is also evidence that a "control paradox" exists in economic theories of bureaucracy (Miller, 2004); in other words, the imposition of hierarchy, monitoring mechanisms, and additional rules and sanctions can result in "inferior outcomes" and decreased innovation (Hirst et al., 2011; Miller, 2004, p. 117).

It is incumbent on hierarchical superiors to engage in trusting behavior to "increase the likelihood that employees will reciprocate and trust them" (Whitener et al., 1998, p. 516). This point carries even more weight within the appointee-careerist nexus, where careerist's expectations of appointee behavior may be premised on "inverse partisan learning"—the notion that careerists learn to anticipate the "tendency [for presidents and their appointees] to transmit organizational philosophy along party lines" (Walcott & Hult, 2005, p. 305). Because careerists may base their approximations of an appointee's trustworthiness on past relations with appointees from administrations of the same party, it will become incumbent upon new appointees to establish their own respective capacity for credible commitment.

Thus, I proposed a theoretical framework that integrates the concepts of "encapsulated interest," "character-based" or "personal" trust, plus Williamson's concept of "embeddedness," as antecedents to intellectual capital capacity. For the readers' convenience, figure 2.1 provided a heuristic model that draws upon these three areas of organization theory. The heuristic illustrated the connection between trust and an organization's capacity to build intellectual capital. Importantly, it showed in ways unappreciated in prior research on the appointee-careerist nexus that this relationship will be moderated by the institutional environment in which actors are embedded. Encapsulated interests are informed by character-based assessments and vice versa. Both interact with different embeddedness attributes of the institutional environment to form a more complete construct of trust than has typically been proffered in the administrative presidency literature (and, for that matter, in public management research).

Politicization (in both structural and cognitive terms) is, in itself, an embeddedness attribute. It negatively affects an organization's capacity to build intellectual capital. To accommodate the cognitive dimension of politicization, I offered an embeddedness attribute I called "stratified trust." I proposed that the relationship between trust and intellectual capital for employees at lower levels of an organization will be conditioned by the level of trust that is established between actors in hierarchically separate relations at higher levels of the organization.

I illustrated four additional propositions on how the complete construct of dyadic trust (i.e., superior-subordinate relationships), as regulated by its institutional environment, will determine the means by which the capacity to build intellectual capital is developed. Trust will increase (1) the accessibility to organizational actors to combine and exchange information, (2) the anticipated value of these exchanges, (3) individuals' motivation to participate in these exchanges, and (4) the capacity of individuals to participate in exchange. In this instance, again, each of these propositions (with trust conceptualized as a product of encapsulated interest, character-based assessments, and embeddedness attributes of the organizational environment) weave together observations and precepts from the fields of organization theory, social psychology, and economics. By integrating these perspectives, I have addressed, in part, Martha Feldman's (1992) concern that other intellectual perspectives (e.g., organization theory) that can help us understand the phenomena that help define the presidency are incorporated into presidency research and executive politics more generally. I proposed that the trust that is established between career executives and political appointees will affect the connection between trust and intellectual capital capacity throughout the organization.

The Significance of Appointee-Careerist Relations

In chapters 3 and 4, I examined the relationship between trust and intellectual capital capacity as trust develops throughout an organization's hierarchical structure, as well as the accompanying impact of politicization, appointee vacancies, and ideology on the development of intellectual capital within agencies. I found that dyadic trust established between employees and their immediate supervisors has a strong correlation with perceptions of intellectual capital capacity, a precondition to effective performance. Moreover, I found that the trust established among high-level agency actors affects perceptions of intellectual capital capacity at lower levels of an agency's hierarchy. Specifically, the trust established between career SES personnel and political appointees has positive effects on perceptions of intellectual capital capacity at the middle-management level of organizations. These subordinate-superior relationships at the executive levels are separate from the dyadic relationships measured at the middle-management levels of organizations in my study, indicating that trust can have "trickle-down" effects on the development of intellectual capital within a hierarchically structured organization. Given the evidence that politicization has a direct negative impact on intellectual capital capacity, these trickle-down effects may be exacerbated under conditions of strategic appointee layering. However, while structural politicization does not have a statistically significant moderating impact on either dyadic trust or TIL, the relative persistence in appointed leadership vacancies has varying moderating impacts on the two forms of trust. Appointee vacancies have a negative impact on TIL while increasing the premium that career middle managers place on dyadic trust in their immediate supervisors (presumably, career executives). This is consistent with Brehm and Gates's (2008) observations emphasizing the capacity of immediate supervisors to insulate their subordinates from political interference and cultivate trust. Under conditions of political uncertainty (here measured in terms of appointee vacancies), SES members may have more capacities for influence than what are generally recognized, in that they are able to minimize the effects of organizational ambiguities on subordinates.

In chapter 5, I provided an empirical test of the impact of appointee-careerist relations on the likelihood of SES-awareness of important decisions within their organizations, with transition activities as the focus of the analysis. I used perceptual and relational measures from a widely distributed National Academy of Public Administration (NAPA) survey of the SES. In this respect, the evidence from this study strengthened that provided by previous studies of appointee-careerist relations. It is the first survey that captures quantifiable evidence of SES members' awareness of important decision-making activities within their own organization at the time of implementation.

The empirical results of chapter 5's study indicated that SES members are more likely to be aware of important decision-making processes in their organization if they have established trust with political appointees. I provided evidence indicating that those career executives who perceive their actions as encapsulating the interests of higher-level political appointees were more likely to have explicit knowledge of transition preparations in their organization.

The analysis in chapter 5 also provides further evidence that a president's (e.g., Clay Johnson's memorandum) mandate is not necessarily self-executing. Indeed, although the data does not allow me to measure appointees' ideological and personal loyalty to the president, the dominant opinion of the literature reviewed in the first two chapters proposes that the Bush administration held to "loyalty-first" standards in appointee placement. If so, the evidence presented in chapter 5, in part, refutes Sperlich's (1969) critique of Neustadt's argument that reliance on "self-executing" commands is a sign of presidential weakness. Sperlich argued that selective recruitment and ideological identification can make self-executing commands implicit within the executive branch. But even with a presumed procedural edict—as opposed to a policy or program change—implementation can still be a problem.

Also of significance from the analysis in chapter 5 are indications that the conventional wisdom regarding the scope, persistency, and nature of the Bush administration's use of jigsaw puzzle management strategies needs some rethinking. Rather than keeping careerists consistently in the dark about the true ends of policy, by definition, the Johnson memo belied this assertion. But more importantly, analysis revealed evidence by the end of the Bush administration (at least) that selectivity based on levels of trust may have guided implementation of this strategy. Granted, significant numbers of respondents (nearly one-fifth) didn't know about transition activities, despite the memo's instructions to be sure they did. But the real message here is not only that old habits die hard but that a paradoxical situation flourished (i.e., a policy designed to encourage appointee-careerist collaboration was implemented in a noncollaborative way).

The analysis indicates that information exchange was predicated on perceived levels of trust—in other words, what Heclo prescribed as a "contingently cooperative" strategy was being carried out by Bush appointees (Durant, 1992; Golden, 2000; Heclo, 1978). We do not know the reasons for that, whether it was a truly new or emergent form of relationship indicated by Pfiffner's cycle of accommodation or whether this notion of "keeping careerists in the dark" was either pragmatically difficult to implement or a canard for political opponents of the Bush administration to pursue for their gain. But the fact that some evidence exists perceptually begs further study.

This is the first study of its kind to grapple with these issues in theoretically grounded and empirically sophisticated ways. The findings beg testing, elaborating, and refining in future study. If confirmed in a procedural policy arena, it seems likely that these tendencies will be even more pronounced in a more contentious policy arena where the stakes are perceived high for all constituencies concerned. Moreover, if, indeed, old "jigsaw puzzle management" habits die hard, it is worth pursuing whether a kind of personal and/or institutional "path dependency" exists in appointee-careerist relations and why or why not. Conversely, if "contingent cooperative" strategies were used at certain points in the Bush administration—presumably one of the most predisposed administrations in history to practice jigsaw management, keeping careerists "in the dark and feeding them manure" (as the saying goes)—perhaps a final stake might be driven in the heart of such theories of administration. And if they were used under certain circumstances and not for others, it would seem useful theoretically and practically to understand the conditions under which they are or are not used.

The Administrative Presidency and Beyond

Given the important methodological and substantive implications that these findings present for scholarship, they offer several areas for future study. First, the analysis in chapter 4 produces evidence that suggests that the relationships established at higher levels of an organization's hierarchy have substantive effects not only on the individual career executives' policy knowledge but on the intellectual capital capacity of entire federal agencies. The explanatory power of variables and insights derived from cognate research fields that produced these findings indicate that students of the administrative presidency should not only follow Martha Feldman's call two decades ago to apply organizational theory to the study of the presidency generally. They should also look to schools of thought within that tradition that have not been pursued as aggressively as they should (e.g., organization theory, social psychology, and generic management studies). While the political dynamics of public organizations, and namely executive agencies, limit the generalizability of management research in the private sector to public organizations, it is a mistake to ignore findings from the cognate fields that can inform the study of the administrative presidency. The analysis of chapter 4 demonstrates that, especially as it pertains to the relationships established at higher levels of the organization (the locus of most appointee-careerist interaction), many of the findings from these cognate fields hold true, and future studies of the administrative presidency would do well to incorporate them.

Second, due to the cross-sectional nature of the analysis in chapter 5, we simply do not know if a blanket jigsaw management strategy was implemented prior to the transition. So, it may have been only when appointees were commanded to work with careerists that conditional cooperation emerged. Nonetheless, the encapsulated interest indicators do measure the history of interactions, while the dependent variable (explicit policy knowledge) measures a distinct policy as it was being implemented over a discrete timeframe. Thus, future research should look to improve on this analysis by undertaking a longitudinal research design that focuses on a presidential mandate as it is being implemented. Such a design could account for the fact that relationships develop over time but may also be contingent on the perceived cooperation of both parties to advancing their individual interests.

Third, my hope is that the promise of the model I presented in chapter 2, incorporating this cognate literature, will prompt others to test, elaborate, and extend to other areas of research in executive politics. More specifically, the book's analysis demonstrates that research that unpacks the interpersonal dynamics of appointee-careerist relations will yield a more nuanced and fuller view of the extent to which presidents can be successful in pursuing administrative strategies. As I detailed, intellectual capital capacity throughout organizations was, in part, dependent on the level of trust established at the executive ranks—one of several embeddedness traits that are measurable and important to the institutional environment of federal agencies. This finding, in particular, seems to merit further analysis by students of executive politics. Importantly, politicization does not present as substantial a direct, or indirect, impact on institutional competence as does stratified trust. This finding is consistent with West's (1995) contention that application of the politicization strategy and the reorganization of the management structures of agencies "only allow the president to influence the general contours of policy implementation rather than specific actions" (p. 88).

Fourth, the negative and direct impact that politicization has on intellectual capital may, at first, seem consonant with structural reform prescriptions put forth by scholars such as Paul Light, the two National Commissions on the Public Service led by Paul Volcker, and the Brookings Institution's Presidential Appointee Initiative Report that the federal government should reduce the overall number of political appointees.[40] Yet, the findings more acutely address why these prescriptions need to be modified and redirected toward the motivations that underlie presidential administrative strategies. The evidence I present in this book implies that simply layering appointees throughout management ranks does not, in and of itself, have as substantial impact on functional competence of federal agencies as previously argued (Lewis, 2008). Rather, I find and argue that it is the interpersonal relations that develop among career and political executives that have the largest impact on institutional competence. These findings indicate that it is necessary to understand the forces that determine how these relationships develop in order to understand the effect that appointee-careerist relations have on organizational outcomes.

Fifth, and more in line with these earlier prescriptions for reform of appointee-careerist relations, the very foundation of administrative strategies paradoxically undermines the legitimacy and effectiveness of their application, because implementation depends on exactly the career bureaucracy presidents seek to circumvent (Durant & Resh, 2010, p. 580). Therefore, it is imperative that research goes beyond principal-agent frameworks that rely on problematic, microeconomic assumptions of human behavior that ostensibly ignore institutional and interpersonal influences (see Carpenter & Krause, 2015, for a nuanced interpretation of this argument). Rather, research should begin to examine the relational dynamics and organizational behavior of the actors involved in these relationships, the context in which these relationships develop, and how these relationships cumulatively impact organizational outcomes. Additionally, research should expand on what I have presented here by operationalizing organizational outcomes in ways that make explicit connections to a president's policy goals.

Sixth, the importance of appointee-careerist relations is not exclusive to the Bush administration or to Republican administrations, generally. Well into the Obama administration's first term, a study from the Government Business Council indicated that the administration's appointees generally lacked both "functional and agency-specific knowledge," were unwilling to collaborate or communicate with career employees, and exercised familiar top-down management approaches intended to control, not facilitate, bureaucratic action: "[Careerists] believe appointees don't understand human resources and procurement rules, saying they presume the 'institution is there as an obstruction' and therefore attempt to 'break organizations.' Appointees have 'unbelievably poor communication with career employees,' one commenter said. Forty percent of managers gave them Ds or Fs on collaboration and communication with their staffs. . . . [One] manager said the result has been 'politicization of normal agency functions.'"[41] Importantly, one might not glean the extent of this politicization through traditional structural measures of the construct. Whereas efforts to maximize the political responsiveness of the SES were perceived when the G. W. Bush administration increased the percentage of SES members who were noncareer to 9.97% of the total ranks, in the Obama administration, noncareer to career proportions fell back down to pre–George W. Bush levels (8.6% in 2013).

Additionally, while his Republican predecessors met collectively with career members of the SES early in their administrations, Obama did not choose to meet with senior career managers and executives in the executive branch until near the end of his second term (in 2014)—to the chagrin of many senior executives. As Senior Executive Association president Charles Bonosaro lamented, "It's always baffled me that a president wouldn't just do this early on, because it sets a tone, not only for the career executives, but also the political appointees, who then get the message that the career executives are part of the team."[42]

Most indications are that career SES personnel have generally come to be seen by the Obama administration as mere conduits of top-down policy decisions from an increasingly large and complex White House staff, without regard to career executives' talents, contributions, expertise, or the difficult conditions under which they serve (e.g., cutbacks, furloughs).[43] This may be a result of an increasing distrust of government generally (by the general population and the short-term politicals delegated to lead it), the increasing partisan divide (such that none other but "loyalists" can be trusted), or a general lack of competence in public management by presidential administrations generally. Nonetheless, as evidenced in this book by the relative failure of White House mandates to be implicitly self-executing, these appointee-careerist relations might inhibit Obama's threat to Congress that he will use all the powers of his office to advance his prerogatives. Indeed, little research on the administrative presidency examines appointee-careerist relations or presidential administrative strategies *across* presidencies. Future research should explore the interpersonal dynamics of appointee-careerist relations, exploiting the variance that appointee-careerist trust has within individual agencies and across organizations and administrations.

Finally, I would like to make an observation that is more normative and more broadly related to the study of executive politics—or, more precisely, the lack of focus of students of the presidency on it. If Carroll's syllogism rings true, it is important to understand how this power is exploited in order to carry out presidential agendas. In an age of legislative gridlock, partisan rancor, and 24/7 punditry, the day-to-day relations of public servants who are "hidden in plain sight" could become paramount to understanding how policy develops (Durant & Resh, 2010). Examinations of principal agent relationships in the bureaucratic politics scholarship that ignore the insights of organization theory, social psychology, and organizational behavior are incomplete at best (Carpenter & Krause, 2015). With a federal bureaucracy issuing a multiplicity of rules for every piece of legislation enacted in any given year by Congress, its relationship to other institutions should not be pigeonholed to a narrow disciplinary perspective. The evidence provided in this study suggests that the trust established at executive levels in federal agencies cannot only affect these personal relationships, but also the extent to which presidential (and congressional) missives are faithfully, effectively, and intelligently implemented is directly and indirectly related to the development of organizational intellectual capital.

Thus, the study of how trust (and its multidimensional nature) and intellectual capital develop (or are thwarted) within the executive branch by misguided or empirically uninformed strategies and reform prescriptions would seem to be a topic that should move front and center on research agendas. As I indicated at the beginning of this book, presidential pursuits of administrative strategies are fueled in part by the public's increasingly irrational expectations of the president. Thus, it seems that today's political environment demands nothing less than the impossible of the American presidency. Generic management studies suggest that through the development of trust and cooperation over the long term, it is more likely that organizations can innovate and achieve the seemingly impossible (Sitkin et al., 2011). Yet, exactly the opposite advice is typically proffered to those charged with leading federal agencies or gleaned from the observations that emerge from narrow understandings of principal-agent theory. According to the evidence marshaled throughout this book, it would also be wise for presidents to heed this. In fact, understanding this relationship seems critical in any effort to advance presidential agendas administratively.

Notes

1. "Dyadic trust" is the term used throughout this book to describe the trust established between two individual actors. In this book, it is used explicitly in terms of trust between an individual subordinate and an individual superior, e.g., employee and manager. "Stratified trust," as explicated in chapter 3, refers to the collective trust established between dyads of career executives and political appointees, i.e., the average dyadic trust established at the highest stratum of a respective organization.

2. C.f. http://www.aspeninstitute.org/policy-work/commission-appointments.

3. At the end of the Bush administration, for instance (according to the 2008 Plum Book), there were 1,141 positions subject to presidential appointment with Senate confirmation (PAS), 314 positions subject to presidential appointment without Senate confirmation (PA), 665 SES general positions filled by noncareer appointments, 121 SES positions filled by limited emergency or limited-term appointments, 1,559 Schedule C Excepted appointments, and 473 positions filled by Statutory Excepted appointment (http://www.gpoaccess.gov/plumbook/2008/index.html). In September 2008 the Bush administration had filled 1,510 Schedule-C appointments (1,215 of which were in cabinet-level agencies) (www.fedscope.opm.gov).

4. As quoted in Pfiffner, 1991.

5. There are several other constraints on the president as well. The president is structurally constrained by the separation of powers system in which the institutional presidency is embedded. While Congress has deferred substantial powers to the executive, the institution and its members retain the power to address threats to their own capacity and repeatedly prevent the adoption of grandiose administrative reforms proposed by presidents to achieve institutional congruence with his goals (Rosenbloom, 1983). At the same time, the president and his advisors possess limited knowledge of the modern administrative state's organizational complexities and hybrid policy domains: "Even if they had the resources to impose any reforms they liked, they would not know how to design an institutional system optimally suited to presidential needs" (Moe, 1993, p. 241). Indeed, this hypothesis has repeatedly been tested and affirmed by countless half-hearted, halting, incremental, ignored, or abandoned attempts by modern presidents to design the executive branch. Presidents are "severely constrained by time" (p. 242). The president's honeymoon quickly wanes, and opposition to his policy proposals and institutional reforms grow by the minute. Changes in the environment call for quick shifts of the president's focus and agenda-setting opportunities are elusive, all while congressional support varies with each two-year electoral cycle (Jones, 1999). Lastly, while presidents are constrained by the path dependency created by past institutional reforms, they are also constrained by their placement in the "political time" of American regime cycles (Skowronek, 2008).

6. Marissa Golden (2000) described politicization as the utilization of "strategic ap-

pointments" and central to the "administrative presidency": "Whereas earlier presidents typically appointed individuals who had ties to agency clients and interest groups and whose loyalties were thus divided, administrative presidents select their appointees strategically, based on their ideological policy congruence with the president" (p. 6).

7. For instance, Dwight Ink (2000), executive director of Carter's Personnel Management Project, argued that evaluations of CSRA have "erroneously" assumed that its intent was to "develop greater political control of the career service" (p. 42). He argued that there were legal safeguards put in place to minimize arbitrary actions and political interference but that these provisions have been "distorted beyond recognition" or ignored (p. 54).

8. The Heritage Foundation purportedly referred to Bush administration policies as emanating "straight from the Heritage playbook" (http://www.rightwingwatch.org/content/heritage-foundation). In fact, one of the report's coauthors (Nesterczuk) was appointed "to oversee the design and implementation of the National Security Personnel System" (Durant, Stazyk, & Resh, 2010b, p. 396) that brought about a vast "reduction of Title V coverage for U.S. civilian personnel" (Pfiffner, 2007, p. 7).

9. Years surrounding the transition from the Clinton administration to the Bush administration were not included in the analysis due to extensive turnover, high rates of early departure preceding the transition, and subsequent delays in filling positions post-transition.

10. Interview conducted October 13, 2010, at American University's School of Public Affairs, Washington, DC.

11. Consistent with the literature examining interpersonal trust in social units such as families, organizations, and institutions, I use the term "dyadic trust" to describe the trust established between two individuals (Larzelere & Huston, 1980; Mayer, Davis, & Schoorman, 1995). However, as Korsgaard et al. (2015) argued, there are three approaches to understanding dyadic trust: "reciprocal trust, wherein one party's trust influences the other party's trust; mutual trust, wherein both parties share a given level of trust that has important consequences for the dyad; and asymmetric trust, wherein each party has a different level of trust, and this disparity has consequences for the dyad" (p. 47). Throughout this study, I explore empirically the concept of dyadic trust exclusively in terms of reciprocal trust, though theoretically I include both mutual and asymmetric accounts in my conceptualization of dyadic trust.

12. Interview conducted at the Department of Agriculture headquarters, College Park, MD.

13. Interview conducted October 5, 2010, in Dupont Circle neighborhood of Washington, DC, with a former Bush appointee at the Department of Education.

14. The "shadow of the future" could weigh heavily into the calculations of both appointees and careerists. It is possible that it devalues the importance careerists attribute to their exchanges with appointees, due to the relatively short tenures of appointees (Wood & Marchbanks, 2007). At the same time, however, the "in-and-outer" status of many appointees precludes any short-term-only expectations in these exchanges. Additionally, as most of the careerists who I interviewed indicated, careerists must maintain a reputation that is consistent across administrations in order to succeed in their respective careers. Although appointees are generally characterized as being focused on short-term policy goals, like presidents, they would also presumably like to protect their legacy in the long-term.

Therefore, it becomes incumbent upon appointees to establish trust in their relations with careerists if they are to see through both short-term and legacy policy goals.

15. Interviews conducted July 20, 2010, at the Department of Education headquarters in Washington, DC, and October 12, 2010, at American University's School of Public Affairs in Washington, DC.

16. Interview conducted July 22, 2010, at a Starbucks coffee shop in Washington, DC.

17. Interview conducted July 22, 2010, at a Starbucks coffee shop in Washington, DC.

18. Interview conducted October 12, 2010, at American University's School of Public Affairs, Washington, DC.

19. Interview conducted October 12, 2010, at American University's School of Public Affairs, Washington, DC.

20. Interview conducted July 22, 2010, at a Starbucks coffee shop in Washington, DC.

21. Interview conducted October 13, 2010, at American University's School of Public Affairs, Washington, DC.

22. Representative bureaucracy theorists refer to "stratification" as the "focal bureaucrats in supervisory positions in public agencies" (Keiser, 2010, p. 1205). According to these theorists, stratification is important to active representation because those bureaucrats with higher authority have more discretion to affect policy implementation (Smith & Fernandez, 2010). I borrow this parlance to refer to the trust established at executive levels in public organizations as "stratified trust," in the sense that the trust established at higher strata will affect the relationship between dyadic trust in supervisors at lower levels of the organization because the discretion that career executives have in affecting policy implementation will be a product of the trust that they have established with their respective superiors.

23. Other embeddedness attributes captured in the proceeding chapters' models will include measures for professionalization, procedural red tape, and technical orientation, among others.

24. Interview with career Senior Executive Service member in the Department of Education, July 20, 2010.

25. However, such analysis potentially overlooks the possibility of the politicization strategy being used in coordination with other tools of the administrative presidency. The authors measure the performance of programs led by either career managers or political appointees using scores from the Bush administration's Program Assessment and Rating Tool (PART). Moreover, the biggest potential problem with each of these studies is that the authors seem to misinterpret the possibility that if there is a political bias in PART scores, it would lean toward appointee-run programs being scored higher than careerist-run programs (however, see Gallo & Lewis, 2012, for more improvements on "overcoming the shortcomings of PART scores in order to make reliable inferences from this measure of federal program performance"; Lewis, 2008, p. 175). These authors contend that PART scores are actually a conservative measure of the positive impact of career management. Although, it stands to reason that a Republican administration might give lower scores to a majority of government programs that regulate certain markets and perform redistributive functions to constituencies outside their base, as well as strategically place appointees who are adversarial to the mission of the programs they lead. For examples of this strategy, see Wood and Waterman, 1994; Golden, 2000; and Durant, 1992. Additionally, PAS once

appointed work at the discretion of the president. If PART is used as a political tool to threaten hated programs, it is unlikely that scores would be inflated as a post-hoc justification of the president's choices for appointment (as the authors claim). Conversely, it is possible that programs that align with the administration's agenda are also assigned lower scores in recognition of the complaints of important constituencies (e.g., Veterans Affairs). Additionally, political appointees are infamous for their short tenures (an average of approximately two and a half years) (Dull & Roberts, 2009; Wood & Marchbanks, 2007). The authors' analyses comprise PART scores up to FY 2004, which would have been the fourth year of PART evaluations. Career executives with consistent exposure to PART over those four years are more likely to have learned how to "manage expectations" (Romzek & Dubnick, 1987) and navigate the subjective and ambiguous nature of the PART questions (Radin, 2004) than a potential array of newly appointed managers. This is especially poignant given the usual high rate of PAS turnover at the end of a president's first four-year term. Therefore, there could be testing threats that are not captured in the authors' models. Additionally, the authors' reliance on 2000 Plum Book data to assess structural effects on 2004 PART scores precludes them from identifying how long a particular program head (in 2004) had been with that program.

26. Interview conducted July 22, 2010, at Starbucks coffee shop in Washington, DC.

27. Interview conducted July 28, 2010, at the Department of Education headquarters, Washington, DC.

28. Starting in 2010, the Federal Human Capital Survey has been changed, in name, to the Federal Employee Viewpoint Survey. Because I use 2006 and 2008 data, I continue to refer to the survey and its data using the former name.

29. Please directly refer to the succeeding tables for information regarding the test statistics for the remaining summed scale measurements in the model.

30. Measures are adapted from previous uses in the public management literature.

31. I also ran a single-level OLS regression, with the level-2 variables included as single-level observations. I then calculated the variance inflation factor (VIF) score to analyze the degree of multicollinearity in the model, because there is no method of calculating the degree of multicollinearity in multilevel models. While there is no formal critical VIF value, a common rule of thumb is that if $VIF > 5$, the multicollinearity is severe. For the single-level OLS regression model, I calculated a VIF score of 2.27, indicating that multicollinearity is not a problem.

32. Interview conducted July 20, 2010, at the Department of Education headquarters, Washington, DC.

33. I do not propose, however, that trust is built only on a rational calculation of future payoff. While trust can be rational, it is at the same time linked to the altruistic sense of generalized reciprocity that often drives human behavior (Bianco, 1994). Additionally, as Brewer evidenced, civil servants are more likely than actors within the private sector to have altruistic goals that are often linked to their perceptions of policy target populations and policy goals (Brewer, 2003). Finally, character-based assessments are critical to a full conceptualization of "trust" (Mayer, Davis, & Schoorman, 1995). Nonetheless, I argue that the operationalization in the present study sufficiently captures a parsimonious account of the construct "trust," i.e., "encapsulated interest." This is in line with Putnam's definition of social capital, with the basis of trust being the "frequent interaction among a diverse set

of people, [tending to] produce a norm of generalized reciprocity" (Putnam, 2000). Consequently, mutual trust can conceptually absorb the additional facets of norms (and the intrinsic awareness of sanctions in violation of those norms), obligations, and expectations.

34. I use the term "moderate" to describe this correlation because of the seemingly perfect association one might suppose in these relationships. In other words, one would expect that a person involved in transition preparations would surely be aware of the activities that are ongoing or being planned (i.e., $r = 1.0$). Nonetheless, I drop this fixed effect from the model due to potential endogeneity issues. Coefficients do not change appreciably with or without its inclusion.

35. As I explained in the model for chapter 4, before I interpret the individual coefficients, I can evaluate the proportion of variation in my dependent variable that is explained by between-agency effects. For this model as well, where $\text{AWARE}_{ij} = \gamma_{00} + u_{0j} + r_{ij}$, I compute the ICC and find that 48% of the variance in my dependent variable is between agencies.

$$\hat{\rho} = \frac{\hat{\tau}_{00}}{\hat{\tau}_{00} + \hat{\sigma}^2} = \frac{0.8754}{0.8754 + 0.95663} = 0.478$$

The fully specified model, in which the individual- and agency-level controls are added, explains approximately 63% of the variation in activity awareness.

36. Interview conducted July 28, 2010, at the Department of Education headquarters, Washington, DC.

37. Interview conducted July 20, 2010, at the Department of Education headquarters, Washington, DC.

38. Available at http://www.huffingtonpost.com/paul-c-light/open-letter-to-the-presid _b_109276.html.

39. Interview conducted July 20, 2010, at the Department of Education headquarters, Washington, DC.

40. See http://www.aspeninstitute.org/policy-work/commission-appointments/Histor ical%20Summaries%20of%20Past%20Commissions%20and%20Reports.

41. Available at http://www.govexec.com/features/0611-15/0611-15s1.htm.

42. Available at http://www.washingtonpost.com/blogs/federal-eye/wp/2014/11/20/ report-obama-to-meet-with-senior-federal-executives-next-month/.

43. Available at https://seniorexecs.org/images/documents/A_Review_of_the_State _of_the_Federal_Career_Executive_Corps.pdf.

References

Aberbach, J. D., & Peterson, M. A. (2005). Control and accountability: Dilemmas of the executive branch. In J. D. Aberbach & M. A. Peterson (Eds.), *The executive branch* (pp. 525–554). New York: Oxford University Press.

Aberbach, J. D., & Rockman, B. A. (1988). Mandates or mandarins? Control and discretion in the modern administrative state. *Public Administration Review, 48*(2), 606–612.

Aberbach, J. D., & Rockman, B. A. (1995). The political views of U.S. senior federal executives, 1970–1992. *Journal of Politics, 57*(3), 838–852.

Adams, J. S. (2005). Equity theory. In J. B. Miner (Ed.), *Organizational behavior I: Essential theories of motivation and leadership* (pp. 134–159). Armonk, NY: M. E. Sharpe.

Agranoff, R. (2006). Inside collaborative networks: Ten lessons for public managers [Special issue]. *Public Administration Review, 66*, 56–65.

Albrecht, S., & Travaglione, A. (2003). Trust in public-sector senior management. *International Journal of Human Resource Management, 14*(1), 76–92.

Anrig, G. (2007, July 24). "Smart regulation" in action. Retrieved from http://tcf.org/commentary/2007/nc1638

Appleby, P. H. (1949). *Policy and administration.* Tuscaloosa: University of Alabama Press.

Arnold, P. (1998). *Making the managerial presidency* (2nd ed.). Lawrence: University Press of Kansas.

Axelrod, R. (1984). *The evolution of cooperation.* New York: Basic Books.

Axelrod, R., & Hamilton, W. D. (1981). The evolution of cooperation. *Science, 211*(4489), 1390–1396.

Balkin, J. (2008, November 12). Obama and the imperial presidency. *The Guardian.* Retrieved from www.guardian.co.uk/commentisfree/cifamerica/2008/nov/12/obama-white-house-barackobama

Ban, C. (2000). The national performance review as implicit evaluation of CSRA: Building on or overturning the legacy? In D. A. Brook & J. P. Pfiffner (Eds.), *The future of merit: Twenty years after the Civil Service Reform Act* (pp. 57–80). Washington, DC: The Woodrow Wilson Center Press.

Ban, C., & Ingraham, P. W. (1990). Short-timers: Political appointee mobility and its impact on political-career relations in the Reagan administration. *Administration & Society, 22*(5), 106–124.

Barnard, C. I. (1938, 1968). *The functions of the executive: Thirtieth anniversary edition.* Cambridge, MA: Harvard University Press.

Barnes, F. (2003, August 15). Big-government conservatism: How George W. Bush squares the fiscally expansive/conservative circle. *Wall Street Journal.* http://www.weeklystandard.com/Content/Public/Articles/000/000/003/017wgfhc.asp

Beckmann, M. N., & Godfrey, J. (2007). The policy opportunities in presidential honeymoons. *Political Research Quarterly, 60*(2), 250–262. doi:10.1177/1065912907301775

Benda, P. M., & Levine, C. H. (1988). Reagan and the bureaucracy: The bequest, the promise, and the legacy. In C. O. Jones (Ed.), *The Reagan legacy: Promise and performance* (pp. 102–142). Chatham, NJ: Chatham House.

Bertelli, A. M., & Lynn, L. E. (2006). *Madison's managers: Public administration and the Constitution.* Baltimore: Johns Hopkins University Press.

Bianco, W. T. (1994). *Trust: Representatives and constituents.* Ann Arbor: University of Michigan Press.

Blau, P. M. (1964). *Exchange and power in social life.* New York: Wiley.

Bohte, J., & Meier, K. J. (2000). Goal displacement: Assessing the motivation for organizational cheating. *Public Administration Review, 60*(2), 173–182.

Boisot, M. (1995). *Information space: A framework for learning in organizations, institutions and culture.* London: Routledge.

Bounfour, A., & Edvinsson, L. (2005). *Intellectual capital for communities: Nations, regions, and cities.* London: Routledge.

Bowen, D. E., & Lawler, E. E., III. (1992, Summer). The empowerment of service workers: What, why, how, and when. *Sloan Management Review,* 73–84.

Bowman, J. S., & West, J. P. (2009). To "re-Hatch" public employees or not? An ethical analysis of the relaxation of restrictions on political activities in civil service. *Public Administration Review, 69*(1), 52–63.

Bozeman, B. (1993). A theory of government "red tape." *Journal of Public Administration Research and Theory, 3*(3), 273–303.

Brehm, J., & Gates, S. (1997). *Working, shirking, and sabotage: Bureaucratic response to a democratic public.* Ann Arbor: University of Michigan Press.

Brehm, J., & Gates, S. (2008). *Teaching, tasks, and trust: Functions of the public executive* (Vol. 10). New York: Russell Sage Foundation.

Brewer, G. A. (2003). Building social capital: Civic attitudes and behavior of public servants. *Journal of Public Administration Research and Theory, 13*(1), 5–26.

Brook, D. A. (2000). Merit and the Civil Service Reform Act. In D. A. Brook & J. P. Pfiffner (Eds.), *The future of merit: Twenty years after the Civil Service Reform Act* (pp. 1–14). Washington, DC: The Woodrow Wilson Center Press.

Brown, T., & Potoski, M. (2006). Contracting for management: Assessing management capacity under alternative service delivery arrangements. *Journal of Policy Analysis and Management, 25*(2), 323–346. doi:10.1002/pam.20175

Burke, J. P. (2002). The Bush transition in historical context. *PS: Political Science and Politics, 35*(1), 23–26.

Burt, R. (1997). The contingent value of social capital. *Administrative Science Quarterly, 42,* 339–365.

Bush, G. W. (2010). *Decision points.* New York: Crown Publishers.

Campbell, C. (1986). *Managing the presidency: Carter, Reagan, and the search for executive harmony.* Pittsburgh, PA: University of Pittsburgh Press.

Campbell, C. (2005). The complex organization of the executive branch: The legacies of competing approaches to administration. In J. D. Aberbach & M. A. Peterson (Eds.), *The executive branch.* London: Oxford University Press.

Carpenter, D., & Krause, G. A. (2015). Transactional authority and bureaucratic politics. *Journal of Public Administration Research and Theory, 25*(1), 5–25.

Carroll, J. D. (1975). Service, knowledge, and choice: The future as post-industrial administration. *Public Administration Review, 35*(6), 578–581.

Carson, P. P., Carson, K. D., Birkenmeier, B., & Toma, A. G. (2006). Looking for loyalty in all the wrong places: A study of union and organizational commitments. *Public Personnel Management, 35*(2), 137–151.

Chandler, A. D. (1962). *Strategy and structure: Chapters in the history of the American industrial enterprise.* Cambridge, MA: MIT Press.

Chang, K., Lewis, D. E., & McCarty, N. (2001). *The tenure of political appointees.* Paper presented at the the 2001 annual meetings of the Midwest Political Science Association, Palmer House Hilton, Chicago, IL.

Cho, Y. J., & Ringquist, E. J. (2011). Managerial trustworthiness and organizational outcomes. *Journal of Public Administration Research and Theory, 21*(1), 53–86. doi:10.1093/jopart/muq015

Chun, Y. H., & Rainey, H. G. (2005). Goal ambiguity in U.S. federal agencies. *Journal of Public Administration Research and Theory, 15*, 1–30.

Clinton, J. D., & Lewis, D. E. (2008). Expert opinion, agency characteristics, and agency preferences. *Political Analysis, 16*, 3–20.

Coase, R. H. (1937). The nature of the firm. *Economica, 4*(16), 386–405. doi:10.1111/j.1468-0335.1937.tb00002.x

Cole, R. L., & Caputo, D. A. (1979). Presidential control of the senior civil service: Assessing the strategies of the Nixon years. *American Political Science Review, 73*(2), 399–413.

Coleman, J. S. (1990). *Foundations of social theory.* Cambridge, MA: The Belknap Press of Harvard University Press.

Colquitt, J. A., Scott, B. A., & LePine, J. A. (2007). Trust, trustworthiness, and trust propensity: A meta-analytic test of their unique relationships with risk taking and job performance. *Journal of Applied Psychology, 92*(4), 909.

Cook, K. S., Hardin, R., & Levi, M. (2005). *Cooperation without trust?* (Vol. 9). New York: Russell Sage Foundation.

Cooper, P. J. (2002). *By order of the president: The use and abuse of executive direct action.* Lawrence: University Press of Kansas.

Cooper, P. J. (2011). The duty to take care: President Obama, public administration, and the capacity to govern. *Public Administration Review, 71*(1), 7–18. doi:10.1111/j.1540-6210.2010.02302.x

Cronin, T. E. (1978). The post-imperial presidency: An imperiled presidency? *Society, 16*(1), 57–64.

Dahl, R. A. (1957). The concept of power. *Behavioral Science, 2*(3), 201–215.

Darley, J. M. (2004). Commitment, trust and worker effort expenditure in organizations. In R. M. Kramer & K. S. Cook (Eds.), *Trust and distrust in organizations: Dilemmas and approaches* (Vol. 7, pp. 127–151). New York: Russell Sage Foundation.

Davis, J. H., Schoorman, F. D., Mayer, R. C., & Tan, H. (2000). The trusted general manager and business unit performance: Empirical evidence of a competitive advantage. *Strategic Management Journal, 21*(5), 563–576.

Dickinson, M. J. (2005). The executive office of the president: The paradox of politicization. In J. D. Aberbach & M. A. Peterson (Eds.), *The executive branch*. London: Oxford University Press.

Dickinson, M. J., & Rudalevige, A. (2004). Presidents, responsiveness, and competence: Revisiting the "golden age" at the Bureau of the Budget. *Political Science Quarterly, 119*(4), 633–654.

Dilulio, J. (2014). *Bring back the bureaucrats: Why more federal workers will lead to better (and smaller!) government.* West Conshohocken, PA: Templeton Foundation Press.

Dirks, K. T., & Ferrin, D. L. (2002). Trust in leadership: Meta-analytic findings and implications for research and practice. *Journal of Applied Psychology, 87*(4), 611–628.

Dirks, K. T., & Skarlicki, D. P. (2004). Trust in leaders: Existing research and emerging issues. In R. M. Kramer & K. S. Cook (Eds.), *Trust and distrust in organizations: Dilemmas and approaches* (Vol. 7, pp. 21–40). New York: Russell Sage Foundation.

Dixit, A. K., & Nalebuff, B. J. (2010). *The art of strategy: A game theorist's guide to success in business and life.* New York: W. W. Norton.

Downs, A. (1967). *Inside bureaucracy.* Boston: Little, Brown.

Dudley, S. (2005). The Bush administration's regulatory record. *Regulation, 27*(4), 4–9.

Dull, M. (2009). Results-model reform leadership: Questions of credible commitment. *Journal of Public Administration Research and Theory, 19*(2), 255–284.

Dull, M., & Roberts, P. S. (2009). Continuity, competence, and the succession of Senate-confirmed agency appointees. *Presidential Studies Quarterly, 39*(3), 432–453.

Dull, M., Roberts, P. S., Keeney, M. S., & Choi, S. O. (2012). Appointee confirmation and tenure: The succession of U.S. federal agency appointees, 1989–2009. *Public Administration Review, 72*(6), 902–913.

Dunn, J. (1990). Trust and political agency. In D. Gambetta (Ed.), *Trust: Making and breaking cooperative relations.* New York: Blackwell Publishers.

Durant, R. F. (1992). *The administrative presidency revisited: Public lands, the BLM, and the Reagan revolution.* Albany: State University of New York Press.

Durant, R. F. (2000). Whither the neoadministrative state? Toward a polity-centered theory of administrative reform. *Journal of Public Administration Research and Theory, 10*(1), 79–109.

Durant, R. F. (2006). A "new covenant kept": Core values, presidential communications, and the paradox of the Clinton presidency. *Presidential Studies Quarterly, 36*(3), 345–372.

Durant, R. F. (2009). Back to the future? Toward revitalizing the study of the administrative presidency. *Presidential Studies Quarterly, 39*(1), 89–110.

Durant, R. F. (2010). Contextual soaking, statistical poking, and the shadows in Plato's cave. *Public Administration Review, 70*(5), 820–824. doi:10.1111/j.1540-6210.2010.02210.x

Durant, R. F., Girth, A., & Johnston, J. (2010). American exceptionalism, human resource management, and the contract state. *Review of Public Personnel and Administration, 29*(3), 207–229.

Durant, R. F., & Resh, W. G. (2010). Presidential agendas, administrative strategies, and the bureaucracy. In G. Edwards (Ed.), *Handbook of the American presidency.* London: Oxford University Press.

Durant, R. F., Stazyk, E., & Resh, W. G. (2010a). Introduction. Symposium: HRM, "big government conservatism," and the personnel legacy of George W. Bush. *Review of Public Personnel and Administration, 30*(4), 372–378.

Durant, R. F., Stazyk, E. C., & Resh, W. G. (2010b). Faithful infidelity, "political time," George W. Bush, and the paradox of "big government conservatism." *Review of Public Personnel and Administration, 30*(4), 379–403.

Durant, R. F., & Warber, A. L. (2001). Networking in the shadow of hierarchy: Public policy, the administrative presidency, and the neoadministrative state. *Presidential Studies Quarterly, 31*(2), 221–244.

Dyer, J. H., & Chu, W. (2003). The role of trustworthiness in reducing transaction costs and improving performance: Empirical evidence from the United States, Japan, and Korea. *Organization Science, 14*(1), 57–68.

Dyne, L. V., Ang, S., & Botero, I. C. (2003). Conceptualizing employee silence and employee voice as multidimensional constructs. *Journal of Management Studies, 40*(6), 1359–1392. doi:10.1111/1467-6486.00384

Edwards, G. C. (2001, Spring). *Why not the best? The loyalty-competence trade-off in presidential appointments.* Washington, DC: Brookings Institution Press.

Eisner, M. A., & Meier, K. J. (1990). Presidential control versus bureaucratic power: Explaining the Reagan revolution in antitrust. *American Journal of Political Science, 34*(1), 269–287.

Ellis, K., & Shockley-Zalabak, P. (2001). Trust in top management and immediate supervisor: The relationship to satisfaction, perceived organizational effectiveness, and information receiving. *Communication Quarterly, 49*(4), 382–398.

Elmore, R. F. (1979). Backward mapping: Implementation research and policy decisions. *Political Science Quarterly, 94*(4), 601–616.

Farquhar, K. W. (1995). Not just understudies: The dynamics of short-term leadership. *Human Resource Management, 34*(1), 51.

Feeney, M. K., & Kingsley, G. (2008). The rebirth of patronage. *Public Integrity, 10*(2), 165–176. doi:10.2753/pin1099-9922100205

Feldman, M. S. (1992). Organization theory and the presidency. In G. E. Edwards, J. H. Kessel, & B. A. Rockman (Eds.), *Researching the presidency: Vital questions, new approaches* (pp. 245–265). Pittsburgh, PA: University of Pittsburgh Press.

Felzenberg, A. S. (2000). The transition: A guide for the president-elect. *Policy Review* (103), 33–45.

Fernandez, S., & Moldogaziev, T. (2011). Empowering public sector employees to improve performance: Does it work? *American Review of Public Administration, 41*(1), 23–47. doi:10.1177/0275074009355943

Finer, H. (1940). Administrative responsibility in democratic government. *Public Administration Review, 1*, 335–350.

Flaherty, K. E., & Pappas, J. M. (2000). The role of trust in salesperson-sales manager relationships. *Journal of Personal Selling and Sales Management, 20*(4), 271.

Folger, R. (1996). Distributive and procedural justice: Multifaceted meanings and interrelations. *Social Justice Research, 9*(4), 395–416. doi:10.1007/bf02196992

Friedrich, C. J. (1940). Public policy and the nature of administrative responsibility. In C. J. Friedrich & E. S. Mason (Eds.), *Public policy: A yearbook of the Graduate School of Public Administration, Harvard University, 1940.* Cambridge, MA: Harvard University Press.

Fukuyama, F. (1995). *Trust: The social virtues and the creation of prosperity*. New York: Simon & Schuster.

Gailmard, S., & Patty, J. W. (2007). Slackers and zealots: Civil service, policy discretion, and bureaucratic expertise. *American Journal of Political Science, 51*(4), 873–889.

Gallo, N., & Lewis, D. E. (2012). The consequences of presidential patronage for federal agency performance. *Journal of Public Administration Research and Theory, 22*(2), 219–243.

Gannon, F. (2010, May 15). Domestic policy initiatives of the Nixon years. *Domestic Policy*. Retrieved from http://domestic.nixonfoundation.org/2010/05/15/the-domestic-policy-initiatives-of-the-nixon-years-2/#more-160

Garson, G. D. (2013). *Hierarchical linear modeling: Guide and applications*. Thousand Oaks, CA: Sage Publications.

Gelman, A. (2006). Multilevel (hierarchical) modeling: What it can and cannot do. *Technometrics, 48*(3), 432–435.

Gelman, A., & Hill, J. (2007). *Data analysis using regression and multilevel/hierarchical models*. New York: Cambridge University Press.

Gelman, A., & Pardoe, I. (2006). Bayesian measures of explained variance and pooling in multilevel (hierarchical) models. *Technometrics, 48*(2), 241–251.

George, A. L. (1972). The case for multiple advocacy in making foreign policy. *American Political Science Review, 66*(3), 751–785.

Gillespie, N. (2012). Measuring trust in organizational contexts: An overview of survey-based measures. In F. Lyon, G. Möllering, & M. Saunders (Eds.), *Handbook of research methods on trust* (Chap. 17). Northampton, MA: Edward Elgar.

Gilmour, J. B., & Lewis, D. E. (2006a). Does performance budgeting work? An examination of the Office of Management and Budget's PART scores. *Public Administration Review, 66*(5), 742–752.

Gilmour, J. B., & Lewis, D. E. (2006b). Political appointees and the competence of federal program management. *American Politics Research, 34*(1), 22–50.

Gimbel, P. A. (2001). *Understanding principal trust-building behaviors: Evidence from three middle schools* (Doctoral dissertation). Retrieved from Dissertation Abstracts International (UMI No. 3018320).

Golden, M. M. (2000). *What motivates bureaucrats? Politics and administration during the Reagan years*. New York: Columbia University Press.

Golembiewski, R. T., & McConkie, M. (1975). The centrality of interpersonal trust in group processes. In C. L. Cooper (Ed.), *Theories of group processes* (pp. 131–186). New York: John Wiley & Sons.

Gouldner, A. W. (1954). *Patterns of industrial bureaucracy*. Glencoe, IL: Free Press.

Graham, J. D. (2010). *Bush on the home front: Domestic policy triumphs and setbacks*. Bloomington: Indiana University Press.

Granovetter, M. S. (1973). The strength of weak ties. *American Journal of Sociology, 78*, 1360–1380.

Granovetter, M. S. (1985). Economic action and social structure: The problem of embeddedness. *American Journal of Sociology, 91*, 481–493.

Granovetter, M. S. (1992). Problems of explanation in economic sociology. In N. Nohria &

R. Eccles (Eds.), *Networks and organizations: Structure, form and action* (pp. 25–56). Boston: Harvard Business School Press.

Greenstein, F. (2005). The person of the president, leadership, and greatness. In J. D. Aberbach & M. A. Peterson (Eds.), *The executive branch* (pp. 218–242). New York: Oxford University Press.

Hall, J. L. (2007). *Direct versus indirect goal conflict and governmental policy: Examining the effect of goal multiplicity on policy change.* Paper presented at the Leading the Future of the Public Sector: The Third Transatlantic Dialogue. University of Delaware, Newark.

Handel, M. J. (2003a). Economic theories of organizations. In M. J. Handel (Ed.), *The sociology of organizations: Classic, contemporary, and critical readings* (pp. 263–268). Thousand Oaks, CA: Sage Publications.

Handel, M. J. (2003b). Organizations as rational systems I: Classic theories of bureaucracy and administration. In M. J. Handel (Ed.), *The sociology of organizations: Classic, contemporary, and critical readings* (pp. 5–16). Thousand Oaks, CA: Sage Publications.

Hardin, R. (1993). The street-level epistemology of trust. *Politics & Society, 21*(4), 505–529.

Hardin, R. (2006a). The street-level epistemology of trust. In R. M. Kramer (Ed.), *Organizational trust: A reader* (pp. 21–47). New York: Oxford University Press.

Hardin, R. (2006b). *Trust.* Malden, MA: Polity Press.

Hargrove, E. C. (2001). Presidential power and political science. *Presidential Studies Quarterly, 31*(2), 245–261.

Heclo, H. (1977). *A government of strangers: Executive politics in Washington.* Washington, DC: Brookings Institution.

Heclo, H. (1978). Issue networks and the executive establishment. In A. King (Ed.), *The new American political system* (pp. 87–124). Washington, DC: American Enterprise Institute.

Heclo, H. (1983). *The executive office of the president.* Occasional Paper. Center for American Political Studies, Harvard University. Boston, MA.

Hedge, D. M. (2009). *The George W. Bush presidency and political control of the bureaucracy.* Paper presented at the APSA 2009, Toronto, ON. http://ssrn.com/abstract=1450715

Heinrich, C. J., & Hill, C. J. (2010). Multilevel models in the study of bureaucracy. In R. F. Durant (Ed.), *The Oxford handbook of American bureaucracy* (pp. 833–867). New York: Oxford University Press.

Henderson, P. G. (1988). *Managing the presidency: The Eisenhower legacy—from Kennedy to Reagan.* Boulder, CO: Westview Press.

Hess, F. M., & McGuinn, P. J. (2009). George W. Bush's education legacy: The two faces of No Child Left Behind. In R. Maranto, T. Lansford, & J. Johnson (Eds.), *Judging Bush* (pp. 157–175). Stanford, CA: Stanford University Press.

Hess, S. (2002). *Organizing the presidency.* Washington, DC: Brookings Institution.

Hill, C. J., & Lynn, L. E. (2005). Is hierarchical governance in decline? Evidence from empirical research. *Journal of Public Administration Research and Theory, 15*(2), 173–195. doi:10.1093/jopart/mui011

Hirsch, F. (1978). *Social limits to growth.* Cambridge, MA: Harvard University Press.

Hirschman, A. O. (1970). *Exit, voice, and loyalty: Responses to decline in firms.* Cambridge, MA: Harvard University Press.

Hirst, G., Van Knippenberg, D., Chin-Hui, C., & Sacramento, C. A. (2011). How does bureaucracy impact individual creativity? A cross-level investigation of team contextual influences on goal orientation-creativity relationships. *Academy of Management Journal, 54*(3), 624–641.

Hissam, M. (2007). The impact of Executive Order 13,422 on presidential oversight of agency administration. *George Washington Law Review, 76,* 1292.

Hosmer, L. T. (1995). Trust: The connecting link between organizational theory and philosophical ethics. *Academy of Management Review, 20*(2), 379–403.

Howell, W. G. (2005). Unilateral powers: A brief overview. *Presidential Studies Quarterly, 35*(3), 417–439.

Huddleston, M. W., & Boyer, W. W. (1996). *The higher civil service in the United States.* Pittsburgh, PA: University of Pittsburgh Press.

Hult, K. M., & Walcott, C. E. (2004). *Empowering the White House: Governance under Nixon, Ford, and Carter.* Lawrence: University Press of Kansas.

Ingraham, P. W. (1995). *The foundation of merit: Public service in American democracy.* Baltimore: Johns Hopkins University Press.

Ingraham, P. W. (2005). The federal public service: The people and the challenge. In J. D. Aberbach & M. A. Peterson (Eds.), *The executive branch.* New York: Oxford University Press.

Ingraham, P. W., Thompson, J. R., & Eisenberg, E. F. (1995). Political management strategies and political/career relationships: Where are we now in the federal government? *Public Administration Review, 55*(3), 263–272.

Ink, D. (2000). What was behind the 1978 civil service reform? In D. A. Brook & J. P. Pfiffner (Eds.), *The future of merit: Twenty years after the Civil Service Reform Act* (pp. 39–58). Washington, DC: The Woodrow Wilson Center Press.

Johnson, C. (2008, July 18). *Transition direction* [Memo to PMC members]. Retrieved from http://transition2008.files.wordpress.com/2008/08/omb-transition-memo-07-18-08.pdf

Jones, C. O. (1999). *Separate but equal branches: Congress and the presidency* (2nd ed.). New York: Chatham House.

Kagan, E. (2001). Presidential administration. *Harvard Law Review, 114*(8), 2245–2385.

Kamensky, J. (2008, August 19). *Bush transition-out plan.* Retrieved from http://transition2008.wordpress.com/2008/08/19/bush-transition-out-plan/

Katz, D., & Kahn, R. L. (1966). *The social psychology of organizations.* New York: John Wiley & Sons.

Katzen, S. (2009, June 23). *Which way the political winds are blowing.* Paper presented at the New Ideas for Risk Regulation, Resources for the Future Conference Center, Washington, DC.

Keiser, L. R. (2010). Representative bureaucracy. In R. F. Durant (Ed.), *Handbook of the American bureaucracy.* New York: Oxford University Press.

Kelman, S. J. (2002). Contracting. In L. M. Salamon (Ed.), *The tools of government: A guide to the new governance* (pp. 282–318). New York: Oxford University Press.

Kerwin, C. M. (2003). *Rulemaking: How government agencies write law and make policy* (3rd ed.). Washington, DC: CQ Press.

Kerwin, C. M., West, W., & Furlong, S. R. (2010). Interest groups, rulemaking, and American bureaucracy. In R. F. Durant (Ed.), *Handbook of the American bureaucracy*. London: Oxford University Press.

Kettl, D. F. (1994). Beyond the rhetoric of reinvention: Driving themes of the Clinton administration's management reforms. *Governance, 7*(3), 307–314.

Kettl, D. F. (2000). *The global public management revolution: A report on the transformation of governance*. Washington, DC: Brookings Institution Press.

Kingdon, J. W. (2003). *Agendas, alternatives and public policies* (2nd ed.). New York: Longman.

Konovsky, M. A., & Cropanzano, R. (1991). Perceived fairness of employee drug testing as a predictor of employee attitudes and job performance. *Journal of Applied Psychology, 76*, 698–707.

Konovsky, M. A., & Pugh, S. (1994). Citizenship behavior and social exchange. *Academy of Management Journal, 37*, 656–669.

Korsgaard, M. A., Brower, H. H., & Lester, S. W. (2015). It isn't always mutual: A critical review of dyadic trust. *Journal of Management, 41*(1), 47–70. doi:10.1177/0149206314547521

Krause, G. A. (1999). *A two-way street: The institutional dynamics of the modern administrative state*. Pittsburgh, PA: University of Pittsburgh Press.

Krause, G. A. (2009). Organizational complexity and coordination dilemmas in U.S. executive politics. *Presidential Studies Quarterly, 39*(1), 74–88.

Krause, G. A., Lewis, D. E., & Douglas, J. W. (2006). Political appointments, civil service systems, and bureaucratic competence: Organizational balancing and executive branch revenue forecasts in the American States. *American Journal of Political Science, 50*(3), 770–787.

Kreps, D. M. (1990). *Game theory and economic modeling*. Oxford: Clarendon Press.

Kumar, M. J. (2002). Introduction. The presidential transition of 2001: Scholars offer expertise and analysis. *PS: Political Science and Politics, 35*(1), 7–8.

Kumar, M. J. (2009). The 2008–2009 presidential transition through the voices of its participants. *Presidential Studies Quarterly, 39*(4), 823–858.

Kumar, M. J., Edwards III, G. C., Pfiffner, J. P., & Sullivan, T. (2000). "The contemporary presidency": Meeting the freight train head on: Planning for the transition to power. *Presidential Studies Quarterly, 30*(4), 754–769.

Langbein, L., & Felbinger, C. L. (2006). *Public program evaluation: A statistical guide*. Armonk, NY: M. E. Sharpe.

Larzelere, R. E., & Huston, T. L. (1980). The dyadic trust scale: Toward understanding interpersonal trust in close relationships. *Journal of Marriage and Family, 42*(3), 595–604.

Lee, J. W., Rainey, H. G., & Chun, Y. H. (2010). Goal ambiguity, work complexity, and work routineness in federal agencies. *The American Review of Public Administration, 40*(3), 284–308.

Lee, S.-Y., & Whitford, A. B. (2008). Exit, voice, loyalty, and pay: Evidence from the public workforce. *Journal of Public Administration Research and Theory, 18*(4), 647–671. doi:10.1093/jopart/mum029

Lewis, D. E. (2005). Staffing alone: Unilateral action and the politicization of the executive office of the president, 1988–2004. *Presidential Studies Quarterly, 35*(3), 496–514. doi:10.1111/j.1741-5705.2005.00261.x

Lewis, D. E. (2007). Testing Pendleton's premise: Do political appointees make worse bureaucrats? *Journal of Politics, 69*(4), 1073–1088.

Lewis, D. E. (2008). *The politics of presidential appointments: Political control and bureaucratic performance.* Princeton, NJ: Princeton University Press.

Light, P. C. (1995). *Thickening government: Federal hierarchy and the diffusion of accountability.* Washington, DC: Brookings Institution.

Light, P. C. (2008). *A government ill executed: The decline of the federal service and how to reverse it.* Cambridge, MA: Harvard University Press.

Long, J. S., & Freese, J. (2006). *Regression models for categorical dependent variables using stata.* College Station, TX: Stata Press.

Lowery, D. (2000). The presidency, the bureaucracy, and reinvention: A gentle plea for chaos. *Presidential Studies Quarterly, 30*(1), 79–108.

Luhmann, N. (1979). *Trust and power.* Chichester, England: Wiley.

Lundin, M. (2007). Explaining cooperation: How resource interdependence, goal congruence, and trust affect joint actions in policy implementation. *Journal of Public Administration Research and Theory, 17,* 651–672.

Luton, L. S. (2009). Administrative "interpretation" as policy-making. *Administrative Theory & Praxis, 31*(4), 556–576.

Lynn, L. E., Heinrich, C. J., & Hill, C. J. (2000). Studying governance and public management: Challenges and prospects. *Journal of Public Administration Research and Theory, 10*(2), 233–262.

Mackenzie, G. C. (1987). *The in-and-outers: Presidential appointees and transient government in Washington.* Baltimore: Johns Hopkins University Press.

Mackenzie, G. C. (2002). The real invisible hand: Presidential appointees in the administration of George W. Bush. *PS: Political Science and Politics, 35*(1), 27–30.

Maranto, R. (1993). *Politics and bureaucracy in the modern presidency.* Westport, CT: Greenwood Press.

Maranto, R. (2002). "Government service is a noble calling": President Bush and the U.S. civil service. In L. D. Feldman & R. Perotti (Eds.), *Honor and loyalty: Inside the politics of the George H. W. Bush presidency* (pp. 97–108). Westport, CT: Greenwood Press.

Maranto, R. (2005). *Beyond a government of strangers: How career executives and political appointees can turn conflict to cooperation.* Lanham, MD: Lexington Books.

March, J. G., & Olsen, J. P. (1976). *Ambiguity and choice in organizations.* Bergen: Universitetsforlaget.

March, J. G., & Simon, H. A. (1993). *Organizations* (2nd ed.). Cambridge, MA: Blackwell Publishers.

Mayer, R. C., & Davis, J. H. (1999). The effect of the performance appraisal system on trust for management: A field quasi-experiment. *Journal of Applied Psychology, 84,* 123–136.

Mayer, R. C., Davis, J. H., & Schoorman, F. D. (1995). An integration model of organizational trust. *Academy of Management Review, 20*(3), 709–734.

Merton, R. K. (1940). Bureaucratic structure and personality. *Social Forces, 18,* 560–568.

Michaels, J. E. (1997). *The president's call: Executive leadership from FDR to George Bush.* Pittsburgh, PA: University of Pittsburgh Press.

Milbank, D., & Nakashima, E. (2001, March 25). Bush team has "right" credentials; conservative picks seen eclipsing even Reagan's. *Washington Post,* p. A1.

Miller, G. J. (1992). *Managerial dilemmas: The political economy of hierarchy.* New York: Cambridge University Press.

Miller, G. J. (2004). Monitoring, rules, and the control paradox: Can the good soldier Svejk be trusted? In R. M. Kramer & K. S. Cook (Eds.), *Trust and distrust in organizations: Dilemmas and approaches* (Vol. 7, pp. 99–126). New York: Russell Sage Foundation.

Miller, G. J., & Whitford, A. B. (2007). The principal's moral hazard: Constraints on the use of incentives in hierarchy. *Journal of Public Administration Research and Theory, 17*(2), 213–233.

Mishra, A. K. (1996). Organizational responses to crisis: The centrality of trust. In R. Kramer and T. Tyler (Eds.), *Trust in organization: Frontiers of theory and research* (261–287). Newbury Park, CA: Sage.

Moe, T. M. (1989). The politics of bureaucratic structure. In J. E. Chubb & P. E. Peterson (Eds.), *Can the government govern?* (pp. 267–329). Washington, DC: Brookings Institution.

Moe, T. M. (1993). Presidents, institutions, and theory. In G. Edwards, J. Kessel, & B. A. Rockman (Eds.), *Researching the presidency: Vital questions, new approaches.* Pittsburgh, PA: University of Pittsburgh Press.

Moe, T. M., & Howell, W. G. (1999). The presidential power of unilateral action. *Journal of Law Economics & Organization, 15*(1), 132–179.

Moffit, R. E. (2001, January 8). *Personnel is policy: Why the new president must take control of the executive branch* (Backgrounder No. 1403). Retrieved from Heritage Foundation website: http://www.heritage.org/research/governmentreform/BG1403.cfm

Moffit, R. E., Nesterczuk, G., & Devine, J. (2001, January 10). *Taking charge of federal personnel* (Backgrounder No. 1404). Retrieved from Heritage Foundation website: http://http://www.heritage.org/research/reports/2001/01/taking-charge-of-federal-personnel

Moynihan, D. P. (2008). *The dynamics of performance management: Constructing information and reform.* Washington, DC: Georgetown University Press.

Moynihan, D. P., & Roberts, A. S. (2010). The triumph of loyalty over competence: The Bush administration and the exhaustion of the politicized presidency. *Public Administration Review, 70*(4), 572–581.

Nahapiet, J., & Ghoshal, S. (1998). Social capital, intellectual capital, and the organizational advantage. *Academy of Management Review, 23*(2), 242–266.

NAPA. (1985). *Leadership in jeopardy: The fraying of the presidential appointments system.* Washington, DC: Author.

NAPA. (1989). *Guidebook for the senior executive service.* Washington, DC: Author.

NAPA. (2009). *Agencies in transition: A report on the views of members of the federal senior executive service.* Washington, DC: Author.

Nathan, R. P. (1983). *The administrative presidency.* New York: John Wiley and Sons.

Nelson, R. R., & Winter, S. G. (1982). *An evolutionary theory of economic change.* Boston, MA: Belknap Press of Harvard University Press.

Neustadt, R. E. (1990). *Presidential power and the modern presidents: The politics of leadership from Roosevelt to Reagan*. New York: Free Press.

Newland, C. A. (1983). A mid-term appraisal—the Reagan presidency: Limited government and political administration. *Public Administration Review, 43*(1), 1–21.

O'Connell, A. J. (2009). Let's get it started: What president-elect Obama can learn from previous administrations in making political appointments. Washington, DC: Center for American Progress.

O'Leary, R. (2005). *The ethics of dissent: Managing guerrilla government*. Washington, DC: CQ Press.

Olson, M. (1965). *The logic of collective action* (2nd ed.). Boston: Harvard University Press.

OMB. (2000). *Stimulating smarter regulation*. Washington, DC: Author.

OMBWatch. (2009, February 4). *OMB Watch applauds Obama's revocation of Bush-era executive order on regulatory review*. Retrieved from http://www.ombwatch.org/node/9662

Ostrom, E. (1998). A behavioral approach to the rational choice theory of collective action: Presidential address, American Political Science Association, 1997. *American Political Science Review, 92*(1), 1–22.

Ostrom, E. (2000). Social capital: A fad or a fundamental concept? In P. Dasgupta & I. Serageldin (Eds.), *Social Capital: A Multifaceted Perspective*. Washington, DC: International Bank for Reconstruction.

Patterson, B., Pfiffner, J. P., & Lewis, D. E. (2008). *The White House Office of Presidential Personnel* (Report No. 2009-27). Washington, DC: The White House Transition Project.

Pear, R. (1992, November 15). Clinton's promise of cleaning house worries some career civil servants. *New York Times*, p. A26.

Pear, R. (2008, September 21). Behind the scenes, teams for both candidates plan for a presidential transition, national desk. *New York Times*.

Perry, J. L., & Wise, L. R. (1990). The motivational bases of public service. *Public Administration Review, 50*, 367–373.

Pfiffner, J. P. (1985). Political public administration. *Public Administration Review, 45*(2), 352–356.

Pfiffner, J. P. (1987). Political appointees and career executives: The democracy-bureaucracy nexus in the third century. *Public Administration Review, 47*(1), 57–65.

Pfiffner, J. P. (1990). Establishing the Bush presidency. *Public Administration Review, 50*(1), 64–73.

Pfiffner, J. P. (1991a). Political appointees and career executives: The democracy-bureaucracy nexus. In J. P. Pfiffner (Ed.), *The managerial presidency*. Belmont, CA: Wadsworth.

Pfiffner, J. P. (Ed.). (1991b). *The managerial presidency*. Belmont, CA: Wadsworth.

Pfiffner, J. P. (1996). *The strategic presidency: Hitting the ground running*. Lawrence: University Press of Kansas.

Pfiffner, J. P. (2007). The first MBA president: George W. Bush as public administrator. *Public Administration Review, 67*(1), 6–20. doi:10.1111/j.1540-6210.2006.00691.x

Pfiffner, J. P. (2009). Presidential transitions. *The Oxford handbook of the American presidency*. Oxford: Oxford University Press.

Pfiffner, J. P., & Patterson, B. (2001). The White House Office of Presidential Personnel. *Presidential Studies Quarterly, 31*(3), 415–438.

Pitts, D. (2009). Diversity management, job satisfaction, and performance: Evidence from U.S. federal agencies. *Public Administration Review, 69*(2), 328–338. doi:10.1111/j.1540-6210.2008.01977.x

Podsakoff, P. M., & Organ, D. W. (1986). Self-reports in organizational research: Problems and prospects. *Journal of Management, 12*(4), 531–544.

Posner, P. L., & Radin, B. (2014). Can presidents be managers? *Government Executive.* Retrieved from http://www.govexec.com/management/2014/12/can-presidents-be-managers/100382/

Pugh, D. S. (1973). The measurement of organization structures. *Organizational Dynamics, 1*(4), 19–34.

Putnam, R. D. (2000). *Bowling alone: The collapse and revival of the American community.* New York: Simon & Schuster.

Radin, B. (2004). *The dark side of the performance movement: Unanticipated consequences or faulty assumptions?* Paper presented at the APPAM Conference, Washington, DC.

Radin, B. (2006). *Challenging the performance movement: Accountability, complexity, and democratic values.* Washington, DC: Georgetown University Press.

Rainey, H. G. (1993). Toward a theory of goal ambiguity in public organizations. In J. L. Perry (Ed.), *Research in public administration* (Vol. 2). Greenwich, CT: JAI Press.

Rainey, H. G. (2003). Understanding people in public organizations: Values and motives. In H. G. Rainey (Ed.), *Understanding and managing public organizations* (pp. 219–247). San Francisco, CA: Jossey-Bass.

Rainey, H. G. (2009). *Understanding and managing public organizations.* San Francisco, CA: Jossey-Bass.

Reagan, R. (1989). *Speaking my mind: Selected speeches.* New York: Simon & Schuster.

Resh, W. G. (2012). Who participates now . . . and why? A case study of modern interest participation and bureaucratic decision-making in the age of e-government. In A. Manoharan & M. Holzer (Eds.), *E-Governance and civic engagement: Factors and determinants of e-democracy* (pp. 315–337). Hershey, PA: IGI Global.

Resh, W. G. (2014). Appointee-careerist relations in the presidential transition of 2008–2009. *Presidential Studies Quarterly, 44*(4), 697–723.

Resh, W. G., & Marvel, J. D. (2012). Loopholes to load-shed: Contract management capacity, representative bureaucracy, and goal displacement in federal procurement decisions. *International Public Management Journal, 15*(4), 525–547.

Rockman, B. A. (1986). The modern presidency and theories of accountability: Old wine and old bottles. *Congress & the Presidency: A Journal of Capital Studies, 13*(2), 135–156.

Rockman, B. A. (2012). The Obama presidency: Hope, change, and reality. *Social Science Quarterly, 93*(5), 1065–1080.

Rogers, R. W. (1995). The psychological contract of trust. *Executive Development, 8*(1, Pt. 1), 15–19.

Rohr, J. A. (1986). *To run a constitution: The legitimacy of the administrative state.* Lawrence: University Press of Kansas.

Romano, L. (2007, August 28). Lonely at the top; for the president, confidants are lacking. *Washington Post.*

Romzek, B. S., & Dubnick, M. J. (1987). Accountability in the public sector: Lessons from the Challenger tragedy. *Public Administration Review, 47*(3), 227–238.

Rose, R. (2005). Giving direction to government in comparative perspective. In J. D. Aberbach & M. A. Peterson (Eds.), *The executive branch* (pp. 72–99). New York: Oxford University Press.

Rosenbloom, D. H. (1983). Public administrative theory and the separation of powers. *Public Administration Review, 43*(3), 219–227.

Rosenbloom, D. H. (2001, December). "Whose bureaucracy is this, anyway?" Congress' 1946 answer. *Ps-Political Science & Politics, 34*, 773–777.

Rosenbloom, D. H. (2010). Reevaluating executive-centered public administrive theory. In R. F. Durant (Ed.), *Oxford handbook of the American bureaucracy* (pp. 101–127). New York: Oxford University Press.

Rosenbloom, D. H., & Kravchuk, R. S. (2005). *Public administration: Understanding management, politics, and law in the public sector* (6th ed.). New York: McGraw-Hill.

Rothstein, R. (2002, November 30). Friends of Bill? Why liberals should let up on Clinton. Retrieved from http://www.prospect.org/cs/articles?article=friends_of_bill_1211994

Rourke, F. (1991). Presidentializing the bureaucracy: From Kennedy to Reagan. In J. P. Pfiffner (Ed.), *The managerial presidency* (pp. 123–134). Pacific Grove, CA: Brooks/Cole.

Rourke, F. (1992). Responsiveness and neutral competence in American bureaucracy. *Public Administration Review, 52*(6), 539–546.

Rubin, E. V. (2007). The role of procedural justice in public personnel management: Empirical results from the Department of Defense. *Journal of Public Administration Research and Theory, 19*(1), 125–143.

Rudalevige, A. (2002). *Managing the president's program: Presidential leadership and legislative policy formulation*. Princeton, NJ: Princeton University Press.

Rudalevige, A. (2006). *The plot that thickened: Inheriting the administrative presidency*. Paper presented at the Annual Meeting of the American Political Science Association, Philadelphia, PA.

Rudalevige, A. (2009). The administrative presidency and bureaucratic control: Implementing a research agenda. *Presidential Studies Quarterly, 39*(1), 10–24.

Salamon, L. M., & Abramson, A. J. (1984). Governance: The politics of retrenchment. In J. L. Palmer & I. Sawhill (Eds.), *The Reagan record: An assessment of America's changing domestic priorities* (pp. 31–68). Washington, DC: Urban Institute.

Sanera, M. (1984). Implementing the agenda. In S. Butler, M. Sanera, & W. B. Weinrod (Eds.), *Mandate for leadership II*. Washington, DC: Heritage Foundation.

Savage, C. (2009, January 11). Democrats look for ways to undo late Bush administration rules. *New York Times*. http://www.nytimes.com/2009/01/12/us/12regulate.html?pagewanted=all&_r=0

Scahill, J. (2007). *Blackwater: The rise of the world's most powerful mercenary army*. New York: Nation Books.

Scherer, M. (2005, January/February). Little big companies: How did corporations like Halliburton get millions in government contracts designated for small minority businesses? *Mother Jones Magazine*.

Seidman, H. (1998). *Politics, position, and power: The dynamics of federal organization* (5th ed.). New York: Oxford University Press.

Seidman, H., & Gilmour, R. (1986). *Position, politics and power: From the positive to the regulatory state.* Oxford: Oxford University Press.

Shapiro, S. (2004). Unequal partners: Cost-benefit analysis and executive review of regulations. Retrieved from http://ssrn.com/paper=590241

Shepsle, K. A. (1992). Bureaucratic drift, coalitional drift, and time consistency: A comment on Macey. *Journal of Law, Economics, & Organization, 8*(1), 111–118.

Shipan, C. (2005). Congress and the bureaucracy. In P. J. Quirk & S. A. Binder (Eds.), *The legislative branch.* New York: Oxford University Press.

Shirley, C., & Devine, D. (2010, April 4). Karl Rove is no conservative, as his memoir shows. *Washington Post.* http://www.washingtonpost.com/wp-dyn/content/article/2010/03/31/AR2010033102630.html

Shoop, T. (1994, January 1). Targeting middle managers. Retrieved from http://www.gov exec.com/reinvent/downsize/0194s1.htm

Simon, H. A. (1964). On the concept of organizational goal. *Administrative Science Quarterly, 9*(1), 1–22.

Simon, H. A. (1997). *Administrative behavior: A study of decision-making processes in administrative organizations* (4th ed.). New York: Free Press.

Simons, T. (1999). Behavioral integrity as a critical ingredient for transformational leadership. *Journal of Organizational Change Management, 12*(2), 89–104.

Simons, T., & Parks, J. M. (2002). *Empty words: The impact of perceived managerial integrity on employees, customers and profits.* Paper presented at the annual meeting of the Academy of Management, Denver, CO.

Sitkin, S. B., See, K. E., Miller, C. C., Lawless, M. W., & Carton, A. M. (2011). The paradox of stretch goals: Organizations in pursuit of the seemingly impossible. *Academy of Management Review, 36*(3), 544–566.

Skowronek, S. (1993). *The politics presidents make: Leadership from John Adams to George Bush.* Cambridge, MA: Belknap Press of Harvard University.

Skowronek, S. (2006). *The presidency and the political system.* Washington, DC: CQ Press.

Skowronek, S. (2008). *Presidential leadership in political time: Reprise and reappraisal.* Lawrence: University Press of Kansas.

Smith, C. R., & Fernandez, S. (2010). Equity in federal contracting: Examining the link between minority representation and federal procurement decisions. *Public Administration Review, 70*(1), 87–96. doi:10.1111/j.1540-6210.2009.02113.x

Spender, J.-C. (1996). Making knowledge the basis of a dynamic theory of the firm. *Strategic Management Journal, 17*(S2), 45–62.

Sperlich, P. W. (1969). Bargaining and overload: An essay on presidential power. In A. Wildavsky (Ed.), *The presidency.* Boston: Little, Brown.

Stinchcombe, A. L. (1990). *Information and organizations.* Berkeley: University of California Press.

Suleiman, E. (2003). *Dismantling democratic states.* Princeton, NJ: Princeton University Press.

Suskind, R. (2004, December 28). The cabinet of incuriosities. *New York Times.* http://www.nytimes.com/2004/12/28/opinion/28suskind.html

Thompson, D. F. (2009). Obama's ethics agenda: The challenge of coordinated change. *The Forum, 7*(1), Article 8.

Thompson, F., & Jones, L. R. (2008). Reaping the advantages of information and modern technology: Moving from bureaucracy to hyperarchy and netcentricity. *International Public Management Review, 9*(1), 148–192.

Tolchin, M., & Tolchin, S. J. (2010). *Pinstripe patronage: Political favoritism from the clubhouse to the White House and beyond.* New York: Paradigm.

Turocy, T. L., & von Stengel, B. (2001). *Game theory.* Draft prepared for the *Encyclopedia of Information Systems.* CDAM Research Report LSE-CDAM-2001-09.

Tversky, A., & Kahneman, D. (1973). Availability: A heuristic for judging frequency and probability. *Cognitive Psychology, 5*(2), 207–232.

Van Riper, P. P. (1958). *History of the United States Civil Service.* Evanston, IL: Row, Peterson.

Walcott, C., & Hult, K. M. (1994). White House organization as a problem of governance: The Eisenhower system. *Presidential Studies Quarterly, 24*(2), 327–339.

Walcott, C., & Hult, K. M. (2005). White House structure and decision making: Elaborating the standard model. *Presidential Studies Quarterly, 35*(2), 303–318.

Warshaw, S. A. (2006, Spring). The administrative strategies of President George W. Bush. *Extensions,* 1–7.

Waterman, R. (1989). *Presidential influence and the administrative state.* Knoxville: University of Tennessee Press.

Waterman, R., & Gill, J. (2005). *When bureaucracy's mission and structure changes: An analysis of the Department of Homeland Security with a hierarchical principal-agent model.* Paper presented at the Annual Meeting of the Midwest Political Science Association, Palmer House Hilton, Chicago, IL. http://www.allacademic.com/meta/p86422_index.html

Weko, T. J. (1995). *The politicizing presidency: The White House Personnel Office, 1948–1994.* Lawrence: University Press of Kansas.

West, W. F. (1995). *Controlling the bureaucracy: Institutional constraints in theory and practice.* Armonk, NY: M. E. Sharpe.

West, W. F. (2005). Neutral competence and political responsiveness: An uneasy relationship. *Policy Studies Journal, 33*(2), 147–160.

Whitener, E. M., Brodt, S. E., Korsgaard, M. A., & Werner, J. M. (1998). Managers as initiators of trust: An exchange relationship framework for understanding managerial trustworthy behavior. *Academy of Management Review, 23*(3), 513–530.

Williams, R. (2009). *Alternatives to logistic regression (brief overview).* University of Notre Dame. Notre Dame, IN. Retrieved from http://www.nd.edu/~rwilliam/stats3/L09.pdf

Williamson, O. E. (1993). Calculativeness, trust, and economic organization. *Journal of Law Economics & Organization, 36*(1), 453–486.

Wilson, J. Q. (1989). *Bureaucracy: What government agencies do and why they do it* (2nd ed.). New York: Basic Books.

Wood, B. D., & Bohte, J. (2004). Political transaction costs and the politics of administrative design. *Journal of Politics, 66*(1), 176–202.

Wood, B. D., & Marchbanks, M. P., III. (2007). What determines how long political appointees serve? *Journal of Public Administration Research and Theory,* mum019. doi:10.1093/jopart/mum019

Wood, B. D., & Waterman, R. (1994). *Bureaucratic dynamics: The role of bureaucracy in a democracy.* Boulder, CO: Westview Press.

Woolston, R. L. (2001). Faculty perceptions of dean transitions: Does trust matter? *Dissertation Abstracts International, UMI No. 3007300.*

Zand, D. E. (1972). Trust and managerial problem solving. *Administrative Science Quarterly, 17*(2), 229–239.

Index

Page numbers in *italics* indicate figures and tables.

Senior Executive Service personnel (*cont.*)
change in number of appointees, 37; as
interim agency leadership, 121; jigsaw
puzzle management and, 16; NAPA survey of, 117; Obama administration and,
157–58; perceptions of transition impediments, 124–25, *126*, 127–32; policy views,
36, 38; reassignment of, 26; role of, 22–24;
transition preparation and, 122–24, *123*.
See also appointee-careerist relations;
career executives/careerists
separation of powers system, 161n5
"shadow of the future," 53
Shapiro, S., 30
Skarlicki, D. P., 76–77
"social embeddedness," 58–59
social exchange theory, 54–55
Spender, J.-C., 60
Sperlich, P. W., 153
stratification, 163n22
stratified trust: definition of, 66–67, 161n1,
163n22; direct and moderating impacts of,
100; intellectual capital and, 74, 76, 77,
105, 151; measurement of, 89–90; moderating effect of, 110–11, *111*; trickle-down
effect of, 113, 152
structural politicization, 148
subversion, fear of, 144–45
superior-subordinate relationships. *See*
appointee-careerist relations; dyadic trust
Suskind, Ron, 14

tacit knowledge, 59–60
TIL. *See* generalized trust in leadership
time and trust building, 61–62
top-down knowledge accessibility and
intellectual capital capacity, 86
transition preparation: appointee vacancies
and, 128–32, *130*; awareness of activities
related to, 131–40, *135, 137*; conditional
cooperation strategy in, 119; explicit
knowledge exchange and, 140–42; impediments to, *129*; information exchange
during, 121–22; jigsaw puzzle management
and, 122–24, *123*; memo issued on,
117–18; overview of, 6–7; perceptions of

impediments to, 124–25, *126*, 127–32;
study of, 116–17; time period for, 121
trust: administrative presidency and, 148–52;
awareness of transition activities and,
138–39, *139*; in context of federal agencies,
2; as context-specific construct, 99, 144;
cycle of accommodation thesis and, 80,
140; in dyadic relationships, 47–55;
information exchange and, 15, 75;
intellectual capital and, 59–63, 94, *95*,
96–98, 156; in interpersonal relations,
40–41; limitations of studies of, 72; middle
management and, 45–47, 77; model of
intellectual capital and, 63, *64*, 65–67;
noncalculative, 49, 65; organizational, 80;
organizational effectiveness and, 10; policy
implementation and, 158–59; role of in
organizations, 40–47; as socially embedded, 56–59; studies on, 40; "trickle-down"
effect of, 5–6. *See also* distrust; dyadic
trust; encapsulated interest; generalized
trust in leadership; interpersonal trust;
stratified trust
trust index, 131–32, 136, 138

vacancies: acting officials in, 62; awareness
of transition activities and, 136, 138;
consequences of, 80; impacts of, 53–54,
101, 148; measurement of, 91–93; perceptions of intellectual capital capacity
and, 105, 109; reasons for, 78; transition
preparation and, 128–32, *130*
vacancy index, 92, 128–29, *130*
vertical coordination, 86, 109
voice, acquiescent, 39
Volcker, Paul, 156

Walcott, C. E., 35, 52, 149
Weber, Max, 41
West, W. F., 30, 65, 71–72, 114, 156
Whitener, E. M., 62
Williamson, Oliver, 58, 62, 63, 65, 74, 151
Wilson, J. Q., 38
Wise, L. R., 51
workforce knowledge and intellectual capital
capacity, 85